POWER

of

OTHERS

About the Author

Michael Bond has been writing on psychology and human behaviour for more than fifteen years as a regular contributor to *New Scientist*, *Nature*, *Prospect*, the *Observer*, the *Daily Telegraph*, the *Financial Times*, and others. During the Arab Spring, he also served as lead researcher for the Royal Society report on science in Egypt. He lives in London.

The
POWER
of
OTHERS

Peer Pressure, Groupthink, and How the People
Around Us Shape Everything We Do

—

MICHAEL BOND

ONEWORLD

A Oneworld book

First published by Oneworld Publications, 2014
This edition published 2015

Copyright © Michael Bond 2014, 2015

The moral right of Michael Bond to be identified as the
Author of this work has been asserted by him in accordance
with the Copyright, Designs and Patents Act 1988

ISBN 978-1-78074-653-1
eISBN 978-1-78074-345-5

Typeset by Tetragon, London
Printed and bound in Great Britain by Clays Ltd, St Ives plc

Oneworld Publications
10 Bloomsbury Street
London WC1B 3SR
England

Stay up to date with the latest books,
special offers, and exclusive content from
Oneworld with our monthly newsletter

Sign up on our website
www.oneworld-publications.com

For Jessica

Contents

List of Illustrations

Acknowledgements

In addition to the many people quoted in this book who gave generously of their time, I would like to thank the following for their help or encouragement: Chloe Courtauld, Basem Fathy, Nasra Hassan, Ruth Mayer, Thomas Pyszczynski, Stephen Reicher, Karim Rizk, Sheldon Solomon, Clifford Stott, Mike Stroud, Ginette Thaler, Jeremy Webb at *New Scientist*, Richard Wolman, my editors at Oneworld, Mike Harpley, Kathleen McCully and Robin Dennis, and particularly my agent Bill Hamilton at A. M. Heath.

Note

All quotations are taken from interviews with the author unless otherwise specified.

Prologue

We may think we're running the show, but most of the time it's the other way round. The situation we are in, and particularly the people around us, hold sway over our thoughts and behaviours far more than we like to imagine.

In almost every area of our lives, we are steered by others. They influence what we wear, the music we like, the food we eat (and how much of it), our voting habits, how we invest our money. They affect our mental state, the ebb and flow of our moods and emotions. They even colour our moral outlook, whether we act good or bad.

The scientific study of these group dynamics, which work beneath our conscious radar, is transforming our understanding of human nature. We are not the autonomous ringmasters we believe we are; we are social through and through. This insight is disquieting because it challenges the way we see ourselves, and how we judge others. It suggests, for example, that character and personality are not a reliable guide to future conduct. It also forces us to confront some awkward questions about the human condition. Is criminality a state of mind? Does evil beget evil? Are heroes born heroic?

Acknowledging such complexities can be difficult. Recall the outcry in July 2013 when *Rolling Stone* depicted on its cover a photograph of Boston bombing suspect Dzhokhar Tsarnaev looking doe-eyed and tousle-haired and a little too boyish and innocent for many tastes. The implication was that alleged murderers should not be shown to look like rock stars, or like their mothers' sons.

Of course they can be all these things. The uncomfortable truth is that people are never the knowable rogues they appear to be. By and large it is their sociability, their compulsive groupishness, that makes it so.

——

There is no doubting the human fondness for groups. We categorize people on the flimsiest of pretexts: the length of their hair, their turn of phrase. Little wonder that much of human behaviour is understandable only at the level of the collective. In 1954, the Turkish-American psychologist Muzafer Sherif demonstrated this scientifically for the first time in his 'Robbers Cave' experiment, pitching two groups of adolescent boys in competition with each other at a summer camp in Oklahoma to study the effect on their behaviour. Within days, they had developed an inter-group rivalry that resembled tribal warfare. Yet the boys were almost identical in background and age: Sherif had conjured up discrimination and intolerance simply by drawing a line in the sand.

In the decades since, social psychologists have demonstrated many times how effortlessly we construct a narrative of 'us' and 'them', and how quickly prejudice can follow. They have shown, for example, that people will instinctively divide themselves according to the colour of their eyes, the colour of their shirt, their preference for a particular artist, whether they over- or under-estimate the number of dots in a pattern, whether a coin lands heads up or tails.

Even when based on such arbitrary criteria, group identities run deep. Mark Levine, now at the University of Exeter, found that Manchester United fans, who had been asked to ponder the virtues of their club, were three times as likely to help an injured stranger in a Manchester United shirt as one in a Liverpool or plain shirt. When he repeated the experiment, this time asking them to think about being a football supporter in general, they were happy to lend a hand whatever shirt the stranger was wearing – so long as it was a football shirt. Group identities are transformative, but they are transitory too. They are also instinctively adopted. 'This impulse ... to sunder all the peoples of the world into belligerent collectivities has existed as long as humanity itself', notes historian David Cannadine in *The Undivided Past*.[1]

Groupishness makes evolutionary sense. In our ancestral environment, natural selection would have favoured individuals who co-operated with each other and were quick to distinguish friend from foe. Group living provided benefits, such as the division of labour and protection from predators and enemies, that made survival and reproduction more likely. These tribal proclivities are knitted into our physiology, moderated by hormones and neurotransmitters such as testosterone, which promotes competitive behaviour, and oxytocin, which boosts people's love for their in-group (but not for all humanity as is sometimes suggested). This helps explain both our innate hunger for social connection and the excoriating effects of loneliness. The presence of others can lead us astray, but their absence can propel us to a far worse place.

Many people find it daunting, sometimes overwhelming, to reflect that they are influenced by those around them in such dramatic and fundamental ways. They worry that they are not in control of their lives, that it is not their hand on the tiller, that they will lose their mind in a mob or that group forces will corrupt them as they have corrupted the victims of so many cults. Much of this fear is based on myth (mobs are neither mindless nor mad). But not all of it. Unquestionably, our group leanings can drag us to the moral depths.

They can make us less tolerant towards those who differ from us, and even split societies apart. They have on countless occasions caused people to favour aggression over negotiation. They can trigger the collapse of banks. They can persuade ordinary people to commit extraordinary acts of brutality. They can turn disaffected loners into mass killers. They can lead us to extreme views and distort our thinking on all kinds of issues. They can make us conform too much to what other people think of us, a serious problem when what other people think of us is negative (this is probably the best explanation for why, in some cultures, girls do worse at maths and science than boys, and why African-American students often under-perform when they think they are being tested on intellectual ability).[2]

Yet they can raise us to heights we are unlikely to reach by ourselves. Most acts of resistance to totalitarian regimes during the twentieth century were communal. Most heroes are not born extraordinary but step up in response to the desperate need of their compatriots, and it's almost impossible to predict who they will be. Armies can make up in camaraderie and solidarity what they lack in numbers. Solidarity is also behind much sporting achievement and has made possible extraordinary feats of adventure and survival in extreme environments. Crowds, contrary to how they are usually portrayed, tend to be highly co-operative and altruistic, to the extent that social psychologist John Drury has dubbed them 'the fourth emergency service'.

Social bonds keenly felt can even help those in isolation: many kidnap victims and solo explorers have kept sane by taking refuge in a world of abstractions far beyond their immediate confines. Furthermore, our social needs can be co-opted to positive ends. The UK government's 'nudge' strategy for recovering unpaid income tax, which involves sending feet-draggers a letter telling them most people pay on time, has improved compliance by some twenty percent. What other people do matters to us at every conceivable level.

The Power of Others is an attempt to illustrate the full extent of all this through stories of behaviour from the outlandish to the everyday. We'll encounter war heroes, polar explorers, London rioters, Arab Spring protestors, American revolutionaries, mountaineers, round-the-world yachtsmen, New York City firefighters, astronauts, suicide terrorists, heroic rescuers of Jews in wartime Europe, lone wolf killers, professional cyclists, kidnap victims and 'supermax' prisoners. We'll hear from the social psychologists whose laboratory and field studies are redefining our ideas about what makes us tick. We'll travel from the refugee camps of Gaza to the streets of Cairo, from Guantanamo Bay to the woody valleys of Vermont.

Above all, we'll learn how to manage our social impulses and vulnerabilities and use them to our own ends: when to follow the herd or go our own way, how to survive a crowd emergency, how self-awareness can help us stand up to prejudice, the secrets to successful brainstorming, how to counter loneliness and alienation, how to avoid the perils of groupthink.

We'll discover that getting your employees to chat and mingle is a more effective way of increasing productivity than having them compete against each other; that it is far easier to dissent when someone else is doing it with you (heroism can be a group activity too); that the sensationalism that sells newspapers also distorts our view of the world and each other. We'll see why all-star teams almost always perform beneath expectations; why there has hardly ever been a suicide bomber who has acted alone; why peer pressure can make intelligent people give ridiculous answers to straightforward questions.

The aim is to shine a light on these endlessly fascinating vagaries of group behaviour, and to demonstrate how they affect us in just about everything we do. Social psychology can teach us a great deal about ourselves; without it, we can never hope truly to understand each other.

1

Emotional Chameleons

Most people in Britain of a certain age remember where they were on the morning of 31 August 1997 when they heard the news that Princess Diana had died in a car crash in Paris. It was our JFK moment. Unexpected and shocking as it was, what followed was in some ways even more bizarre. Huge numbers of Britons grieved as if they had known her personally. Tens of thousands queued through the night at St James's Palace in London to sign a book of condolence. Around a million lined the route of her funeral cortège to Westminster Abbey. Outside the gates of her home in Kensington Gardens the floral tributes lay so deep that those at the bottom began to decompose.

At the time I was living near Kensington, and I remember the day she was killed, which was a Sunday, walking through the gardens and watching all the downcast people standing at the gates looking at the flowers and laying their own bouquets, and starting to feel a little sad myself where before there had been only a kind of astonishment, and thinking, what is going *on* here? I saw strangers embrace in commiseration. On the television, some newsreaders looked close to tears. The writer Carmen Callil likened it to the Nuremberg Rallies:[1] in this cult of mourning, there was only one way to feel.

Looking back, it seems clear what was going on. Psychologists know it as emotional contagion: an unthinking synchronization of mood and feeling that can propagate across whole groups. In this case, as in many, there is little doubt it was provoked by relentless media coverage that set the tone for the nation through sentimental commentary and extravagant coverage of what in the beginning was sporadic public grief. It was a case of the 'dominant opinion monopolizing the public scene', as cultural studies expert James Thomas put it.[2] Yet emotional contagion is an inevitable consequence of human social behaviour. Like chameleons that change colour with their surroundings, we imitate automatically. Before we explore how that works, consider another example of how quickly emotions – in this case fear – can spread through a community, and how dramatic the effects can be.

On Wednesday, 10 December 1930, a New York City merchant walked into the branch of the privately held Bank of United States on Freeman Street in the Bronx and asked a teller to dispose of the stock he held in the bank. When the manager tried to discourage him, insisting it was a sound investment, the merchant left and spread the story among his business colleagues that the bank was in trouble. Within a few hours, hundreds of people had turned up at the branch seeking to withdraw their money. By the time it closed its doors at 8 p.m., the crowd had swelled to twenty thousand. Three thousand customers had taken out some $2 million, including a man who queued for two hours to remove his measly two bucks.

The Bank of United States never re-opened. The rumours had resulted in runs at other branches, and the bank's directors feared that large mobs would gather the next day and bleed the business dry. Early on Thursday, they closed down the entire operation and handed over the remaining assets to Joseph Broderick, New

York State Superintendent of Banks, for safekeeping. It was the right decision. By 9.30 a.m., eight thousand agitated customers were standing in the rain outside the Freeman Street offices, and thousands more outside the fifty-eight other branches in the Bronx, Brooklyn and Manhattan. At the bank headquarters at 535 Fifth Avenue, mounted policemen had to ride flush to the walls to keep the crowds away.[3]

At the time, the Bank of United States was the largest commercial bank in terms of dollars on deposit to fail in the country's history. Its collapse was a considerable blow to the public's confidence in the economy, coming as it did just thirteen months after the Wall Street crash known as Black Tuesday. The economist Milton Friedman and others have argued that it accelerated a crisis in banking that helped transform what had been an ordinary, cyclical recession into the Great Depression.[4] Another three hundred banks closed their doors before the end of the year.

The run on the Bank of United States was fuelled by the contagious fear that the institution could not pay out. Like all bank runs, it represented a collective loss of faith in how the banking system worked and in the value of credit – a term derived from the Latin *credere*, to believe. Such fear becomes a self-fulfilling prophecy regardless of whether the rumour that triggered it is true: no bank carries all its deposits in cash. Collective fear is hard to ignore and the pattern has been repeated many times since the Great Depression. A recent example was September 2007, when thousands of worried customers queued to withdraw their savings from the ailing British bank Northern Rock after reading reports in newspapers and blogs that others were doing the same, even though the Bank of England had already agreed to support it.

It is easy to scoff at such herdishness, yet it is not as mindless as it appears. When you see large numbers of people losing faith

Fig. 1 Depositors gather in the rain outside the
Bank of United States, December 1930.

in the system, it makes sense to get your investment out fast. Even
if such behaviour is not well founded, an institution that has lost
its reputation is highly likely to fail. The flipside is that we are just
as liable to follow the herd when it is running after something we
want – or think we want. In January 2012, Apple was forced to
delay the launch of its newest iPhone in China 'for safety reasons'
after a riot broke out among hundreds of desperate customers
outside its flagship store in Beijing. Fear of missing out can be just
as motivating as fear of financial ruin.

It feels like we are in the driving seat in our daily lives, making
decisions autonomously, experiencing emotions that we ourselves
generate, choosing what we believe in (and what we don't). Mostly
this is an illusion. Four decades of research into how people decide

4

to do what they do has shown that we are highly susceptible to the winds of social influence – indeed, it is impossible to escape them, short of living in hermitic isolation (and even that may not immunize us, as we'll see in a later chapter).

To understand why, let's start with the epitome of social ritual, a good meal. 'In food, as in death, we feel the essential brotherhood of man', runs a Vietnamese proverb, a notion that recently has acquired scientific credibility thanks to the work of a group of Dutch behavioural researchers led by Roel Hermans. Hermans and his team built an experimental restaurant in their lab at Radboud University in Nijmegen to test the extent to which people feed off each other – in behavioural terms – while sharing food. (This is the kind of experimental protocol that makes psychology such a popular subject among university students.) They set up a small table, dressed it with plates, cutlery, glasses and napkins, and placed two chairs facing each other. They hid a CCTV camera in a nearby lamp to allow them to observe the diners from an adjacent room. They then served evening meals to seventy pairs of young women – presumably undergraduates grateful for a free meal – and recorded the amount each diner consumed, the number of times she placed food in her mouth and the precise time at which she did so.

Three thousand, eight hundred and eighty-eight mouthfuls later, they found not only that how much each woman ate depended on how much her companion ate, but that each couple's eating was highly co-ordinated. In other words, the women were more likely to put fork to mouth simultaneously than separately, particularly at the beginning of the meal.[5] The researchers realized they were observing a classic case of social mimicry, a ubiquitous phenomenon where one individual unwittingly imitates the mannerisms of another. Known as the chameleon effect, it appears to improve communication and rapport. Hermans thinks it might explain many common social dining quirks, such as why we tend to eat more in the presence of others,[6] and why drinking partners often sip their drinks simultaneously,[7] especially when each is focused on what the other is saying. This can work even when the interaction is virtual: the next time you watch a film with a glass in hand, observe how often you raise it in sync with the actors on the screen.[8]

This type of behavioural orchestration carries on well below our level of conscious awareness, which makes it particularly tricky for those of us trying to moderate what we put in our mouths. Like bank runs and public grief, overindulgence is contagious. 'People have less control over their eating than they like to imagine', says Hermans. When I ask him what we can do to counter this, he declares: 'Decrease mindless eating!' Easier said than done. To be fully mindful about our eating – to savour every flavour to the exclusion of all else – we'd have to dine alone. Hermans thinks it's more a question of learning to be aware of the external factors that influence our habits, though he stops short of encouraging people to override their mimicking instinct. 'I'm not sure whether I would advise therapists to even go there, since it is such a big part of our social lives.'

Studies of eating behaviour raise as many intriguing questions as they answer. The women who took part in Hermans's experiment had an average age of twenty-one, were of 'normal' weight, did not know each other, and were three times as likely to mimic each other during the first ten minutes of the meal as during the final ten. Would the effect have been the same if they had been older, or male, or if they had been friends before they sat down together? Or if the pairs had been of mixed age, gender or weight? Or if they had been forbidden from talking? We don't know. The display of mimicry at the start of each encounter may have been an unconscious attempt by the women to get along with each other. If so, and if this is a general trait, you might expect less imitation at family meals where everyone knows each other well and more at, say, business lunches.

Shortly after talking with Hermans, I went to lunch with a fellow reporter whom I had not seen for a year, expecting our eating behaviour to resemble the flamingo's spectacularly synchronized mating dance, since it was in both our interests to go the extra mile. Instead, he hoovered up his food, leaving me stranded. I spent the rest of the meal worried that he didn't like me, even though we don't know enough yet about the psychology of mimicry to make such tender judgements. It's possible of course that he was very hungry.

Or he could just be very selfish. Studies show that selfish people are not great synchronizers. Joanne Lumsden, who studies social cognition at the University of Aberdeen, has discovered that people who approach an encounter aiming to secure the best possible outcome for themselves mirror the movements of their partner about half as frequently as those concerned about the mutual benefits to both.[9] The most likely explanation, she says, is that co-ordination requires you to pay attention to the other person, and if you are focused only on yourself you do that less.

Mimicry is the breath of social interaction. We do it without thinking, and without it anything beyond superficial communication would be impossible. All of us inadvertently copy the facial expressions, postures, manner of speech and other tics and quirks of those we are with all the time. And we do it at remarkable speed.

An experiment carried out in 1966 with students at the University of Pittsburgh revealed that people emulate each other's body movements within twenty-one milliseconds.[10] Compare that to the average human reaction time – how long it takes to press a button in response to the flash of a light – which is around ten times as slow, and you can see that there is nothing conscious about the way we mimic. It is a primitive, innate response: all primates do it, including human infants, who start to shadow their mother's facial gestures when they are just a few hours old. It leads to a remarkable flow during social encounters. If you watch a slowed-down film of two people in conversation, the co-ordination between their movements and postures looks almost balletic, the more so the greater the rapport between them. As Hermans observed, this applies even to an exercise as apparently mechanical as eating.

But mimicry is not just about body language. It works across our whole behavioural repertoire. As the death of Princess Diana and the history of bank runs have shown, even emotions and moods – the very architecture of our inner world – are 'catchable'.

One of the pioneers of the study of contagious emotions is Peter Totterdell, professor of psychology at the University of Sheffield. Totterdell didn't set out to look at contagion; he began by investigating circadian rhythms in shift workers, such as nurses and police officers, to see how their state of mind changed over the hours they were on the job. One day he noticed that the workers' moods were changing hand-in-hand, fluctuating as one. He has since observed this pattern in accountants, security workers, teachers, assembly line workers, customer service staff – and professional cricketers.

Cricket is an exasperating sport for those not accustomed to its arcane ways and the improbable length of time it can take to get a result (up to five days). This is precisely the reason it appealed to Totterdell as an environment in which to measure the ebb and flow of relationships among colleagues – in this case, players on the same side. He enlisted the members of two professional cricket teams who were drawn against each other in the English County Championship. He issued them with pocket computers and asked them to record their moods and what they were feeling at various points in the game. It turned out that each player's happiness at any one time was strongly linked to that of his teammates, regardless of whether or not things were going in their favour.[11] It was as if they were all plugged into a giant hubble-bubble, inhaling the collective mood like smoke.

Emotional contagion appears to be a natural feature of all our social interactions. In 2008, the social scientists Nicholas Christakis and James Fowler investigated a network of several thousand friends, relatives, neighbours and work colleagues in Framingham, Massachusetts, whose residents have been tracked by epidemiologists since 1948 as part of a multigenerational heart study. They noticed not only that happy people were clustered together in this network, meaning they were more likely to be friends with each other, but also that their chances of being happy increased the better connected they were to other happy people.[12] Christakis explained: 'Most people will not be surprised that people with more friends are happier, but what really matters is whether those friends are happy.'[13]

The idea that people can pass on emotions and moods such as anger or anxiety, or even more enduring states of mind such as contentment or sadness, is hardly new to science. More than three decades ago, an experiment at the University of California showed that when small groups of people sit facing each other without talking for two minutes, everyone in the group ends up adopting the mood of the most expressive person – the one who exhibits feelings most visibly through facial expressions, gestures and body movements.[14] Other studies have found similar effects in diverse everyday environments. For instance, if you're sharing a living space with someone suffering from mild depression, you're at risk of becoming progressively more depressed the longer you live with them – you pick up their negative vibes.[15] Likewise, bank tellers and retail staff really can lift the mood of customers by smiling at them and asking them how they are. When customers respond in kind, which they usually do, that rubs off on the staff.[16] It leads to a virtuous circle of reciprocated jollity and, more to the point if you're a bank or shop manager, increased sales. Some retailers have taken this to heart: the high-end fast-food chain Pret a Manger requires its staff to effuse ebullience and 'authentic happiness'. Recent studies have shown that such feelings can transmit not just from one person to another, but across entire social worlds of friends and work colleagues.[17]

Much of the time our emotions stem from things that happen to us directly. You might be feeling upbeat because of the spring sunshine on your face, anxious because you're thinking about a presentation you're due to give, or sad after remembering a friend who passed away. But if you experience strong feelings in a social situation and can't pinpoint how they arose, there's a strong chance you've picked them up from those around you. The converse is also true: you may well be dealing your emotions out to others.

Psychologists believe it is even possible consciously to influence people by forcing a display of a specific emotion. One of the most effective ways is to 'deep act', according to Stéphane Côté, who studies behaviour in the workplace at the University of Toronto. Deep acting involves bringing to mind a past occasion in which you felt a genuine emotion.[18] It is akin to the techniques used by method actors to feel their way into a character. So, if you wish to appear confident and positive, think of a time when you successfully applied for a new job, or a friend paid you an unexpected compliment, or you won a prize at school. If you wish to appear conciliatory, think of an empathic conversation you had with someone you care deeply about.

Nonetheless, the most infectious emotions are those that are honestly felt. Emotional displays that are unashamedly visceral can affect all who witness them. At the victory parade held to celebrate the end of the 2012 London Olympics, I was standing in Trafalgar Square with thousands of others facing a huge TV screen that had been set up beneath Nelson's Column. We were watching an interview with the Paralympian volleyball player Martine Wright, who was talking about her rehabilitation following the loss of her legs and eighty per cent of her blood in the London terrorist bombings of 7 July 2005, the day after London was awarded the Games. Suddenly she started to cry. Turning to look at the crowd, I could see her sadness mirrored on the faces of hundreds who had their eyes to the screen, an almost instantaneous outbreak of emotional contagion. It was hard not to catch it.

Mimicry allows for social choreography, but it is the door to something much deeper. It helps us understand other people's minds. When we emulate the look on someone's face, we begin to experience the emotion behind the expression – a phenomenon observed by Charles Darwin in *The Expression of the Emotions in Man and Animals*, published in 1872. Darwin noted that manipulating our facial muscles profoundly affects the way we feel.

A decade later, the philosopher William James proposed that emotions are a mental perception of a change in the body, an idea recently expanded by the neuroscientist Antonio Damasio and others. Damasio argues that the physical sensations of an emotion – racing pulse, contracting muscles, dilated pupils, for example – precede their representation in the brain.[19] In other words, physiology determines feeling. Such 'embodied cognition' was inadvertently demonstrated in the 1970s by University of California psychologists Paul Ekman and Wallace Friesen while they were developing a technique for categorizing facial expressions.[20] To determine how facial muscles control expression, they videotaped themselves pulling faces using some ten thousand combinations of muscle actions. Afterwards, Ekman described how it felt:

> I found that when I made certain expressions, I was flooded with strong emotional sensations. It wasn't just any expression, only the ones I had already identified as universal to all human beings. When I asked Friesen if this was happening to him also, he reported that he, too, was feeling emotions when he made some of the expressions, and they often felt very unpleasant.[21]

Little wonder that actors sometimes get lost in the characters they portray. This is Kirk Douglas recalling how he got too close for comfort to Vincent van Gogh, whom he played in the 1956 film *Lust for Life*:

> I felt myself going over the line, into the skin of Van Gogh. Not only did I look like him, I was the same age he had been when he committed suicide. Sometimes I had to stop myself

from reaching my hand up and touching my ear to find out if it was actually there. It was a frightening experience. That way lies madness.[22]

You don't have to be an actor or an experimental psychologist to appreciate why mimicking someone's physical appearance can tell us about their mental state. It is easy to manufacture emotions using body postures, movements and vocalization patterns. Try sadness. A guaranteed way to momentarily offset the joy of a sunny morning is to slouch across the bedroom with the inner corners of your eyebrows slightly raised and the corners of your lips pulled down while humming the Beatles' *Eleanor Rigby* (or talking in pitch intervals that correspond to a musical minor third).[23]

There is a modern antidote to this kind of emotional super-stimulation: botulin toxin-A, or Botox. Applying this powerful nerve poison to certain muscles in the face can help arrest the development of wrinkles in the skin, but because humans use these muscles to express emotions, this beauty regimen can also disrupt the way we feel. In 2010, a team of psychologists at the University of Wisconsin-Madison tested this on a group of women who were seeking Botox treatment to reduce their frown lines. Before the treatment, the researchers invited the women to the lab so they could time them as they read various emotionally leading statements on a computer, such as 'You spring up the stairs to your lover's apartment' (designed to make them feel happy); 'You open your email in-box on your birthday to find no new emails' (sad); and 'Reeling from the fight with that stubborn bigot, you slam the car door' (angry). Two weeks later, after the women had had their corrugator supercilii muscles at the inner ends of their eyebrows temporarily paralysed, they re-took the test. The Botox had no effect on how quickly they reacted to the happy sentences, but it slowed their reaction to the sad and angry ones. Since they could not properly express these emotions on their face, it took them longer to process them in their brain. Not being able to frown actually seemed to slow their cognition.[24]

This finding has been corroborated by functional magnetic resonance imaging (fMRI) research in which German women who had received Botox injections in their frown muscles showed decreased activity in their amygdala, a brain region critical to emotions, when asked to pull an angry face.[25] The takeaway message has less to do with Botox as a beauty treatment than with how important emotional expression and mimicry are to social interaction: if your face is lagging behind the conversation, the person you are talking to will get the impression you are disinterested. It may even darken their view of you. David Havas, who led the experiment at the University of Wisconsin, suspects that because the toxin impairs the ability to produce micro-expressions, 'people who get Botox are perceived as less likeable'.[26]

In spite of the part it plays in public grief, bank runs, fuel crises, health scares and other behaviours we would rather do without, emotional contagion appears to have a strong evolutionary function: it increases co-operation within groups. 'If people are in the same mental state when they're interacting socially, they're going to be able to co-ordinate their activities more smoothly and effectively', says Peter Totterdell.

The benefits of this kind of social harmony have been demonstrated with great effectiveness by computer scientist Alex Pentland and his colleagues at the Human Dynamics Laboratory at the

Massachusetts Institute of Technology (MIT). The team has developed a technique they call 'reality mining', in which they monitor people's behaviours, body movements, conversational patterns and other interactions using data from their mobile phones and specially designed electronic devices such as Bluetooth location sensors and accelerometers. In Pentland's words, reality mining is:

> just like data mining, where you go in and look at data and try and find patterns and make predictions and understand what's going on, except instead of being applied to text and web pages and things that are already digital, we're trying to find patterns in real life. [This way] you can tell a lot about people: where they go, who they hang out with, even whether they're having a good time.[27]

One of their most valuable observations for businesses and other organizations is that cohesion and communication among office workers – the extent to which they talk, mingle and share things – is a strong predictor of how productive they are. In one Chicago IT company, employees who were in the top third in terms of group cohesiveness were more than ten per cent more productive than average. And at a Bank of America call centre in Rhode Island, the most accomplished operators were those who talked to their co-workers the most. 'Much of the important information about how to be successful and productive at a job is likely to be found in the break room', explains Pentland.[28] He has found that high-performing teams have a buzz about them – literally a hum of conversation. What's important is not what they are talking about, but how engaged all the members are.[29] Consider Pentland's advice to team-builders, based on the data he has gathered: 'Individual reasoning and talent contribute far less to team success than one might expect. The best way to build a great team is not to select individuals for their smarts or accomplishments but to learn how they communicate and to shape and guide the team so that it follows successful communication patterns.'[30] This suggests companies that allow staff to work from home will lose out in the long run. By the same measure, performance-related pay, aimed at boosting individual motivation, can be counter-productive because it fosters competition among co-workers and reduces the incentive to work as a team. This is not just about the flow of ideas that comes from uninhibited interaction; it's also about the added motivation that comes from sitting and socializing with people you know, and hopefully like.

Between March 2010 and June 2011, Pentland's lab carried out its 'Friends and Family' study, which continually tracked the behaviour of 130 adults living in a young-family residential community next to MIT. The study collected mobile phone-based data such as a person's location, movement, proximity to others, communication patterns and use of online apps, and a mass of additional information including Facebook activity, financial statements and self-reported daily mood and sleep patterns. Needless to say, this blatant invasion of privacy took place with the participants' full consent. Among the most intriguing findings: residents were more likely to share mobile apps with people they spent time with face-to-face; were more likely to engage in incentive programmes that awarded them for taking exercise if the benefits (in this case small financial rewards) were shared with others; and mixed with fewer people in a less diverse social set when their income levels fell (as Pentland describes it, the richer a person is, the more their curiosity will permit them to explore).[31] A good chunk of the variation observed in the Friends and Family study is due to emotional and behavioural contagion – people copying what others do. 'When in Rome, you do as the Romans do', says Pentland.

Mimicry makes good survival sense. As social networks expert Duncan Watts explains: 'The world is too complicated for each individual to be able to solve problems on their own. We rely on information that is encoded in our social environment. We assume other people know things we don't.' This explains our gullibility in the face of crowds, as illustrated beautifully by the psychologist Stanley Milgram in 1969. Milgram arranged for his collaborators to stand in a busy New York street and stare up at a sixth-floor window while he counted the number of passers-by who did the same. He discovered that the more collaborators he started off with, the more likely it was that people would stop and follow their gaze.[32]

Such persuasion is hard to resist. Would you walk on by?

———

Elaine Hatfield is more aware than most people of the infectiousness of emotions. She has been studying social interactions, relationships and intimacy for forty years, more than thirty of them as a professor of psychology at the University of Hawaii. Yet that hasn't made her any less susceptible. In the early 1990s, when she was working as a psychotherapist, she noticed that her clients were instilling 'perplexing emotional reactions' in her. And not only her clients. One day, she and her husband were invited to dinner at the home of two local artists. Over the course of the evening she became so sleepy she could hardly hold her head up. Afterwards she sent a note of apology to their hosts, who promptly arranged a repeat dinner. When the day came the same thing happened: half an hour into the meal, Hatfield started to nod off. Later she discussed it with her husband, who was a psychotherapist too, and they worked out what was going wrong:

> Susan is filled with energy – and anxiety. Her conversation is a battery of long-stored-up grievances and complaints. She is not uninteresting, however: if one had only to listen to Susan, the dinner would probably have worked out ... Dealing with Susan's husband, Harry, on his own would not have been a problem either, although he is profoundly depressed and says nothing: [we] talk to depressed people all day, and would simply have questioned him about his life. The trouble was that there were two of them. When caught between the Scylla of hysteria and the Charybdis of depression, Elaine – busily sponging up both contradictory emotions – had nowhere to go but asleep.[33]

Hatfield and her husband dealt with the problem in uncompromising fashion: they elected never to visit the couple again.

Some of us are especially prone to the moods of those around us. We are more likely than others to be lifted up by a friend's exuberance or floored by their melancholy. Women are generally more empathic than men and therefore more open to emotional contagion, as are extroverts of both sexes, who tend to be highly focused on the people with whom they are interacting. Indeed, the inward gaze of introverts and depressives insulates them, to some extent. How susceptible you are to someone's mood can depend a lot on the nature of your relationship with them. The more important they are to you, the more likely you will soak up their vibe, since you will be more engaged or invested in what they are saying and how they are feeling. Mothers are highly vulnerable to the emotions of their children,[34] and lovers to the emotions of their partners. As Hatfield attests, not even professional therapists are immune.

Emotional contagion may explain why many couples who have been together for years begin to resemble each other more as the years go by: they have mimicked each other's expressions and mannerisms so often that their lines and wrinkles have started to match. (Recent insights into the emotions of animals suggest this might also apply to dogs and their owners.) Imitation is indeed a form of flattery: one study of married couples found that those who had grown most alike in physical appearance by their silver wedding anniversary enjoyed the greatest marital accord.[35]

Just as people vary in the extent to which they absorb moods and behaviours, so some of us are better at spreading our emotions to others. No doubt you know such people: they are charismatic, exuberant, expressive in face and posture. It is hard not to be infected by them. John F. Kennedy, Martin Luther King, Ronald Reagan and Bill Clinton fit the bill. As does Dean Moriarty, Jack Kerouac's tragic hero in *On the Road*:

> Dean's intelligence was every bit as formal and shining and complete, without the tedious intellectualness. And his 'criminality' was not something that sulked and sneered; it was a wild yea-saying overburst of American joy; it was Western, the west wind, an ode from the Plains, something new, long prophesied, long a-coming (he only stole cars for joy rides) ... Dean just raced in society, eager for bread and love; he didn't care one way or the other.[36]

Is it possible to parry the effects of contagion, to hold a shield up against other people's mood clouds? This is almost impossible if you are fully caught up in the encounter. Your best bet is probably to back off by paying less attention, staying detached or emotionally zoning out[37] – 'thinking and daydreaming in the face of horror', as Hatfield puts it rather dramatically. Or try monitoring and managing your emotional responses as you listen. The drawback is that you run the risk of appearing rude (think of the Botox effect).

On the other hand, trying to increase empathic feelings or social cohesion by consciously exaggerating your mimicking behaviour is fraught with danger. Recall how quickly we copy the movements of others. Trying to ape that can easily look phoney or plain weird. Frank Bernieri at Oregon State University has done extensive research on how synchronized movement relates to rapport, filming people as they interact during debates, conversations or interviews and then analysing the video clips.[38] He says postural mimicry is 'an automatic process, like one's blood pressure and heartbeat. I have seen no good evidence that one can control this intentionally.' He has found that it is possible to wilfully imitate someone during a conversation without them consciously noticing, but that this will not increase their affinity for you. For reasons that are not yet clear, forced mimicry does not appear to convey the same emotional messages as the real thing. Best not to try it on dates or in job interviews.

———

Emotional contagion is a variation of what social scientists call an 'information cascade', where the inclination to copy – automatically and without reflection – causes large numbers of people to think and act the same way. Information cascades can have a powerful effect on behaviour: consider the public mourning that

How susceptible are you?
The emotional contagion scale

This scale will give you an idea of how sensitive you are to the emotions of people around you. The higher your score on the fifteen questions, the more susceptible you are, and the more likely to 'catch' the moods of others.

Use the following key:

4.	*Always*	=	Always true for me.
3.	*Often*	=	Often true for me.
2.	*Rarely*	=	Rarely true for me.
1.	*Never*	=	Never true for me.

1. If someone I'm talking with begins to cry, I get teary eyed.

2. Being with a happy person picks me up when I'm feeling down.

3. When someone smiles warmly at me, I smile back and feel warm inside.

4. I get filled with sorrow when people talk about the death of their loved ones.

5. I clench my jaws and my shoulders get tight when I see the angry faces on the news.

6. When I look into the eyes of the one I love, my mind is filled with thoughts of romance.

7. It irritates me to be around angry people.

8. Watching the fearful faces of victims on the news makes me try to imagine how they might be feeling.

9. I melt when the one I love holds me close.

10. I tense when overhearing an angry quarrel.

11. Being around happy people fills my mind with happy thoughts.

12. I sense my body responding when the one I love touches me.

13. I notice myself getting tense when I'm around people who are stressed out.

14. I cry at sad movies.

15. Listening to the shrill screams of a terrified child in a dentist's waiting room makes me feel nervous.

Source: R.W. Doherty, 'The emotional contagion scale: a measure of individual differences', *Journal of Nonverbal Behavior* 21 (1997), 131–54. Reproduced with kind permission of Elaine Hatfield.

followed the death of Princess Diana, or outbreaks of collective hysteria such as the one in Shelkovsk, Chechnya, in December 2005, when dozens of pupils and teachers suffered seizures, breathing difficulties and convulsive fits that seemed to have no organic cause. Cascades shape the decisions we make every day: what music we listen to, what clothes we wear, which phones we buy, which YouTube clips we watch, which charities we support, which Facebook comments we 'like'.

More significantly, they can also influence how we vote. In countries where elections are held sequentially – such as in the American presidential primaries – or in places where voting closes in some districts before others, the knowledge that a particular candidate already has the edge over rivals can persuade people to back that candidate when, without that information, they might have gone for someone else.[39] We are easily won over: how can 95,000 voters in New Hampshire (traditionally the first primary) be wrong! Opinion polls published in the run-up to an election can have a similar effect. For this reason, the UK and Germany prohibit the release of exit poll results until polling stations have closed, and Singapore has banned exit polls altogether. France, Israel, Italy and Russia have gone even further, restricting the release of all opinion polls in the days (or in Italy's case, a full two weeks) before an election.

Cascades feed on information, but they are driven by emotion. As Duncan Watts says:

> You want to do the same thing as other people, not because you think it's better – although you may – but because what matters is doing things together. We all want to belong to a group, and identify with other people in that group. One way to do that is have a common set of cultural references and shared tastes. Liking the same songs, movies, sports, and

books not only gives us something to talk about, but makes us feel like we're part of something larger than ourselves.

Marching in step with lots of other people might feel emotionally fulfilling but it doesn't help us much if they all turn out to be wrong. The chances of that, if you think about it, are discomfortingly high, since everyone who joins in solely under the sway of social influence leaves their own independently acquired knowledge at the door. In the absence of new information, the quality of collective decision-making is bound to diminish as the group gets bigger. The sheer weight of numbers can make an information cascade look like a sure bet, yet it is often a case of the blind leading the blind.

Consider the speculative housing bubble in the US that many economists believe triggered the 2008 global financial crisis. From 1997 to 2006, home prices in the US as a whole increased by eighty-five per cent in real terms.[40] During the same period, sub-prime mortgages, which are lent to home-buyers with a poor credit history, grew from five per cent of the mortgage market to around twenty per cent.[41] Many people were buying houses thinking them a safe, long-term investment, swept along on a cascade of optimism that prices would continue to rise and that owning a home would guarantee financial security or better. In 2005, when this ebullience was still in full swing, the Yale University economist Robert Shiller and his colleague Karl Case asked home-buyers in San Francisco how much they expected their houses to increase in value. The average prediction was fourteen per cent a year, a remarkable rate of return in any financial climate. About a third of respondents had ridiculously extravagant expectations, some of them anticipating fifty per cent annual growth. 'On what did they base such outlooks?' asked Shiller. 'They had observed significant price increases and heard others' interpretation of such increases.'[42]

Throughout our evolution, humans have been vulnerable to this kind of contagious thinking, but today we are increasingly at its mercy. This is due partly to the ability of social networking tools such as Twitter, Facebook and YouTube to disseminate information – and emotions – quickly and widely, and partly because we are more exposed than ever to vivid and emotive imagery that distorts our understanding of the world (and makes it difficult for us to make sensible decisions about the risks).[43] In the year after the 9/11 terrorist attacks on the US, many Americans chose to travel by car rather than take an aeroplane, thinking they would be safer. The result was that an additional 1,600 people died in road accidents over that period, six times the number killed in the hijacked aircraft.[44] Simply watching news coverage of the anniversary of 9/11 is enough to make people think another attack is more likely, according to University of Wisconsin psychologist Corrine Enright.[45] Fear and anger trump reason every time, and graphic media throws emotional faces in front of us on a regular basis, feeding our most ancient intuitions. As author and probability specialist Nassim Nicholas Taleb has observed, 'We are not rational enough to be exposed to the press.'[46]

Without doubt, information cascades can be a force for good. They helped spur the anti-apartheid movement in South Africa, precipitated the fall of communism in Eastern Europe and have brought environmental awareness into the mainstream. But too often they are disruptive and damaging. When faced with an epidemic of compelling opinion, how should we respond? The key is to figure out whether those who are already caught up in the emotion of the moment really know what they are doing. Are they using knowledge that they already possess, or that they accessed independently? In this case they could be worth listening to. Or are they simply going with the emotional flow and following the herd as it gallops off into the sunset? If so, remember, safety in numbers does not apply here.

For many people, information cascades and contagious emotions conjure up deep-held anxieties about the madness of crowds and the mindlessness of those swept up in them. Next, we'll explore the colourful history of this fear of the mob and meet the modern-day psychologists who are striving to dismantle it and expose it for what it is: a politically convenient myth. In crowds, people behave in extraordinary ways – but they are not the ways you might have imagined.

2

Crowd Smarts

———

Joseph Priestley was about as unconventional a polymath as there has ever been. Not only did he discover oxygen, invent soda water, become one of the most famous scientists of his era and befriend the American president Thomas Jefferson, he was also a dissenting clergyman, a theologian, a philosopher, a teacher, a scholar of English grammar and a political commentator. According to his modern biographer, Robert Schofield, he was 'a leading luminary of the Enlightenment in an extraordinary variety of subjects'.[1] Yet all that counted for little on 14 July 1791, when an angry mob burned down his home in Birmingham and, ultimately, forced him to spend the last ten years of his life in exile in America.

How did it come to this? For all his achievements and influence, the British Establishment found Priestley objectionable on several counts: he rejected the divinity of Jesus, a blasphemous position;[2] he favoured the separation of church and state; he supported the colonists in the American War of Independence; and he hailed the French Revolution as a break for civil liberty, a view that quickly soured in England as people began to fear that the unrest would spill across the Channel. It seems he crossed the line when he helped organize a banquet at a Birmingham hotel to mark the second

27

anniversary of the fall of the Bastille. Scenting an opportunity, his opponents – who included an attorney, a magistrate and several members of the local clergy – organized a riot.

The mob they raised wreaked havoc for three days, beginning in the finest traditions of public disorder by throwing stones and mud at diners as they left the hotel. After learning that Priestley had stayed away, they set fire to the chapel where he presided as minister, to cries of 'church and king' and, a little confusingly, 'no popery' (Priestley was no Catholic). They advanced to his home on the edge of town. 'After supper', he later wrote, 'when I was preparing to amuse myself, as I sometimes did, with a game of backgammon, we were alarmed by some young men rapping violently at the door.'[3] Taking refuge at the house of a friend a few miles up the road, he and his wife could hear 'all that passed at [our home], every shout of the mob, and almost every stroke of the instruments they had provided for breaking the doors and the furniture'.[4]

Priestley lost forty years of personal diaries and letters, his unpublished memoirs, all his religious manuscripts, a register of his experiments in chemistry and physics, his library and his laboratory with its many scientific instruments. By the time government troops arrived from London three days later, the rioters had desecrated or burned down four dissenting chapels and the homes of twenty-seven reformist sympathizers. Priestley did not feel free or safe in England again, and within three years he had moved his family to a new home in rural Pennsylvania. He never went back.

The Priestley riots, as they became known, reinforced the popular idea that people who marched en masse could be persuaded to do anything to anybody. Since the storming of the Bastille, when a thousand-strong crowd overran the prison garrison and decapitated the governor, the urban mob had been recast in the public imagination as a political force that was either an expression of the will of the people or a demonic and fearsome animal, depending on your outlook.

It certainly terrified plenty of intellectuals. The Whig parliamentarian Edmund Burke, whose long friendship and political alignment with Priestley took a dive with the Bastille, spoke for many when he anticipated civilization being 'trodden down under the hoofs of a swinish multitude'.[5] His somewhat overwrought depiction of the agitators in Paris as 'the unutterable abominations of the furies of hell'[6] found favour several decades later with the French historian Hippolyte Taine, for whom they resembled a 'howling horde' and a 'tame elephant suddenly become wild again'.[7]

The scientific view of that era was no less kind. French criminologist Gabriel Tarde likened even the most civilized of crowds of the nineteenth century to 'a monstrous worm whose sensibility is diffuse and who still acts with disordered movements according to the dictates of its head'.[8] His Italian counterpart Scipio Sighele invoked the psychology of hypnotism to try to explain why crowds could so easily be induced to behave with common purpose. Ideas and emotions once implanted can spread like 'microbes', he suggested, and therefore all crowds must be pathological and predisposed to evil.[9]

By far the most influential of this new breed of crowd analysts was the doctor, social psychologist and all-round intellectual eccentric Gustave Le Bon. Scarred, like Taine, by his experiences during the Paris insurrection against the French government in 1871, Le Bon set out to find a scientific understanding of how people behave when they are gathered together in large numbers. He diagnosed a kind of paralysis of the brain and (like Sighele) the emergence of a special hypnotic state in which the individual becomes the slave of his unconscious impulses, inclined to follow suggestion without thinking:

He is no longer himself, but has become an automaton who has ceased to be guided by his will. Moreover, by the mere fact that he forms part of an organised crowd, a man descends several rungs in the ladder of civilisation. Isolated, he may be a cultivated individual; in a crowd, he is a barbarian ... a grain of sand amid other grains of sand, which the wind stirs up at will.[10]

Today, this is still the prevailing view of crowd behaviour among politicians, commentators and the public at large. Most of us are convinced that crowds inhabit a psychological shadowland of primordial instincts and unrestraint, where individuals are stripped of their identity and led unthinking to violent and irrational acts. 'The dominant trait of the crowd is to reduce its myriad individuals to a single, dysfunctional persona. The crowd is stupider than the averaging of its component minds', declared columnist Will Self after the UK riots in 2011.[11] The purpose of this chapter is to show how this sentiment came to prominence; and why, according to modern-day social psychologists, it is profoundly misplaced.

———

Le Bon was not the first to articulate the madness of crowds but he was first to popularize the idea. His thesis *La psychologie des foules* was reprinted twenty-five times in France in the twenty-five years following its publication, and sixteen times in English.[12] It was eventually translated into seventeen languages. This seems extraordinary when you look at how far scientifically he was out of step with his contemporaries. He believed, for example, that the size of the skull was a reliable indicator of intelligence; that because Caucasians had bigger heads than other races their brains were consequently more developed; and that women represented an inferior form of human evolution 'closer to children and savages than to an adult, civilised man'. Distinguished women did exist, he accepted, 'but they are as exceptional as the birth of any monstrosity, as, for example, of a gorilla with two heads; consequently, we may neglect them entirely'.[13]

Le Bon's prejudices and methods were criticized by his colleagues but this did not appear to damage his public reputation as an authority on mob psychology. His ideas about the primitivism and stupidity of crowds struck a chord far beyond his academic circle among a European middle class who had grown fretful about the destabilizing effect of urban riots and public demonstrations. Sigmund Freud used Le Bon's analysis as a starting-point for his own thinking on the subject, kicking off his book *Group Psychology and the Analysis of the Ego* with a discussion of Le Bon's 'deservedly famous' thesis.[14] Many public figures echoed Le Bon's fears of the herd mentality. 'Look at a crowd when it roars down a street in anger', implored the writer and politician Hilaire Belloc in 1910.[15] 'You have the impression of a beast majestic in its courage, terrible in its ferocity, but with something evil about its cruelty and determination.'[16]

It was only a matter of time before a manipulative leader tried to appropriate Le Bonian theory for his own dark ends. In the early twentieth century *La psychologie des foules* became something of a bible of totalitarianism. Lenin, Stalin, Mussolini and Hitler all embraced its concepts of hypnotic action, anonymity and the collective mind. Lenin is said to have kept a heavily marked copy on his desk; Mussolini professed high regard for it in his autobiography. What these men coveted most was advice on leadership, and they found plenty to chew on. After characterizing a crowd as 'a servile flock that is incapable of ever doing without a master',[17] Le Bon went on to suggest three tools a leader might use to persuade the masses to adopt an idea: affirmation, repetition and contagion. In other words, if you stated something clearly enough and repeated it enough times it would spread of its own accord. Add to that the charismatic, admiration-inducing quality that he called 'prestige', and the people are yours.

Fear of the atavistic mob became as deep-set in popular literature as it did in political discourse. In *A Tale of Two Cities* (1859), Charles Dickens depicts the revolutionary throng that storms the Bastille as a raging flood being sucked towards a vortex: 'With a roar that sounded as if all the breath in France had been shaped into the detested word, the living sea rose, wave on wave, depth on depth, and overflowed the city.'[18] Likewise for Jack London in *The People of the Abyss* (1903), his account of life in the east end of London, 'the miserable multitudes' thronging the grimy streets are akin to 'so many waves of a vast and malodorous sea, lapping about me and threatening to well up and over me'.[19] Elsewhere, the mob takes the form of a monster or an army of zombies. Émile Zola's coalminers striking in protest at their appalling conditions in *Germinal* (1885) are transfigured into a vengeful swarm, 'their eyes shining, their mouths open, a band of people in heat'.[20]

Such themes persisted in American fiction throughout the twentieth century: for William Faulkner, Harper Lee, John Steinbeck and the like, the lynch mob was as irrational and non-thinking as the political crowd was for Le Bon. 'I feel ... like I been walking in my sleep', exclaims the protagonist of Steinbeck's *The Vigilante* (1938) after emerging from the front line of a mob that had taken a man from jail and hung him from an elm tree. Half an hour earlier he had been fighting for his chance to pull on the rope; now 'a cold loneliness fell upon him' as he tried to come to terms with what he had done.[21]

As we shall see, social psychologists have recently done much to disprove the notion that people in crowds are dysfunctional automata. They have been working to overturn not only the popular Le Bonian understanding of crowd behaviour, but also its scientific counterpart, known as 'deindividuation theory'. This holds that individuals subsumed within crowds lose their self-awareness, become disinhibited and relinquish responsibility for their actions. In 1969, the Stanford University psychologist Philip Zimbardo claimed that deindividuation explains why people are often more aggressive when they are allowed to hide their identities (we will explore Zimbardo's controversial Stanford Prison Experiment in the next chapter).[22] Since then the theory has been used regularly to explain the unruliness of crowds, but some psychologists are not convinced. They point out, for example, that individuals in crowds are generally not anonymous to one another, only to outsiders, and that rather than lose their identities they adapt to what is going on around them.

It is important to bring these arguments into the public conversation, for the myth of mindless mobs is too often used by public figures to shore up dubious theories of social or political behaviour. For example, the American political commentator Ann Coulter has tried to shoot down the entire liberal social and economic agenda by claiming that Democrats (but not Republicans) are beholden to the groupthink and recklessness of crowds. 'The same mob mentality that leads otherwise law-abiding people to hurl rocks at cops also leads otherwise intelligent people to refuse to believe anything they haven't heard on NPR', she writes in *Demonic: How the Liberal Mob Is Endangering America*.[23] Guess who she has acknowledged as the main inspiration behind this fantastical assumption? Gustave Le Bon, no less.[24]

Stephen Reicher is one of those rare people who sound so genial and accommodating on the phone that they may as well be there in person. No surprise, perhaps, for sociality is his meat and drink. He is de facto leader of a small group of British social scientists who, over the last few decades, have been rewriting the textbook on the dynamics of crowds, reaching for a better understanding of the complex social and psychological factors involved. Their findings suggest a mechanism very different to the one established by Le Bon and his followers. Instead of mindlessness and madness, they see mostly coherence and co-operation. Instead of deindividuation, they see shifting identities. Their work is beginning to have a major influence on the way governments and police forces understand and deal with public gatherings.

Reicher's journey into crowd psychology started in 1975, in his first year as an undergraduate at Bristol University, when two important things happened. First, he came across Henri Tajfel, a pioneering social psychologist and the first to explain group behaviour in terms of social identity. Tajfel was a survivor of the Holocaust, the horror, that as Reicher says, 'hangs over all postwar social thought', and which has motivated several generations of Jewish psychologists seeking to understand how and why it happened. We will meet many of them in this book.

The second thing was Reicher's first 'crowd event', the occupation of a campus building by hundreds of students campaigning for women's access to university. This he recalls as 'an incredibly intense and educational intellectual experience', one that contradicted both what he was learning in his psychology course about the supposed irrationality of crowds, and the claim by the university's vice-chancellor that the students were an over-emotional mob who hadn't thought things through. 'That struck me really powerfully: the contrast between the reality as I experienced it, the theories I came across, and the active use of those theories to try to discredit and delegitimize a collection action.'

Five years later, while still at Bristol studying for his PhD, he got the opportunity to test out his thinking for real. On 2 April 1980 he turned on the radio to discover that a riot had broken out down the road in St Pauls, a deprived area with deepening unemployment and racial tension, exacerbated by stop and search laws that were seen as unfairly targeting the Afro-Caribbean community. The police had raided a popular local cafe on the suspicion that it had been selling alcohol without a licence. This provoked an angry demonstration, which evolved into a running battle between residents and police. Twenty-one police vehicles ended up destroyed or damaged, twenty-two officers hospitalized, one hundred and thirty people arrested and several buildings looted or burnt.

Into this walked Reicher, notebook in hand. The first thing he noticed was that far from being indiscriminate, as deindividuation theory and the traditional understanding of crowd behaviour would have predicted, the violence was highly selective, directed specifically at the police. He recalls:

I was standing there and I clearly wasn't from St Pauls, and people would come and check me out and when they discovered I wasn't a police officer they were incredibly friendly. It had this characteristic of many riots, which is that on the one hand they look dangerous, like your life is under threat, but at the same time they seem carnivalesque, and people are in many ways much more sociable than they would otherwise be.

He noted a bizarre atmosphere of normality: amid the burning cars and the flying bricks, people were walking home from work and families were out shopping and standing around chatting as if brick-throwing and car-wrecking were customary in that neighbourhood.

Reicher noticed something else. Despite the claims of a senior police officer that the violence was initiated and premeditated by 'emotional psychopaths and subversive anarchists', he found no evidence of planning or leadership. It seemed clear that the riot had started spontaneously, and that the participants considered themselves a community defined by their opposition to an oppressive police force.[25] As he commented in his published study: 'It is difficult to see how classic theories of the crowd could deal with these [characteristics]'.[26]

Three decades and dozens of demonstrations, protest marches, environmental actions, football matches and street riots later, Reicher and various colleagues have built a new model of crowd behaviour that would have Gustave Le Bon twitching in his grave. They argue that rather than surrender their rationality and self-awareness, people in crowds define themselves according to who they are with at the time – anti-war protestors, fans of a particular football club, environmental activists – and that this 'social identity' determines how the crowd behaves. Furthermore, social identities are shaped as much by the situation people are in – whether or not they feel threatened, for example – as by what they have in common.[27]

By this reckoning, it makes little sense to blame the chaos at the anti-poll tax protests in London on 31 March 1990 on thugs or opportunists who incited others to violence (though such people were undoubtedly present). The 250,000 who turned out that afternoon already shared a sense of outrage at the government's plans for a flat-rate community charge, despite being from a hugely diverse spectrum of backgrounds and interest groups, many of them previously antagonistic. They characterized what is known as a 'psychological crowd', all identifying with a common theme. When police officers tried to disperse protestors with batons, the psychology of the crowd changed. Peaceful demonstrators, who up to then had balked at confrontation, suddenly found themselves a target of what they considered indiscriminate police violence. And they began, together and perfectly rationally, to see conflict with the police as legitimate. The result was the 'Battle of Trafalgar', a riot that raged until 3 a.m. the next morning.

Reicher says this model of crowd behaviour fits every case of public disorder in the past three decades where data have been collected, from the so-called Battle of Westminster between students and police in November 1988 and the anti-M11 link road campaign of the mid-1990s to the 2009 G20 London summit protest (where a bystander, Ian Tomlinson, died after being pushed to the ground by a police officer) and the 2011 UK riots (more on them later). It also squares with the most thorough investigation of urban unrest ever conducted: the Kerner Commission report into the urban riots in Detroit, Chicago, Los Angeles and other US cities between 1965 and 1967. The Kerner report concluded that the key factor behind the unrest was widespread economic marginalization of black communities. It also noted that the typical rioter was better educated than the average in their communities, more socially integrated and less likely to have a previous criminal record.[28]

The implications of this go far beyond academic debate. If crowd violence stems from the social norms of the majority rather than the actions of the criminal few, then the traditional approach to public order policing – send in the riot squad – is likely to make things worse. In the UK and in some European countries (less so in the United States),[29] this argument is starting to sink in and police forces are leaning towards a more sensitive approach to crowd management. Much of the credit for this lies with another British psychologist, one whose academic background is anything but conventional.

———

Clifford Stott's approach to studying crowd behaviour is, by his own admission, 'very unusual'. He calls it ethnography, the field study of human culture; also 'direct participant observation'. You could call it jumping in at the deep end of a large turbulent pool. It has generally involved immersing himself in groups of football supporters – often England fans at away games – and recording what they do, feeling what they feel, drinking what they drink (beer), singing when they sing and, because these are England fans whom European police tend to regard as hooligans one and all, trying to avoid the arc of a truncheon or a night in a cell. The experience, he admits, can be 'horrific. As a researcher in the middle of a group of England fans some of whom on a personal level you would thoroughly detest, the sense of alienation and isolation is profound. Because you're studying it you can't just come out of it, but you can't fully engage with it either.' Inevitably there are physical consequences: he has been tear-gassed, baton-charged, water-cannoned, pelted with missiles, sent tumbling down steps in crowd surges and detained as a suspected hooligan.[30]

There are professional consequences too. Stott says his preference for field research rather than lab-based experimentation has led to him becoming 'incredibly marginalized' by the academic community. Many high-impact psychology journals – those whose papers are regularly cited by other academics – will not consider work that is not based on experiments, which makes it impossible for him to figure in the standard measure by which academics are judged and to exploit traditional avenues of funding. This is partly a dispute over informed consent, considered a fundamental principle of experimental research, but clearly impractical when you're studying large crowds. 'How do you stand in a stadium full of 10,000 people studying it and get informed consent? It makes no sense.'[31]

His stand-off with academia is ironic when you consider that Stott has arguably had a greater impact on public policy than just about any social psychologist alive. As it happens, he is accustomed to being outside the mainstream. He left school at sixteen with no qualifications, having felt so alienated by the school system that he set out to fail his exams. 'I was really quite a problematic child', he says. He signed up for unemployment benefit, before realizing at eighteen that he wanted to do something with his life. So he went back to college, took two A levels in a year and passed into Plymouth Polytechnic (now Plymouth University) to study psychology.

He is engaging to talk with, partly because of his eloquence, partly because he swears more than any academic I have met. 'I piss a lot of people off', he says. He doesn't laugh much. His close-cropped hair and deadpan delivery give the impression he could assimilate into any crowd. He acknowledges that the street skills he developed during his defiant youth have proved useful in his field research. This can mean 'sitting in a bar in some corner of a foreign land with a group of Manchester United hooligans, and the next day sitting in a room with the assistant commissioner of the Metropolitan Police, and pulling both interactions off'.

Stott has been present, Dictaphone in pocket, at some of the most significant episodes of football violence involving England fans in Europe, including the World Cup finals in Italy in 1990 and France in 1998. He has little doubt that most football violence is best understood in terms of broad group identities rather than the influence of a hooligan minority. At the tournaments in Italy and France, for example, the vast majority of England fans started off peaceful, but together changed their song when local police began targeting anyone wearing an England shirt. 'Even when collective conflict did occur, it was not some explosion of mindless violence', notes Stott in his book *Football Hooliganism, Policing and the War on the English Disease*.[32]

The same theoretical approach can explain why Scottish football fans rarely get into trouble despite drinking heavily. Non-violence has become part of their identity. By avoiding conflict, they help differentiate themselves from the English and even punish those within their ranks who get aggressive. As one Scottish supporter remarked during France98: 'The best way to piss the English off is to behave, and have a good laugh with the other fans as well. It makes them look bad.'[33] Because Scottish fans are renowned internationally for their adherence to non-violence, their relationship with the police is markedly different from that of English fans. Needless to say, such nuances tend to be lost on politicians and the media in Britain, who simply blamed the disturbances during France98 on 'opportunistic thugs', 'hooligan generals' and those 'beyond reason and rational appeal'.

In 2001, Stott and his collaborators, who included Dutch behavioural scientist Otto Adang, presented their research to the Portuguese Public Security Police (PSP) in the hope the PSP would take the findings on board in time for the European football championships, due to be held in Portugal for the first time in 2004.

They advised the PSP to drop the riot squad tactics used at most previous tournaments in favour of a lower-profile, firm-but-friendly approach. They stressed the importance of targeting only the instigators of trouble rather than everyone who happened to be present, and of interacting with the different fan groups to gauge how their cultural and social norms were affecting their behaviour.

Fortunately the Portuguese were receptive. They developed a training programme to ensure that all PSP officers understood the theory and how to translate it into non-confrontational policing. The result was an almost complete absence of disorder at England games during Euro2004. English hooligans seeking conflict, who were there in some numbers despite the British government's banning orders, ended up being marginalized by their own fans. Stott says the best moment of his career was when the PSP's senior commander stopped him in the street in Albufeira at the end of the tournament, patted him on the back and told him the plan had worked. 'It was like, fuck yeah, we've done it!'[34]

Today, the social identity model of crowd behaviour is the framework by which all UEFA matches in Europe are policed – though in Russia and in Eastern Europe it is still only tacitly applied. Stott is now working to take it beyond football. After the death of Ian Tomlinson at the G20 protest in 2009, Her Majesty's Inspectorate of Constabulary (HMIC), the UK's independent police inspectorate, asked him to write a report on how to apply crowd psychology to public order policing.[35] Many of his recommendations were then adopted by HMIC in its Adapting to Protest review,[36] which should herald a radical new approach to crowd control in the UK – less kettling, more communication. One outcome has been the creation of liaison units within police forces in London and elsewhere that send officers in distinctive uniforms into protest crowds to establish contact (not, as some activists suspect, to spy on them). This is a significant challenge given the police's credibility problem, though Stott says liaison officers were used successfully around fifty times during the 2012 Olympics and the plan is to use them 'at every protest in London'.[37]

Since Stott started working with the police, he has found himself alienated by a whole new set of institutions. The civil action groups that monitor police behaviour, which used to support him when he was mixing with protesters, now see him as a traitor. One of them even accused him of developing state-sanctioned mind control techniques to undermine social movements, warning of 'a new era of repression based on the relatively new "science" of crowd psychology'.[38] Another tried to have him thrown out of a meeting with the UN Special Rapporteur on human rights. He has become an outsider all over again. What this really illustrates, he says, is that questions of social identity are bound up with questions of ideology and the dynamics of power. 'This isn't just about science. It's also about democracy.'

———

As an example of how outdated, unscientific thinking still dominates the public discourse on crowds, look no further than the reaction to the riots that took place in London and other towns and cities in Britain between Saturday 6 and Tuesday 9 August 2011, the most serious episode of civil unrest in the UK for several decades. It was triggered by the death of twenty-nine-year-old Mark Duggan in Tottenham, north London, shot by police whose failure to properly inform his family what had happened led to a community-wide anti-police uprising in Tottenham and Hackney. The next day, rioting kicked off in other parts of London and then in Birmingham, Liverpool, Leeds, Nottingham, Bristol, Salford,

Manchester and elsewhere in Britain, this time aimed not so much at confrontation with police as theft and vandalism of high-street shops and shopping malls.

Afterwards, the government, opposition politicians and sections of the media skipped over thirty years of research into crowd psychology and invoked classic Le Bonian explanations, characteristic of those used to describe the Priestley riots and the French Revolution. 'Criminality, pure and simple', pronounced prime minister David Cameron.[39] 'Outrageous behaviour by the criminal classes', blustered justice secretary Kenneth Clarke.[40] Home secretary Theresa May pinned most of the violence on 'career criminals',[41] while Tottenham MP David Lammy blamed 'mindless, mindless people'.[42]

Many of these commentators assumed that a typical rioter likely had a previous criminal record, a notion that was repeated several times by the government over the following months. Yet as social psychologist John Drury and historian Roger Ball have demonstrated, this interpretation is flawed.[43] Although government statistics show that around seventy-five per cent of those arrested during the riots and brought to court had previously been cautioned or convicted, it is unlikely that this group is representative of those who took part. Amid intense government pressure to make arrests, the police, by their own admission, first rounded up those whose pictures were already in their databases and who could be identified by CCTV. 'Obviously the ones that you know are going to be arrested first', acknowledged Tim Godwin, acting commissioner of the Metropolitan Police at the time, before the House of Commons Home Affairs Committee in September 2011.[44] Around 4,960 were arrested, but the Met Police have since revealed that some 2,650 individuals captured on CCTV during the London riots will never be identified because the images are too poor or because they covered their faces.[45] Many rioters were never photographed. Another popular misconception – that the violence was orchestrated by gang members – is undermined by a Home Office report stating that only thirteen per cent of those arrested overall were affiliated to a gang,[46] and that 'where gang members were involved, they generally did not play a pivotal role'.[47]

The breakdown of social order is any government's worst-case scenario and not something for which it will rush to accept responsibility. Pointing the finger at known criminals and gangs, or a 'feral underclass', as Kenneth Clarke put it[48] – effectively pathologizing the entire episode as authorities down the ages have done – is a convenient way of disowning the problem. But it is a dangerous conceit, for it makes it difficult to explore how the disorder developed and any underlying social dynamics that contributed to it. Behind the vandalism, arson, thuggery and opportunistic looting that wrecked businesses and caused an estimated £200 million in property damage over those four days, there was legitimate long-term disaffection with which entire communities identified and which made it easy for people to join in the rioting once it had started.

A large part of that disaffection centred on the police. Many of those interviewed about their role in the disorder by both the Reading the Riots project run by the London School of Economics and the *Guardian* newspaper,[49] and the Riots Communities and Victims Panel set up by the government,[50] spoke of their dissatisfaction with the way police engaged with their communities. They were frustrated in particular at being subjected repeatedly to stop and search, a modern inevitability for black youths in inner-city districts. For these people, at least, it was an 'anti-police' riot, a chance to even the score.

Without such grievances, the riots may never have happened. 'You can have anti-police riots without looting, but you can't have looting without anti-police riots', suggest Reicher and Stott in *Mad Mobs and Englishmen*, an analysis of the psychology behind the violence.[51] There is no doubt that it evolved into more than a kick at authority. Plenty of participants admitted taking advantage of the breakdown in law and order to steal goods they could not normally afford. It was also at some level a class war: high-end stores were disproportionately targeted. The dynamics and causes seem deeply complex, but it's clear that the participants had not lost their minds; indeed they appeared empowered and full of intent. As Reicher said: 'Explaining the disorder in terms of the pathologies of those who took part – they must be either mad or bad – flies in the face of all we know about crowds and riots.'[52]

There's another reason the populist, knee-jerk response was inadequate, even irresponsible. It provoked a demand from politicians and the public for anyone involved to be disciplined with unusual severity, one to which judges and magistrates readily acquiesced. In many cases, judgment appeared to be driven less by the content of individual crimes and offenders' criminal histories as by a broad deep-rooted fear of the power of the mob. Individuals were punished not only for their personal transgressions, but also for committing them as part of a nation-wide collective, a factor that in the view of one Manchester crown court judge took them 'completely outside the usual context of criminality'.[53] The general aim was deterrence rather than justice. As a result, average sentences for those convicted in the twelve months following the riots were more than four and a half times longer than for those convicted of similar crimes in 2010 – 17.1 months compared with 3.7 months. Of those brought before the courts, 846 were children between the ages of ten and seventeen, 233 of whom were given custodial terms averaging eight months.[54] One youth court magistrate interviewed by the Reading the Riots project talked of 'the rulebook being torn up'.[55] How else to explain cases such as that of Danielle Corns, sentenced to ten months in custody for stealing two left-footed trainers, which she soon abandoned, and Ricky Gemmell, sentenced to sixteen weeks for shouting abuse at a police officer? Both had excellent character references and no previous convictions.

Many of the judges and magistrates involved in the riot proceedings made clear that punishment should take into account the public sense of outrage at the violence. Following the trial in April 2012 of Darrell Desuze, convicted of killing pensioner Richard Mannington Bowes after punching him while he tried to put out a fire, Justice Saunders remarked that 'the offence of manslaughter is always serious but this case is the more serious because it was committed within the context of widespread civil disorder'. He then argued that since the judgments passed by the courts in the immediate aftermath of the riots (and later approved by the Court of Appeal) were severe, it was important that courts in subsequent cases applied comparable sentences 'even though the initial wave of public condemnation for their behaviour may have passed'.[56] Desuze was jailed for eight years.

It is standard judicial practice to apply more severe sentences to those taking part in public disorder, partly as a deterrent against anarchy, partly in recognition of the fact that criminal behaviour is always more alarming and potentially more disruptive when conducted collectively. Did the judiciary go too far in this case? The British public appears to think so: opinion surveys suggest widespread unease with the punishments handed down to non-violent offenders, an unusual state of affairs since the public generally views criminal courts as too lenient.[57] It seems questionable to factor into sentencing the febrile public mood when this was partly stoked by politicians and media commentators peddling emotive and unscientific ideas about the craziness and inherent criminality of rioters.

The whole episode suggests that the new science of crowd psychology is at odds with the legal understanding of social behaviour. The courts almost always view collective action as a greater crime, even though in some circumstances the dynamics involved – in particular people's innate tendency to identify with and adopt the norms of those around them – could arguably be seen as a mitigating factor. On the other hand, it demonstrates the high value we place on maintaining social order, knowing how swiftly it can break down. And as Reicher points out, the notion that people can have different identities in different contexts poses profound issues for the legal system. 'How can you punish someone if the subject in the crowd is different to the subject in the dock?'[58]

Another area where the science is out-running the common understanding of crowds is the behaviour of people during emergencies. Recent research into mass disasters suggests that acts of helping and heroism are often the norm rather than the exception.

When a group of Islamic suicide terrorists exploded four bombs on London's transport system during morning rush hour on 7 July 2005, killing fifty-two and injuring more than 700, hundreds of passengers were trapped in the dark in the soot-filled underground tunnels with no way of knowing if they would be rescued, nor if further explosions were imminent. From this chaos and carnage, there emerged some remarkable stories of human co-operation. Consider these statements from three people who were there:

> I remember walking towards the stairs and at the top of
> the stairs there was a guy coming from the other direction.
> I remember him kind of gesturing; kind of politely that I

should go in front – 'you first' ... And I was struck I thought
God even in a situation like this someone has kind of got
manners really. Little thing but I remember it.[59]

I am still surprised at how calm the whole scene was. One
wonderful chap stood up and said that we didn't know if we
were getting out or not, but that we should remain calm and
keep talking to one another. The effect this had on us was
extraordinary. We all had these almost out of body conversations with our neighbouring passengers, although you could
still feel the negative feelings and see people's eyes darting
about looking for a sign that we were getting out ...[60]

I felt that we're all in the same boat together ... and then for
the feelings that I was feeling could well have been felt by
them as well 'cos I don't think any normal human being could
just calmly sat there going oh yeah this is great ... it was a
stressful situation and we were all in it together and the best
way to get out of it was to help each other ... yeah so I felt
exactly I felt quite close to the people near me.[61]

These vignettes seem surprising if you compare them with the
traditional way emergencies are reported, which makes much of
the irrational panic and unthinking individualism that supposedly
goes on. Commentators convinced of the stupidity of crowds
often point to disaster scenarios to make their case – a stampede
of pilgrims, the crush of a football crowd, the blind scramble for
the exits in a burning nightclub. But the stereotype fails when
you look at the evidence. In a crisis, people in a group are far
more likely to help one another than panic and fight to escape.
Solidarity wins out over selfishness. A group of psychologists who

interviewed survivors of the London bombings, led by John Drury at the University of Sussex, concluded that panic and disorder were rare and eclipsed by what they called 'collective resilience', an attitude of mutual helping and unity in the midst of danger.[62]

There are many documented examples of this behaviour. In 2008, Drury's team talked to survivors of eleven tragedies from the previous forty years, including the 1989 Hillsborough football stadium crush, when ninety-six Liverpool supporters died of asphyxia after being trapped in overcrowded pens, and the IRA bombing that killed six outside Harrods in London in 1983. In each case, most of Drury's interviewees recalled feeling a strong sense of togetherness during the crisis, and an inclination to help strangers.[63] Without such co-operation the casualty rates could have been far higher, says Drury. He likes to refer to crowds as 'the fourth emergency service', an attitude that he says is not shared by most police, emergency planning authorities or crowd safety professionals.[64] In Drury's view, it is wrong-headed to blame crowd disasters on the behaviour of the crowd. More often the real problem is poor organization – too many people in one place – or inadequate venue design.

The academic interpretation is approximately this: a crisis, or even a minor incident such as a train breaking down in a tunnel, creates a psychological crowd out of what was previously an aggregate of strangers. You suddenly share a common fate, and thus a common identity, with the people suffering around you, or with all those passengers you were doing your best to ignore. Your sphere of interest ramps up from the personal to the group. A survivor of the Hillsborough tragedy expressed it thus:

I think everyone would accept that one had really gone beyond the definition of identifying the person as a supporter

of football ... at this point, they're just human beings struggling, to be fair ... I don't think anyone saw Liverpool fans
and Notts Forest fans ... People stopped being supporters
of a football team and were just people.[65]

How reckless, then, was the *Sun* newspaper when four days after
Hillsborough it printed a front page story accusing drunken
Liverpool fans of attacking rescue workers, urinating on the dead
and picking the pockets of victims, giving air to the idea that the
disaster was caused by hooliganism. The allegations, which derived
from a local MP and unnamed senior police officers attempting to
apportion blame, were all subsequently proved false.[66] To this day,
the *Sun* is despised in Liverpool.

The madness of crowds is often taken as a reason to avoid them.
Yet often during emergencies it is people's disinclination to panic
that can put them at higher risk. Engineers designing evacuation
procedures used to assume that people respond immediately they
hear an alarm, smell smoke or feel their building shake. But that
is not what happens. Often the challenge is getting them to move
quickly enough.

When the hijacked planes hit the World Trade Center towers in
New York on 9/11, most of those inside prevaricated rather than
heading for the nearest exit, according to several studies on how
people responded.[67] Even those who managed to escape waited
an average of six minutes before moving to the stairs. Some hung
around for half an hour, waiting for more information, collecting
things to take with them, securing papers in drawers, changing
their shoes, going to the bathroom, finishing emails, making phone

calls or shutting down their computers. When they did leave, they walked down the stairs with little urgency and considerably more slowly than the building's safety experts had predicted.[68]

No doubt more people would have escaped from the World Trade Center had they acted more quickly. Likewise, many have died in stricken aircraft burning on the ground because they sat in their seats too long before trying to escape. The report of the official investigation into an aircraft fire at Manchester airport on 22 August 1985, when fifty-five people died, stated: 'The major question is why the passengers did not get off the aircraft sufficiently quickly.'[69] John Leach, who studies disaster psychology at the University of Oslo, has found that during serious emergencies such as fires or ferry sinkings most people tend to 'freeze' rather than think about how to save themselves. The reason, he says, is that their state of bewilderment makes it harder for them to process new information. They cannot think properly about what they should do.

Here is some advice if you're caught in an emergency and unsure what to do: move! Except that if you're in a crowd it is likely to be a bit more complicated. Once the sense of collective unity kicks in, you'll feel less disposed to going it alone and you may be unwise to do so: one of the conclusions of Drury's research is that acting individualistically in an emergency can lead to competitive and disruptive behaviour, which reduces everyone's chances of survival. On the other hand, it is clear from the 9/11 attacks, the 1993 bombing of the World Trade Center[70] and numerous aircraft accidents that large groups mill around longer than small groups before settling on an escape plan, since it takes them more time to build a consensus. So, take the bull by the horns: make it clear to those around you that you're heading for an exit and that you want them to come with you. Then hasten ye all.

How to survive a crowd emergency

You're in a crowded place when something goes wrong. Perhaps your train has broken down in a tunnel, or the building you're in starts filling with smoke, or you're on a protest march that turns violent. The following three steps, derived from psychological studies on crowd behaviour, could help save your life:

1. Remember that your natural response to an emergency is likely to be shock and bewilderment and that this can cause you to freeze. Do your best to override this: engage your brain and look for a way out.
2. Co-operate with those around you, don't compete with them. Altruistic behaviour is very common during disasters and will increase your chances of survival.
3. Rehearse an exit strategy in your head beforehand. You should do this whenever you enter an unfamiliar place or situation. You'll be far less likely to dawdle when something goes wrong if you've mentally gone through the motions.

The solidarity and altruism of crowds are rarely noted by those who report on them, yet they are increasingly recognized by psychologists and other students of behaviour. 'It is only in a crowd that man can become free of [his] fear of being touched', noted Bulgarian intellectual Elias Canetti in 1960. 'All are equal there; no distinctions count, not even that of sex. The man pressed against him is the same as himself.'[71] The warmth of feeling within crowds quickly became apparent to Reicher during his study of the St Pauls riots in Bristol in 1980. 'It wasn't like the papers say. This absolute mad mob', one of his interviewees remarked. 'Everyone was together. They were looking at each other the whole time. It was black and white and all ages and that was fantastic.'[72]

More recently, Reicher and his colleagues demonstrated that the positive experience of taking part in a large gathering – in this case the annual Magh Mela Hindu pilgrimage in northern India that attracts millions of devotees – can improve people's sense of well-being and even their physical health, an effect that lasts for weeks.[73] The Magh Mela is renowned for being crowded, noisy and unsanitary, yet none of this appears to diminish the psychological boost that derives from close social interaction.[74] This will come as little surprise to anyone who attended the London Olympics in 2012, during which even the most cynical and pessimistic of Brits found themselves caught up in a carnival of friendliness and harmony.

Positive crowd experiences are worth celebrating because so often when we unexpectedly find ourselves communing with a bunch of strangers the circumstances are hardly appetizing – rushing for a train, for example, or standing in a stationary queue outside a store. One of the aims of the New York City-based prank collective Improv Everywhere is to make shared experiences fun, which it does by causing 'scenes of chaos and joy in public places'. Since August 2001, it has staged more than a hundred impromptu street shows, including a fake U2 concert on a New York rooftop, a 'freeze scene' in which one hundred and fifty actors froze in place for five minutes in the middle of Grand Central Station, and the 'no pants subway ride' held every year one midwinter day in sixty cities around the world. Most on-lookers who witness these events become warmly conspiratorial in their astonishment, just as the organizers intend. Founder Charlie Todd says the events 'encourage people to socialize with one another to try to figure out what the hell just happened'.[75]

Occasionally, the solidarity of crowds can change the course of history. Take the Egyptian revolution of 2011. The dynamics of this uprising – what triggered it, how it was organized, who led it – have been much debated, with little agreement, but the background is well known. Despite years of oppression and a long list of economic, social and political grievances, Egypt's protest movement had had little success in persuading the masses to join its calls for reform. Everything changed on 6 June 2010, when twenty-eight-year-old Khaled Said was beaten to death by police officers in Alexandria, which led to the 'We Are All Khaled Said' Facebook movement and a nationwide outcry over the brutality of the state. Seven months later, the government eroded any legitimacy it had left by so blatantly rigging the parliamentary elections that the Muslim Brotherhood, the largest opposition group (then and now), 'lost' eighty-seven of the eighty-eight seats they had won in the 2005 elections.

Despite this, the Egyptian revolution would likely never have happened – at least, at the time it did – if Tunisia's protest movement hadn't ousted president Zine El Abidine Ben Ali on 14 January 2011, after a month of social and political unrest. 'It's impossible to over-state the impact of the Tunisian model', writes Cairo-based journalist Ashraf Khalil in his revolution chronicle *Liberation Square*. 'Simply seeing that it could be done – that a sustained public and peaceful mass movement could force out an entrenched dictator – changed everyone's perceptions instantly. After that, all bets were off.'[76]

Egypt's response to the Tunisian upheaval began with a day of mass protest on Tuesday, 25 January 2011, the traditional Police Day holiday. Basem Fathy, one of the youth activists who helped co-ordinate the demonstrations in Cairo, says they expected a few hundred protestors to show up, a thousand at most. 'Instead I found thousands and thousands of people in the streets, and most of them had never been involved in politics before. Nobody expected this.'

Fathy takes satisfaction in having proved so wrong the many domestic and foreign analysts (among them writers for the *Economist*, the BBC, *Time* and *Foreign Policy*) who argued that such a thing could never happen in Egypt. And he is keen to deflate the idea, also embraced by the foreign press, that the revolution was driven by social media. 'You cannot describe this as a Facebook revolution', he says. 'The people who were fighting the police on the front lines in Tahrir Square, I don't believe any of them had Facebook accounts.'

While Facebook and Twitter were used to great effect, in particular to help motivate Egypt's young middle class, they were not as ubiquitous as many reports made out. A survey of 1,200 Egyptians who took part reveals that only fifty-two per cent had Facebook accounts and sixteen per cent used Twitter. Almost half of those questioned said they learned about the protests through face-to-face contact with a friend, acquaintance or relative. Only twenty-eight per cent got their information through Facebook, and less than one per cent through Twitter (though five per cent used Twitter to pass on news from the street).[77] The march that reached Tahrir Square on 25 January, which began in the alleyways of the working-class neighbourhood of Bulaq al-Dakrour in western Cairo, was organized not via tweets or Facebook updates but by paper flyers distributed in the streets.[78]

After three days, with the crowds in Tahrir swelling by the hour, the government cut access to the Internet and then to mobile phone networks in the hope that this would make it impossible for protestors to co-ordinate. Instead it inspired some innovative tactics. Satellite TV channels began broadcasting news to radio, enabling drivers listening in their cars to pass it on to demonstrators. Abdallah Hendawy, a youth activist in Alexandria, described how he helped organize rallies by writing protest plans on banknotes and circulating them in stores and on buses. Meanwhile Cairo reverted to 'a surreal word-of-mouth storyteller society', writes Khalil in *Liberation Square*. 'If you were walking on the street and you saw protestors coming in the other direction, you asked them where they were coming from and what the situation was like there. It was intimate and even pleasant.'[79] The intimacy remained right up until Hosni Mubarak resigned the presidency on 11 February.

Social revolutions, like complex life forms, have multi-layered evolutionary histories that resist tidy explanations. The sociologist Duncan Watts compares their dynamics to those of chaotic systems in which the smallest fluctuations can lead to unfathomable changes. The problem with this butterfly effect, he notes, is that 'by the time we notice the gathering storm, the butterfly itself has vanished in the mists of history'.[80] Yet watching them as they develop can teach us a great deal about the nuances of human behaviour, and about how our identity and our state of mind are tied to those around us.

After the violence and the loss of life in the early days of the Egyptian revolution, most of those who remained in Tahrir Square had the time of their lives. They felt something in the crowd they had rarely or never felt before. 'The revolution was the greatest event I will live through in my life', science journalist Mohammed Yahia tells me, a refrain I have heard many times. 'It was a piece of paradise', says Fathy. 'No one thought whether you were Christian or Muslim, poor or rich'. The journalist Ursula Lindsey remembers it like this:

Once you saw that crowd, you just felt the tide was on your side. You felt so right. It made people feel fantastic. People were high on it, seeing they were part of such a big group. It was an endless, mind-opening, affirming experience. You saw the evaporation of fear, this elation, because so many people were with you. Those eighteen days brought out the best in people. People gave the best versions of themselves.

Fig. 2 Tahrir Square, Cairo, 11 February 2011,
the day President Mubarak resigned.

The view that we adapt our identities in crowds rather than abandon them – that we can even 'give the best versions of ourselves' – contradicts the popular belief that crowds are mad and dangerous, akin to Gabriel Tarde's 'monstrous worm'. But it has science on its side: from the altruism of disaster victims to the solidarity of revolutionaries, the evidence for the sanity of crowds is overwhelming. The French Revolution notwithstanding, crowds can be as much a driver of positive change as a threat to the social order. Over the last quarter-century they have forced the abandonment of unfair tax regimes, thwarted the destruction of cherished natural environments, ousted dictators and brought about political and economic change across entire regions. They evoke, says Reicher, 'the ever imminent possibility of resistance. Crowds can do awful things, but they are the way the powerless have a voice. They are the way change happens.'

Yet the identities and behaviours that people adopt in crowds are transitory and short-lived. Like desert flowers, they bloom only under specific conditions. According to numerous reports, Tahrir Square was remarkably free of sexual harassment during the revolution, usually a constant threat in public places in Egypt. 'Gender barriers were suspended and that was very liberating', says Lindsey. 'Women felt comfortable and free.' But this changed right after Mubarak resigned, when many people joined the throng for the first time; the feeling of unity dissolved and old behavioural norms re-emerged. Women were no longer safe in the crowd.

The deeper you look into the relationship between individual behaviour and the social environment, the more it confounds our usual expectations about human nature. For example, one of the key questions for social psychologists is how people who are neither psychopathic nor mentally disturbed come to commit atrocities simply by allowing themselves to conform to what is going on around them. It turns out that even at the moral extremes, group forces play a critical role.

3

Breaking Bad

'Nothing is easier than to denounce the evildoer; nothing more difficult than to understand him.' Dostoevsky's observation never rang more true than during the showcase trial of Nazi war criminal Adolf Eichmann in 1961, held in a converted theatre in Jerusalem. Here was the embodiment of Nazi brutality: the man who co-ordinated the transportation of hundreds of thousands of Jews to the death camps in Eastern Europe and the Soviet Union during the Second World War, who did more than anyone to help implement Hitler's Final Solution. The hundreds present at the trial and the millions watching on television strained to see the evil in the face of this balding, thin-necked bureaucrat in his bulletproof glass booth. 'We have all stared; from time to time we stare again', wrote Martha Gellhorn, reporting for the *Atlantic Monthly*. 'We are trying, in vain, to answer the same question: how is it possible? … What goes on inside him? Who is he; who on God's earth is he?'[1]

People seeking some kind of revelation about the nature of evil will not find it in Eichmann's face. In the video recordings of his testimony he looks impassive, often dispassionate, always organized. He polishes his thick-rimmed glasses, attends to the books

Fig. 3
Adolf Eichmann.

and personal effects on the small table in front of him. He flicks away dust with his handkerchief like a waiter chasing crumbs. Occasionally he runs his tongue around the inside of his mouth, appears to chew his lower lip. The affectations of a mass murderer? Of a common man?

It would be reassuring if we could point to the non-human-ness in the Eichmanns of the world, the monstrousness that marks them out. During the trial, the chief prosecutor, Gideon Hausner, did his best to portray the Nazi lieutenant colonel as a perverted sadist. 'He was born human, but he lived like a beast in the jungle!' But Eichmann's normality was the elephant in the courtroom. The Reverend William Lovell Hull, who served as his spiritual counsellor throughout the trial and witnessed his execution, described him as a 'very ordinary, normal man; that is the mystery of him'.[2] Avner Less, the police officer who interrogated Eichmann for eight months after his capture in Argentina by Israeli agents, remarked on how 'utterly ordinary' he seemed.[3]

The historian David Cesarani put it directly: 'As much as we may want Eichmann to be a psychotic individual and thus unlike us, he was not.' Cesarani points to Eichmann's normal upbringing, his education, his social life, his very conventionality. There was no turn towards brutal anti-Semitism in his youth. The truth, he says, is that 'Eichmann was not "hard-wired" to become an accomplice to atrocities. The key to understanding Adolf Eichmann lies not in the man, but in the ideas that possessed him, the society in which they flowed freely, the political system that purveyed them, and the circumstances that made them acceptable.'[4]

People who do evil things are often considered psychopathic or disturbed, yet this is rarely the case. Eichmann's psychological profile showed no signs of sadism, bigotry or depravity. A group of psychologists who examined his Rorschach record, a test of personality and emotional functioning in which subjects are asked what they see in a series of inkblots, found a socially distant, intellectually pretentious person and no psychopathology.[5] Others found him 'far less psychiatrically disturbed and closer to normal than almost everybody would have thought'.[6]

How does that fit with Eichmann's own assessment of his actions? While he did not deny that the Holocaust happened nor his role in it, he presented himself as a 'little cog', a powerless 'carrier out of orders'. He was merely doing his duty, he said; if he was guilty of anything it was failing to question his superiors. This was probably a ruse, for it was clear from his testimony that he was fully aware of the consequences of his actions, for example that most of the 437,000 Hungarian Jews he deported to Auschwitz would be gassed. Despite this he went right ahead, with considerable enthusiasm and resourcefulness.

The German political theorist Hannah Arendt called the mystery of Eichmann's motivation 'the greatest moral and even legal challenge of the whole case'. How could someone who started off so normal end up orchestrating such horror? Eichmann's testimony was, for Arendt, proof of the 'banality of evil'. Many of the grossest crimes, she argued, are committed unthinkingly and without reflection by people who are not innately bad but who willingly surrender their moral judgement to the situation in which they find themselves. They give themselves up to clichés and trite opinions. 'This new type of criminal ... commits his crimes under circumstances that make it well-nigh impossible for him to know or to feel that he is doing wrong.'[7]

Arendt's conclusions remain controversial. Her critics claim that her theory does not tally with the evidence heard by the court, or with biographical material unearthed recently, which show that Eichmann, like most of the Nazi killers, carried out his orders with creativity, even zeal, and that he was proud of his genocidal achievements. When charged with carrying out the Final Solution, he 'bent to his fresh task with all the managerial skills at his disposal', asserts Cesarani. 'He was educated to genocide and chose to put what he learned into operation.'[8]

The debate over Arendt's thesis has centred largely on what others have supposed she meant, rather than on what she actually said. The phrase 'the banality of evil' came to stand for the idea – still prevalent among some social psychologists, historians and philosophers – that there is an Eichmann in each of us, that given the right conditions we will all fall to evil. Arendt insisted this was a misunderstanding, and that by 'banal' she did not mean commonplace. The notion that Eichmann exists in everybody would be as untrue as its opposite, that he exists in no one, she said.[9] In a lecture given two years after Eichmann was hanged, Arendt stressed that being an unthinking cog in a machine makes people no less responsible for their actions, and that the proper question to ask is not why you obey the machine, as a child or a slave might obey it, but why you *support* it.[10]

———

As the trial of Adolf Eichmann was wrapping up in Jerusalem in August 1961, the young American social psychologist Stanley Milgram began a series of now-infamous experiments at Yale University in New Haven to test how far ordinary people would go when asked by an authority figure to inflict pain on others. Most people, he discovered, would go all the way. The timing of the study was no coincidence. Milgram was the son of Jewish immigrants from Eastern Europe. As a child growing up in the Bronx, he had been acutely aware of the suffering of his fellow Jews under Hitler, who came to power the year he was born. At his bar mitzvah, when he was thirteen, he made a short speech in which he hoped for 'a new era for the Jewish people … May there be an end to persecution, suffering and war.'[11] He was deeply aware of the debate over Eichmann's trial and he hoped his experiments might give 'scientific expression' to his postwar generation's concerns about the power of authority.[12] He was not alone in this: understanding how people are led to act immorally, despite their best intentions, became a particular priority for many Jewish academics after the atrocities of the Second World War. Yet Milgram was about to stir things up in a way he could not have imagined.

His aim was to understand how and when ordinary people submit to or defy authority in the face of a clear moral imperative. However, the volunteers who took part in the initial set-up – men who had all been recruited through an advertisement in the local newspaper – believed they were helping to test the effect of punishment on learning and memory.[13] It was a beautifully orchestrated if ethically dubious sleight-of-hand. The recruit arrived at the lab where he was greeted by the experimenter – an actor dressed in a grey lab coat – who assigned him the role of 'teacher'. He introduced him to the 'learner', another actor, who sat strapped into a chair with an electrode attached to his wrist. The experimenter then led the teacher into another room and placed him before an impressive-looking shock generator machine with a row of thirty switches ranging from 15 to 450 volts in 15-volt steps. The teacher's task was to read a series of word pairs to the learner through the intercom – 'blue box; nice day; wild duck', for example – ask him to recall the associations, and administer a shock each time he gave a wrong answer, starting at 15 volts and increasing with every subsequent error.

In the most famous version of the experiment, the learner would start grunting when the shocks reached 75 volts, which suggested to the teacher that he was in pain. At 120 volts he would shout out, at 135 he would groan, at 150 he would demand the experiment be stopped, and at 270 he would respond to every flick of the switch with agonized screams. Finally, at 330 volts, he would fall silent, apparently incapacitated. In reality, the learner never received any shocks – his complaints were merely a ruse to test the teacher's resolve in sticking to the experimenter's demands that he carry on.[14]

The results astonished Milgram. 62.5 per cent of the volunteers continued dispensing shocks right up to the maximum voltage.[15] They ignored the victim's grunts, groans, complaints, shouts and screams and they ignored their own obvious moral conflict about what they were doing. Milgram recalled one man progressing through the test at a slow, steady pace with a 'sad, dejected expression' on his face. Another broke into fits of giggles as he racked up the voltage, later explaining this as 'a sheer reaction to a totally impossible situation ... being totally helpless and caught up in a set of circumstances where I just couldn't deviate and I couldn't try to help'. Many carried on even after the learner appeared to lose consciousness; very few dropped out once they had hit 330 volts. 'Good God, he's dead; well, here we go, we'll finish him', was how one of the recruits remembered thinking at the time. 'I just continued all the way through to 450 volts ... I figured: well, this is an experiment, and Yale knows what's going on, and if they think it's all right, well, it's all right with me.'[16]

The ingenuity of Milgram's obedience study lay not so much in the stark baseline statistics described above, which made international headlines when they were first published, but in the forty or so variations that he conducted to tease out the nuances of people's tendency to conform. For example, he found that the volunteers were more likely to administer high voltages if the learner was out of earshot as well as sight, and less likely if learner and teacher were put in the same room, or if the teacher was obliged forcibly to hold the learner's hand onto a shock plate while he flicked the switches – though remarkably, in this condition, thirty per cent found the stomach to apply the full 450 volts.

Milgram tried every permutation he could think of. He switched the experiment to the basement of his Yale lab to see if less salubrious surroundings would encourage more disobedience. They didn't. He used a range of actors for the roles of experimenter and learner to test whether the participants would respond differently to different personalities. Again, no effect. He removed the experimenter from the lab and had him give instructions remotely by telephone – this made a dramatic difference, reducing the number of fully obedient subjects threefold. He tried recruiting women as subjects instead of men, finding they were equally acquiescent, in spite of agonizing more about what they were being asked to do. He changed the institutional context by relocating the lab to the nearby industrial city of Bridgeport to remove any sense of awe or authority that an Ivy League university might impart. This reduced the proportion of fully compliant subjects by about half. He replaced the official-looking experimenter with an apparently ordinary man directed to act on his behalf. Most participants found it easier to disobey him and dropped out early. Worth noting is that in each variation, most of those who refused to see the experiment through quit at the critical stage when the victim first asked them to stop, usually at 150 volts.

What Milgram demonstrated above all was the extent to which people's behaviour depends on context. He was concerned with how we respond to authority, but in two of his less well-known variants he explored the power of peer pressure. In the first of these, the volunteer was joined by two other teachers, both of whom, unbeknown to him, were confederates of the experimenter. The three were told to work together in instructing and punishing the learner. But when the machine ticked up to 150 volts, one of the confederates refused to carry on. A few steps later, the other dropped out too, leaving the volunteer alone to apply the punishment. In this version, 62.5 per cent dropped out at the same time as the second confederate, or earlier, and only 10 per cent carried on to the full

450 volts. Here was evidence that it becomes less daunting to defy authority when your peers do it too.

Unfortunately for society, Milgram found that it also works the other way round. In a further experiment, Milgram gave the task of operating the machine to someone else, leaving the volunteer with a more bureaucratic role, one step removed from the action – the equivalent, he insinuated, of shuffling transportation papers or loading ammunition for the firing squad. In this case, more than ninety per cent of volunteers stayed the course, collaborating right up to the maximum voltage.[17] Being an accessory to violence is easier on the conscience than pulling the trigger.

Some have tried to dismiss Milgram's results as peculiar to their era, a time when people were less attuned to the deleterious effects of authoritative systems. But while modern ethical rules make it almost impossible to repeat his study precisely, various approximations have been carried out over the past five decades, and most of them have yielded similar results.[18] Only one offered a different view: an experiment conducted on Australian women in 1974 in which eighty-four per cent of the subjects refused to obey their orders. Tempting though it may be to interpret this as a comment on the obstinacy of the Aussie female, the researchers believe it reflected the anti-authoritarian Zeitgeist prevalent on college campuses at the time, and – since the victim in this version was also a woman – an inclination for women to identify with other women and gang up against an authoritarian male experimenter.[19]

Milgram himself found the results of his obedience experiments 'terrifying and depressing'. He claimed that they demonstrated the human tendency to surrender moral responsibility to the whim of large, bellowing institutions. 'I once wondered whether in all of the United States a vicious government could find enough moral imbeciles to meet the personnel requirements of a national system of death camps, of the sort that were maintained in Germany. I am now beginning to think that the full complement could be recruited in New Haven', he fretted to a colleague.[20] He aligned himself with Hannah Arendt, remarking that her concept of the banality of evil came 'closer to the truth than one might dare imagine'.[21]

Arendt, for her part, did not engage in the discussion of Milgram's study, fearing that his findings reinforced the erroneous idea of an 'Eichmann in everyone'. She did not believe that obedience alone could explain the heinous crimes of Nazi Germany, nor other campaigns of terror. What Milgram showed, however, was that ordinary people are capable of extraordinary cruelty, and that certain conditions make it much more likely they will succumb.

———

Milgram was not the first postwar scientist to highlight the transforming effect of social pressures on judgement and behaviour. His experiments were strongly inspired by his PhD supervisor at Harvard, the pioneering psychologist Solomon Asch, who caused a sensation in the 1950s when he demonstrated that people will often adopt the view of the majority even when it is patently wrong. Asch's research set-up was as novel as Milgram's and, for his subjects, just as disconcerting.

The volunteer turned up at the lab and was asked to sit with six to eight other people, all of whom were Asch's associates. The experimenter then placed two large white cards before the group. One of the cards showed a single vertical black line; the other had three vertical lines of various lengths, one of them identical to the line on the first card. The participants were asked in turn to identify the line that matched.

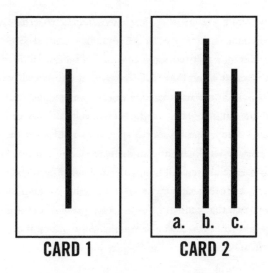

Fig. 4 Solomon Asch's line experiment.

For the first couple of rounds, the answers were straightforward and predictable: the task seemed as mundane as it looked. However, in twelve of the remaining sixteen rounds, the associates deliberately called out wrong answers, choosing lines that were clearly shorter or longer than the reference line. What Asch wanted to know was how the volunteers would respond in those twelve rounds – would they continue to trust the evidence of their own eyes or would they conform to the (incorrect) majority opinion. Although the task was extremely easy, seventy-six per cent of the volunteers conformed at least once, and only a quarter of them answered correctly every time. On average, about a third succumbed to persuasion on each round.[22]

Asch worried deeply about the social implications of what he had observed. 'That reasonably intelligent and well-meaning young people are willing to call white black is a matter of concern. It raises questions about our ways of education and about the values that guide our conduct', he wrote.[23]

A few years later, Read Tuddenham, a psychologist at the University of California, carried out a similar conformity test on students, asking them to judge the veracity of various highly improbable statements about life in America. The outcome was just as disquieting. When the students took the test in isolation, their responses were sensible enough, but when Tuddenham tricked them into believing that those who had gone before them had answered the questions in a certain way, they simply followed what others had done. Even more bizarrely, they reported that they had relied solely on their own judgement, when it was clear they had put all reason aside. They ended up agreeing, for example, that sixty to seventy per cent of Americans were over age sixty-five; that male babies had a life expectancy of twenty-five years; that men were on average eight to nine inches taller than women; that most Americans ate six meals a day and slept only four to five hours a night; that the distance between San Francisco and New York City was six thousand miles; and that most people would be better off in life if they never went to school.[24]

Most people are convinced that they can resist peer pressure. But remaining independent in the face of a majority is a great deal harder than you might think. There are often good reasons to conform. Standing alone can invite ridicule or ostracism, something all of us are keen to avoid. Better to swallow your convictions than be laughed at or cold-shouldered. Moreover, as we saw in the first chapter, the views of others can carry disproportionate weight, since we tend to assume they know things that we don't – to the extent that we trust their eyesight, or their general knowledge, over our own. It would be strange if we *weren't* pulled by the majority, to some extent, even when most of those around us are behaving like a bunch of idiots.

Thankfully, there is a grand exception to this rule. Like his student Milgram, Asch conducted variations on his line experiment in order to understand better the social factors behind our conformity. In one of these he introduced a 'truthful partner' into the group – someone who was also in the dark about the real nature of the experiment, or a researcher who had been instructed to answer correctly rather than incorrectly. This had a substantial effect, reducing the number of mistakes by three-quarters. It seems it takes only two to form a dissenting alliance. What's more, Asch found that the volunteer made fewer errors even when the partner was primed to give an answer that was flagrantly wrong, so long as it differed from the majority's. This suggests that *any* kind of dissent encourages people to think more independently.[25]

Asch's line studies have been replicated many times over the past half-century with considerable deviation in the results, leading some academics to argue that group-driven compliance is strongly dependent on cultural and historical context. In 1996, two social scientists at the University of Sussex conducted a meta-analysis of 133 Asch-type studies carried out in seventeen countries.[26] First, they found that people in so-called collectivist cultures such as Japan, China and Brazil, where family and social goals are considered more important than personal ambitions and the need to fit in is paramount, tend to fall in with the majority more than those in individualistic cultures prevalent in Europe and the US. Second, they concluded that levels of conformity had decreased since the 1950s, at least in the US. This could be because today's university students (who are usually the guinea pigs in human psychology experiments) are more inclined to question the status quo and think independently than those studying in the corseted climate after the Second World War.[27]

In that postwar era, the study of conformity and obedience was behavioural science's undomesticated frontier-land. Experimenters grappled with fundamental questions of human nature in ways that had never been tried and could never be repeated today. One of the few torch-bearers of that time who is still working is Stanford University psychologist Philip Zimbardo, a class-mate of Milgram's at James Monroe High School in the Bronx.[28] Milgram, who died in December 1984 at the age of fifty-one, was the smartest in their class, says Zimbardo, though he claims that he himself was the most popular. 'Stanley later told me, when we met ten years later at Yale University, that he wished he had been the most popular, and I confided that I wished I had been the smartest.'[29]

Zimbardo is undeniably popular, especially among students of psychology. At the Association for Psychological Science's annual convention in New York in May 2006, I watched a thousand people cram into an auditorium to hear him talk about why apparently good people turn evil, his academic calling for some four decades. Afterwards, the younger half of the audience surged towards the stage, many of them to seek his autograph. 'You are watching the Mick Jagger of psychology', murmured the man next to me. Zimbardo's charisma is also evident from the reviews of him on RateMyProfessors, a website for American college students, where he is described as 'inspirational', an 'awesome teacher' and 'a showman'. Some students felt he was 'full of himself', and one even noted that he 'look[ed] like the devil' – a comment that Zimbardo would no doubt have enjoyed given the subject of his 2008 book *The Lucifer Effect*, and given the substance of his recent work: how to promote moral heroism as an antidote to evil, to help people recognize 'the bright white line of goodness'.

Over the course of his career, Zimbardo has thought a great deal about evil. The study that made his name, the Stanford Prison Experiment, remains the most notorious exploration of institutionalized badness ever conducted in a lab. His aim was to investigate the social dynamics of prison life and the effect that being a prisoner or a prison guard would have on a person's psychology. But instead of studying a real prison, which would have been a logistical challenge, he decided to build a replica in the basement of Stanford's psychology building. It was the summer of 1971, the year the *New York Times* started publishing the Pentagon Papers on the US government's conduct of the Vietnam War. Institutional authority was under the spotlight as never before.

Zimbardo and his team recruited twenty-four male university students, all of them physically and psychologically fit. They conducted personality tests on them and then randomly assigned twelve as prisoners and the other twelve as guards. They did their best to make the fake prison feel authentic: the guards sported full uniform, mirrored sunglasses and batons, and were instructed to control the prisoners and make them feel as powerless as possible. The prisoners in turn wore uncomfortable smocks and stocking-caps, and a heavy chain around one ankle. They were confined to their cells day and night and addressed only by their ID numbers.[30]

The experiment was meant to last two weeks, but Zimbardo had to call it off after six days. The basement lab had become, as he put it, 'a hellhole'. 'In less than a week, the experience of imprisonment undid (temporarily) a lifetime of learning; human values were suspended, self-concepts were challenged, and the ugliest, most base, pathological side of human nature surfaced.'[31] Confronted with this authoritarian environment, the students assumed their respective roles with startling conviction. A third of the guards became tyrannical, finding ever more sadistic ways to dehumanize and humiliate their charges: depriving them of sleep, confining them to solitary, chaining them together on toilet runs, forcing them to simulate sodomy on each other. The prisoners responded either with blind obedience – they turned into 'servile, dehumanized robots'[32] – or with deepening confusion, hysteria and depression. Three of them were so traumatized that they had to be let out before the experiment was four days old.

Afterwards, everyone involved seemed astonished at how they had behaved. 'I was dismayed that I could act in a manner so absolutely unaccustomed to anything I would really dream of doing', recalled one of the volunteer guards two months later. 'And while I was doing it I didn't feel any regret, I didn't feel any guilt. It was only afterwards when I began to reflect on what I had done that … I realized this was a part of me I hadn't really noticed before.'[33] Even Zimbardo, who took the role of the prison's superintendent, morphed into character, parading around with his hands clasped behind his back and adopting traits he usually abhorred. He later apologized for the suffering the study caused and for not pulling the plug earlier – he did so only after Christina Maslach, a graduate student he was then dating (they would later marry), became horrified at what she saw and confronted him.[34]

Zimbardo extended our understanding of conformity beyond Asch's line experiments and Milgram's shock machine. Here was an institution – albeit an artificial and unusually sadistic one – that transformed everyone caught up in its reach beyond what they would have expected. The participants became characters they didn't recognize, and there seemed to be no predicting from their personalities how strongly their moral compass would be deflected. 'Good' people became sadistic, 'balanced' people became pathologically withdrawn, and the most abusive guards were on average no more Machiavellian than the least. 'Most of us can undergo significant character transformations when we are caught up in the crucible of social forces', writes Zimbardo in *The Lucifer Effect*. 'What we imagine we would do when we are outside that crucible may bear little resemblance to who we become and what we are capable of doing once we are inside its network.'[35]

Thirty-three years later, the Stanford Prison Experiment became news once again. On 28 April 2004, Zimbardo was flicking through TV channels in a hotel room in Washington DC when he stopped at a channel showing a photograph of grinning American soldiers posing beside a pyramid of naked Iraqi prisoners. He found himself watching a slideshow of perversity: a female soldier leading a naked prisoner via a leash around his neck; prisoners being forced to masturbate or simulate oral sex; a hooded man with electrodes attached to his fingers standing precariously on a box. He had stumbled on CBS's breaking news report about the conditions at Iraq's Abu Ghraib prison.[36] The images triggered a 'shock of recognition' in Zimbardo. 'It was as though the worst-case scenario of our prison experiment had been carried out over months under horrendous conditions, instead of in our brief, relatively benign simulated prison.'[37]

The scandal led to the court-martial of eleven US military police personnel for physical, sexual and psychological abuse of Iraqi inmates. Zimbardo was appointed as an expert witness on the defence team of one of the accused, Staff Sergeant Ivan 'Chip' Frederick, who was in charge of the night shift when many of the abuses took place and was allegedly an enthusiastic participant. In preparing his testimony, Zimbardo conducted several long interviews with Frederick, as well as extensive psychological tests. He found no hint of mental pathology or sadistic tendencies. 'In many ways this soldier was an American icon: a good husband, father and worker, patriotic, religious, with many friends and a history of having lived a most normal, moral small town life.'[38] He argued that it would be wrong to judge Frederick's actions without considering the situational powers in play: the lack of proper oversight by or intervention from superiors; the highly stressful and often frightening working conditions; an escalating culture of moral depravity; and a power structure that encouraged the dehumanization of the prisoners.

Zimbardo's assessment made little impression on the military judge at the trial. Though Frederick pleaded guilty, he was sentenced to eight years in prison on charges of conspiracy, dereliction of duty, maltreatment of detainees, assault and indecent acts, one of the longest sentences meted out (he was released on parole after three years). It was a reminder that psychologists have much to do to persuade judges and others that social processes play an important role in the production of evil.

Abu Ghraib is an especially disorienting case when viewed in the light of research by Yale University psychologist Irving Janis forty years previously. In 1963, Janis demonstrated that members of a cohesive military unit can quite easily adopt collective codes of delinquent conduct such as looting, rape or torture when they feel resentful towards the higher-level leadership, or have no effective means of communicating their grievances.[39] There is little hope that such arguments would ever amount to a successful defence. 'Our society tends to focus on individual psychology', says Zimbardo. 'All our institutions – in war, law, religion, medicine – are based on this concept.'[40]

Decades of experimental behavioural research has taught us that individual psychology is unlikely to account for most of the world's atrocities. In 2003, an ambitious analysis of 25,000 social psychology studies, stretching back to the start of the discipline a hundred years ago and involving some eight million subjects, found that social context consistently plays a major role in shaping behaviours and attitudes.[41] How do these effects play out in the real world? For the rest of this chapter, we'll consider the group and cultural forces behind one particular example of institutionalized horror, perhaps the most lethal and certainly the most confounding of all instruments of terror: suicide terrorism.

———

The Israeli settlement of Karnei Shomron in the West Bank is one of the most contentious places on earth to live. Built in 1977 on occupied Palestinian territory, it is considered illegal – along with all other Israeli settlements – by every government except Israel's. Most of the time it doesn't feel that way to those who live there: the streets are lined with date palms, eucalyptus and neatly trimmed hedges, the white-washed homes overlook limestone hills, and the community is so closely bound that many people leave their doors unlocked. But sometimes the precarious reality of their situation comes knocking.

In October 2002, two years into the violent second Palestinian intifada against the Israeli occupation,[42] I travelled through the northern West Bank to Karnei Shomron, to meet a woman whose life had been derailed by these politics in the worst way imaginable. Eight months earlier, Ginette Thaler's sixteen-year-old daughter Rachel had been blown up by a Palestinian suicide bomber in the pizzeria in the settlement's open-air shopping mall. She died in hospital eleven days later without regaining consciousness. Ginette's fourteen-year-old son Leor, who had been standing close to his sister, was gravely injured: nails in his throat, shrapnel in his stomach and leg, a damaged gall bladder and perforated eardrum. His best friend Nehemia, and Keren, a friend of Rachel, were killed too. The bomber was eighteen years old.

We met in the pizzeria where it happened, Ginette's idea. To anyone other than her it looked like just another fast-food joint with its plastic tables and unremarkable decor. Ginette was cheery and talkative, a natural smiler. The mall was quiet, the day bright and warm and children were sitting on the bar-stools sucking on colourful ice creams. Then the TV flashed up news of another suicide bombing in Ariel, a settlement ten miles to the south-east, and I caught Ginette's sharp intake of breath.

She suggested we drove to the other side of the settlement to see Rachel's friend Hanni, who was hurt in the blast and remembers everything. Ten minutes later, we were sat around the dining-room table in Hanni's home, contemplating a huge vase of fantastically coloured lilies, like something from a magician's hat. A few months ago, Hanni was in intensive care up to her eyes in bandages, but now she looked unblemished. She talked easily. She described the bomber. His light-coloured skin. How he had come up the steps into the pizzeria and stood before their table. How he had stared at them, and Rachel had laughed. 'Then he ran into the middle of the restaurant and I thought he was going to the bathroom.' Ginette asked where all the children were sitting, so Hanni found some paper and a pencil and drew a plan of the pizzeria and the tables as they were arranged that day. She drew a line to show where the bomber came in, where he stopped next to them, his final dash. Then she said something Ginette didn't know: 'Rachel was screaming. Just for a second. Then it was quiet. It was so quiet it was freaky.'

Later, in her home, Ginette showed me a picture of Rachel taken a few days before she died: cropped boyish hair, red T-shirt, sharing a joke with a friend. I asked her about the bomber, whose name was Sadek Abdel Hafeth: what she knew about his family, whether she ever thought about his mother. She said: 'This is the mother of a kid who finds a way of coming into our town, standing by a group of kids, then blowing himself up. As a mother, she has to have had some influence. I am a mother, but this is worlds apart.' I asked if she had seen a picture of Sadek. She had not, but she owned a video tape of his testimony, filmed by the terrorist group that sent him, the Popular Front for the Liberation of Palestine (PFLP). She had never watched this tape, which a German TV company had sent her, and neither had her son Leor. She proposed that the three of us watch it together. The commentary was in German, which none of us spoke, but the images were clear enough. Sadek was in combat uniform, clutching an AK47 to his chest in a classic martyr's pose. 'He looks like a boy', said Ginette. 'I feel sick looking at that. He looks like a young kid. This is what doesn't make sense.'

After leaving Ginette, I set out to find the family of Rachel's killer. With the help of a local Palestinian group, I tracked them down to Qalqilya, a dusty, low-rise town on the western edge of the West Bank a few miles from Karnei Shomron. An olive tree guarded the door of the house, and beyond the tree on the panelling of a neighbouring building someone had put up posters of Sadek, hunkered down in jeans and T-shirt, the AK47 resting on his right knee. The gun looked too big for him.

His father, Abu Mahmoud, was friendly but reluctant to talk. Sadek's death had brought his family endless trouble, he said. Any day now he expected the Israeli army to demolish his house, the standard response to a suicide bombing. He had moved all the furniture out. Nevertheless he invited me inside and walked me round the white-washed walls. I asked him how long he had known that Sadek was involved with the PFLP. He said: 'I learned this at the same time that I learned he had died: on the local TV news.'

———

We like to imagine that suicide terrorists are different from the rest of us, psychologically, biologically or in any other way. We assume that they are homicidal or suicidal; that they are poor, uneducated or ignorant with no hope for the future; that they are religious (Islamic) fanatics; that they are full of rage. Such notions, most of the time, are way off the mark. Studies carried out by a handful of field researchers over the past two decades suggest that suicide terrorists are spectacularly ordinary. As with many other people who have committed atrocities, the critical factor determining their behaviour is not so much their personal background or character as the way they are influenced or manipulated by a group. Suicide terrorists acting alone are almost unheard of.

One of the first people to acknowledge the significance of social forces in the radicalization of suicide bombers was Ariel Merari, a retired professor of psychology at Tel Aviv University who has been studying terrorism and political violence for three decades. Merari is a careful, methodical analyst and observer of human nature, and he is quick to acknowledge that his thinking on suicide terrorism has swung dramatically since he started investigating the phenomenon in 1983, when the first modern systematic campaign of suicide attacks began in Lebanon. At that time, he speculated that the bombers were already suicidal and had volunteered as a way of circumventing the religious and social taboo in Palestinian society over killing yourself.

Then he started looking more closely into the background of certain suicide terrorists, including 'altruistic suicides' such as the ten IRA members who died after spending weeks on hunger strike in the Maze prison in Northern Ireland in 1981. 'This gave my speculative view a good shake', he says. 'It didn't make much sense to assume all those ten IRA guys were suicidal. I took it to mean there were other powers, such as social commitment, that could explain this phenomenon. But I couldn't be sure because I had no access to suicide bombers.'

His luck changed in 1997, when he received a call from Nasra Hassan, who worked for the United Nations in the Middle East and had been posted to Gaza for four years with the UN Relief and Works Agency for Palestine Refugees in the Near East (UNRWA). Some months after arriving, she discovered that the best friend of her landlord's son had died carrying out a suicide attack in Israel. She started wondering about his motives. 'I remembered seeing this guy hanging around', she recalls. 'I knew a lot of people from the Palestinian militant groups through my work and I began to realize that I could find out what the story was. I just couldn't understand, and still don't, how they could choose this path.' Around this time some Israeli friends put her in touch with Merari, and they arranged to meet in his university office.

Merari told her he needed profiles of the Palestinian bombers, who they were, what they were like. She said she could help. Being a Pakistani Muslim, and through her work with UNWRA, which has provided jobs, distributed food and run schools for Palestinian refugees throughout Gaza and the West Bank since 1950, she had a level of access to the families of terrorists that Merari, being an Israeli Jew, would never get. So together they drew up a questionnaire that Hassan would use in interviews with friends and family to build a profile of the dead bombers, a process known as psychological autopsy.

It covered a lot of ground: their age, parental background, education, occupation; their hobbies; as a child what they dreamt of doing when they grew up; how popular they were, who they hung out with; who they were closest to within their family; whether they were more or less religious than their relatives; their favourite sura in the Qur'an; any history of mental illness or trauma; their personality, whether they were aggressive, submissive, compassionate; whether they or any of their relatives had ever been arrested by the Israeli army; whether they were motivated by revenge; who their heroes were.

Over the following year, Hassan used this questionnaire to profile thirty-four out of the thirty-six Palestinians who had blown themselves up between 1993 and 1998, visiting their homes and befriending their closest relatives. This was a remarkable feat. I asked Merari how she had managed it. 'She is a smart lady', he laughed. 'She knows how to talk to people. She is good at convincing people. She has this ability to establish a rapport with people of all walks of life and cultural backgrounds. She did great work.'

In 2003, I had tried to interview Hassan about her endeavours in Gaza and she politely turned me down. When I contacted her again in early 2012 she reminded me of this and apologized, explaining she had become fed up with journalists misusing her data. She no longer works for the UN, preferring to focus all her energies on her terrorism project, researching suicide terrorism in the context of Islam. She is simultaneously writing two books based on her field studies. Since working with Merari she has expanded her database, which now holds profiles on more than 400 Muslim suicide terrorists from Pakistan, Afghanistan, Kashmir, Bangladesh, the Palestinian Territories and elsewhere. During 2012 and 2013, I talked with her on the phone many times, and she was always assertive and eloquent, flush with anecdotes and observations and, like Merari, meticulous about how she interpreted them. She is worried about how others will interpret them. 'Everyone wears the goggles of their own discipline', she says.

Hassan is neither psychologist nor social scientist, though few researchers have as much experience as she has interviewing Muslims accused of suicide terrorism. She interviewed Sheikh Ahmed Yassin, founder and spiritual leader of the Palestinian militant group Hamas, several times before he was killed by an Israeli missile in Gaza in 2004; likewise Abu Daoud, the Palestinian who masterminded the operation that led to the kidnap and death of eleven Israeli athletes at the Munich Olympics in 1972; and one of Pakistan's most feared militants, whose jailers offered her a mask 'so he or his people could never go after me' (she declined). I asked her if she had ever felt frightened or threatened. She replied:

> At no point. I am not interrogating them on behalf of the CIA or Mossad or any national security. I tell them who I am and what I am doing and they all feel comfortable because most of my questions are posed through the aperture of Islam and I use their words directly. This gives them the assurance that they will not be misquoted.

Merari and Hassan's study of Palestinian terrorists was the first methodical analysis of suicide bombers based on evidence from people who knew them well. These are the bare statistics of what they discovered. Of their thirty-four subjects – who were all male – the youngest was eighteen and the oldest thirty-eight; thirty-one were single, and out of those who were married two had children; their educational attainments ranged from elementary school to university degree, though compared with the general Palestinian population they were above average; three of the families were very poor, nine were poor, seven were assessed as lower-middle-class, twelve as middle-class, and three were wealthy; twenty-three families characterized their sons as very religious; sixteen of the thirty-four had lost friends or family in the struggle against Israel, sixteen had been wounded or beaten in clashes with Israeli soldiers and eighteen had been detained in Israeli jails, though none of the families thought their son's suicide had been triggered by a specific personal event; none of them had been hospitalized on mental grounds, suffered from psychotic episodes, mood disorders or any psycho-pathological conditions or were involved in criminal behaviour; none of them told their families what they were going to do.[43]

When I asked Merari what all this added up to, he remarked: 'They looked pretty normal.' Hassan highlighted the sheer diversity of the sample:

> I made profiles of all types: very young, much older, very mature, very serious, very playful, very religious, not at all religious, big football players, jokey types, very funny types, rich, poor, middle class, very educated, those who had barely finished school or hadn't finished school. Nothing surprised me. They were as varied as others in their societies.

This apparent ordinariness of suicide bombers can be a hard concept to grasp, since the stereotype held up by most commentators stresses depravity, fundamentalism, insanity or all three. It is well established among psychologists, however.[44] Since Merari and Hassan's research in Gaza, several studies have made clear that poverty,[45] lack of education, desire for revenge and mental illness are largely irrelevant in determining whether someone will sacrifice themselves for a cause, and that religious devotion, while critical in certain cultural contexts, is not a necessary condition.

Merari's work with Hassan turned his head to the overriding impor-tance of group pressures on behaviour. As we shall see, there are nuances to this sociological landscape: his more recent research implies that certain personality characteristics can make people more likely candidates than others. But he stresses that suicide terrorism is above all an organizational phenomenon, in the sense that for it to happen an organization – however small or marginalized – must decide to embark on it. This decision tends to be strategic: terrorist groups resort to martyrdom operations when they are overwhelmingly outgunned, when conventional methods against the enemy aren't working, or – according to Bruce Hoffman, an expert in terrorism and counter-insurgency at Georgetown University – as a way of making political ground or competing against rival organizations.[46]

Once a group has set its mind to suicide terrorism, how does it go about recruiting? More critically, why do so many apparently normal young men volunteer? How does someone like Sadek Abdel Hafeth, who worked in a mechanical repair shop and who unbeknown to his father was radicalized by the PFLP while he was at college in Ramallah, go from student to suicide-killer in just a few weeks?

The process is more straightforward than you might think, as I discovered on my first venture into Gaza, a twenty-five-mile ribbon of land on the eastern coast of the Mediterranean, which in 2002 was home to 1.2 million Palestinians, now close to 1.8 million. At least half of them live in refugee camps where the population density is among the highest in the world. I visited in March – shortly after Rachel Thaler was killed in Karnei Shomron – which turned out to be the bloodiest month of the intifada. Palestinians were blowing themselves up at a rate of one every two days in Jerusalem and Tel Aviv, on buses and in cafes, hotels and supermarkets, and among crowds of pedestrians. More than 130 Israelis died in suicide attacks that March, more than two-thirds of them civilians. Meanwhile,

Israeli fighter jets bombed Gaza and the West Bank, targeting anyone suspected of being involved in terrorism and any places used by them, though the Palestinians claimed the reprisals were indiscriminate: out of 238 Palestinians killed that month, at least 83 were non-combatants.[47]

Driving south into Gaza City from the Israeli border, one of the first things I noticed was the graffiti. It is hard to miss, stencilled or painted on walls, or on banners strung across the road. The posters that cover the sides of buildings show not pop stars as they might in London or New York, but young men with guns. I asked my driver what it all meant. '*Al-shuhada*', he said. The martyrs. The martyrs, I quickly learned, are the war heroes of the Palestinian resistance. These are the men – occasionally women – who died for their community, the greatest sacrifice, their deeds glorified in the streets, on the news, in coffee shops and school playgrounds. Little wonder that during the second intifada, when Hamas and other groups were regularly sending suicide attackers against Israel, the number of applicants far exceeded what was required. Hassan refers to the 'huge industry' that surrounded suicide bombing: the group that organized a martyr's mission would also arrange his funeral, distribute pamphlets celebrating his courage, film his final video testament and arrange accommodation for his family if the Israeli army destroyed their home.

To hear how Palestinian terrorist groups argued the case for martyrdom, my Palestinian escort took me to see Mahmoud Al-Zahar, a co-founder of Hamas and today the most senior Hamas leader in the Gaza Strip, all those above him having been assassinated.[48] He is a physician and he received me in his surgery in Gaza City: a small, dimly lit room with a desk, a bed, scant medical supplies. He sported a brown leather jacket and grey scarf, a small beard and a neat, solemn appearance. He did not laugh or smile during my

Fig. 5 Mural commemorating the martyrs, Gaza.

time with him. He seemed placid apart from the feverish tapping of his right heel. I asked him how Hamas justified sending suicide bombers to kill Israeli citizens. He stared at me, the tapping of his heel quickening. He replied mechanically, as if reciting from a medical textbook:

> It is not suicide. Suicide is not allowed in Islam. It is the highest form of martyrdom. All Israelis are potential soldiers. They are all potential killers of Palestinians. When Israelis kill our women and children, are they not terrorists? You've heard the saying, an eye for an eye, a tooth for a tooth.[49]

Scott Atran, a researcher at the University of Michigan who studies, among other things, the anthropology of religion and terrorism, has heard this kind of rationalization from terrorist leaders many times.

In his search for a scientific understanding of terrorist behaviour, he has met killers, jihadi masterminds and would-be martyrs in Gaza, Indonesia, Kashmir, Morocco and elsewhere and has conducted fieldwork that would make most researchers quake, much of it documented in his 2010 book *Talking to the Enemy*.[50] He admits he finds it addictive: 'There's a daredevil high to this sort of fieldwork.'

On at least two occasions he has come close to being killed. One of these was on the Indonesian island of Sulawesi,[51] 'the jihadi capital of the world', where he was working with another well-known terrorism researcher, Rohan Gunaratna, the author of several books on the Tamil Tigers who now heads a terrorism research group at Nanyang Technological University in Singapore. A few days into their mission, Gunaratna received a text message from one of his informants warning that Atran was about to be 'eliminated' – no doubt someone had discovered he was American. 'Rohan says to me, they're going to, you know, kill you. I say, are you kidding? He says, no I'm not, but we have enough time for two or three more interviews.' Later I asked Gunaratna about this incident. 'Yes, Scott was a bit afraid', he laughed. 'I told him not to worry about it. I made him comfortable. Naturally one has to be extremely careful'.

None of this appears to have discouraged Atran. His challenge as an anthropologist, he says, is to 'analyse awe-inspiring behaviours alien to our culture', such as terrorism. Yet what his field research appears to be saying is that in many aspects it is not so alien. Earlier in his academic career, Atran presumed that extreme acts could be explained by character and personality. 'For Americans bred on a constant diet of individualism, the group is not where one generally looks for explanation.' But the more he talks to terrorists and their friends and families and studies the dynamics of their communities, the more convinced he is that the prime driver is social. 'Terrorists don't kill and die just for a cause. They kill and die for each other.' Moral perspectives aside, these are bands of brothers like any other. In psychological terms, says Atran, suicide terrorism and war heroism are two sides of the same coin.

The paraphernalia of martyrdom that adorn the streets of Gaza – the graffiti, posters and songs that hail the latest *shahid* – are not peripheral to the phenomenon. They are central to it. 'It is easy to understand that when everyone says suicide bombers are national heroes ... many youngsters would find it rather appealing to join their ranks. But in a situation where the majority of the community is opposed to terrorism in general, and to suicide attacks in particular, very few would find this option attractive', notes Merari in his book *Driven to Death*.[52]

In the late 1990s, the average rate of support for suicide attacks among the Palestinian public was 23.9 per cent. After the start of the second intifada in September 2000, the number in favour tripled, reaching 73.7 per cent in April 2001.[53] Atran, whose own surveys in Gaza and the West Bank towards the end of the intifada found eighty per cent in favour of suicide bombings, says the support was across the board: doctors, lawyers, aid workers, teachers, mothers with young children, people who had held jobs in Israel and even those actively working for peace endorsed it as much as militants. One woman told him: 'I know it's wrong, but after I see a martyrdom action on TV, after what we've been through, I can't help but feel joy.' I recalled watching television in a cafe in Palestinian east Jerusalem when a news flash announced an attack on a bus in Tel Aviv and watching an elderly Palestinian man in front of me raise his hands in celebration, as if his home team had netted a winning goal.

Such a radicalized social milieu explains why militant groups have no trouble finding willing martyrs. Atran tells me of the moment during one of his forays in Gaza, in which it dawned on him just how easily young men could find themselves drawn to this option. It was September 2004, and he was visiting the family of Nabil Masood, an eighteen-year-old who a few months earlier had been sent by the Al-Aqsa Martyrs' Brigade on a suicide mission to the Israeli port of Ashdod. (This attack, which killed eleven Israelis and injured twenty more, prompted Israel to launch an all-out offensive against Hamas in Gaza and to assassinate its leader, Ahmed Yassin.) Nabil's distraught father, who inevitably learned of his mission only after he was dead, said his son had been upset at the death of two cousins, both of them Hamas militants, but that he had loved life, was a model student and had even won a scholarship to study at a British university. 'Why do you think he did it?' Atran asked him. 'For his cousins and his friends', replied the father. 'He died for the people he loved.'

One of the most vivid examples of the role of peer-group influence in persuading young men to sign up for martyrdom is the story of the Jihad Mosque football team, whose players lived in the Abu Katila neighbourhood of the southern West Bank town of Hebron. During 2002 and 2003, at least six of them died in suicide operations organized by Hamas. All were friends or members of the same Qawasmeh clan; all loved football and practised and played together regularly. After 2003, the team largely disbanded. Then in February 2008, Mohammed Herbawi and Shadi Zghayer, two close friends from Hebron who had played for the Jihad Mosque's junior team when the seniors were volunteering for Hamas five years earlier, decided they would follow the same path. They killed a seventy-three-year-old woman during a suicide attack on the Israeli town of Dimona. A few days later, Atran met Herbawi's devastated mother in Hebron, who told him: 'He still loved football and he still loved those boys. That is why he did it.'

The Hebron football boys were not the first nor the last to have been radicalized through sport. A significant number of Al-Qaeda or Al-Qaeda-inspired terrorists played football together, including the group that killed 191 people on Madrid commuter trains in March 2004. The British 7/7 bombers went white-water rafting. This is not to say that football or white-water rafting is radical-izing in itself – rather, that group dynamics are one of the major drivers of terrorism. As we will see in a later chapter, team sports and recreational pursuits are among the most effective ways of reinforcing social cohesion.[54]

The recognition that sane, rational people can be persuaded to kill themselves while killing others is not a satisfactory explanation for why so many have done it. There is a road to travel from agreeing to blow yourself up to actually pressing the button. A person could volunteer in the heat of the moment and change their mind as the day of reckoning approaches.

Terrorist groups use various devices to ensure that a recruit stays the course. For Islamic groups such as Hamas and those inspired by Al-Qaeda, religious devotion is a key motivator. Yet religion is not a prerequisite for radicalization.[55] The PFLP, which sent Sadek Abdel Hafeth to bomb the Karnei Shomron pizzeria in 2002, is a Marxist-Leninist organization whose cause is overtly nationalistic rather than Islamic. And prior to the start of the Iraq war in 2003, by far the most effective perpetrators of suicide terrorism were the Liberation Tigers of Tamil Eelam (LTTE), a secular group fighting for an independent Tamil homeland in the north and east of Sri Lanka. Around a third of the LTTE's recruits were women.[56] This implies that the role of ideology and gender in the radicalization process is strongly determined by culture.

The suicide bombers of the LTTE belonged to an elite division known as the Black Tigers. From their formation in 1987 until the LTTE's defeat by the Sri Lankan army in May 2009, more than 330 Black Tigers – a third of them women – died in suicide operations against the Sri Lankan military and government. They had a fearsome reputation. They were responsible for the assassination of Indian prime minister Rajiv Gandhi in 1991 and Sri Lankan president Ranasinghe Premadasa in 1993, and for numerous devastating attacks on military bases, airports, ports, telecommunications centres and other strategic and civilian sites. Since the end of the war and the dismantling of the rebel army, the Sri Lankan government has been running an assessment and rehabilitation programme for captured Tamil fighters.[57] As a result, we now know a fair bit about the recruitment and radicalization of LTTE cadres, including the Black Tigers. Two things are immediately apparent: religion played no part in the process, and LTTE leaders were adept at exploiting the power of group influence.

One person who knows a great deal about this is Amali (not her real name), a Sri Lankan psychologist who is helping to debrief former LTTE recruits before returning them to their communities. Rohan Gunaratna, Atran's researcher-in-arms on his Indonesia trip and an LTTE expert, tells me Amali's task is 'exceptionally difficult', adding that she has likely talked to more terrorists, including failed suicide terrorists, than any other researcher.

Amali says one of the questions she set out to answer was this: 'How do you groom a person who doesn't think of doing anything destructive, who gets up in the morning with their family and goes to work every day, and turn them into someone who could place a bomb where hundreds of civilians and children will die and not have regret?' After assessing close to 12,000 LTTE cadres, she has learned that the LTTE leadership radicalized the Black Tigers by establishing a culture of martyrdom similar to that in Gaza and the West Bank. Recruits were publicly celebrated, their families given special status when they died. They were trained in independent cells of five or six, and each cell was run like a family, dedicated to its leader. You might expect that this kind of special treatment would make Black Tigers the hardest of all to reintegrate. Not at all, says Amali, for once they emerge from their bubble they quickly see that things are very different from what they were led to believe. Their singular world view can easily be refuted.

The women who join the Black Tigers were thought to be influenced by the same social forces as the men.[58] But Gunaratna, who himself has debriefed many Tamil fighters, has noticed that they differ in one respect. Because women are generally more sociable, he says, they are more likely to volunteer for martyrdom if one of their relatives or friends does, and they are also quicker to make a collective decision to return to normality once the fight is over.[59] 'Once they are indoctrinated they are very committed to the path, very team-spirited. They lose their femininity. Once they abandon the cause, they come back to their lives together, they become women again.' On his visits to Tamil rehabilitation centres, he has found that the most popular educational course chosen by female Black Tigers is beauty treatment.

———

Amali's sobering appraisal – at one point she says, 'I think you can turn almost anybody into a terrorist, if the conditions are right' – suggests that a cult of martyrdom is largely a result of social and cultural conditioning. However, a recent set of studies shows that individual characteristics can certainly play a role.

In 2002, Merari obtained permission to carry out psychological profiling on fifteen would-be suicide bombers who had been detained by Israeli security forces before they managed to blow themselves up. He wanted to see if they had any characteristics that set them apart from other terrorists, or from other Palestinians. He assembled a large team that included Arabic-speaking clinical psychologists and experts on Palestinian society. Four out of the fifteen would-be bombers they interviewed had tried to detonate their explosives but were thwarted by faulty equipment; the rest were caught before reaching their targets. They also assessed a group of captured non-suicide terrorists, and fourteen regional commanders from groups such as Hamas and Islamic Jihad who had been in charge of organizing suicide missions and despatching the bombers.

What Merari found surprised him. While none of the suicide terrorists were psychotic or had any history of mental illness – they were still relatively 'normal' – most had certain personality traits that Merari believes could have made them more likely to volunteer or be recruited. Either they were what psychologists call 'dependent-avoidant' – easily swayed by public opinion, inclined to acquiesce to authority – or they were impulsive and emotion-ally unstable. Most had some sense of being social failures: they feared rejection and were eager to please. They were not 'typical Hollywood monster murderers', he says. It was hard to hate them. Two-thirds of them confessed that they had hesitated somewhere along the way. 'They were youngsters. They were not arrogant or aggressive. They had no air of malice about them. They were guys who tried to be important, they wanted to be somebody. Because everybody in their society was saying how great these attacks are and how patriotic the martyrs are, they found it difficult to say no.'[60]

He felt no such sympathy for the organizers. Psychologically they were very different: manipulative rather than dependent, more sophisticated, more self-confident, more egotistical. These are people who were willing to send others to their deaths but reluctant to volunteer themselves. Still, he managed to detach himself from the terrible things they had done while interviewing them, 'like a doctor who has to operate on a serial murderer. I was interested in understanding what made them tick, how did they explain to themselves what they were doing. I talked to some of them for many hours. They have a point of view. But they did not express remorse.'[61]

In my conversations with mothers of Israeli children killed by suicide terrorists, they often appeared more outraged at the organizers of the attacks than at the bombers. Aviva Raziel lost her sixteen-year-old daughter Michal on 9 August 2001, when a twenty-two-year-old Palestinian called Izz ad-Din al-Masri blew himself up in a restaurant in downtown Jerusalem, killing seven children and eight adults and wounding one hundred and thirty. It was one of the worst atrocities of the second intifada. The bomber's controller, who guided him to Jerusalem from his West Bank home, was Ahlam Tamimi, a twenty-year-old female student at Bir Zeit University. 'A pretty girl', said Aviva when I asked her what she knew about her. 'I'm angry at both of them, but when I saw her photograph in the paper I couldn't believe that somebody who looks like that could be so evil.'

Tamimi was caught and given sixteen life sentences – fifteen for the Israeli victims and one for the bomber. But in October 2011 she was released, along with more than a thousand other Palestinian prisoners, in exchange for the Israeli soldier Gilad Shalit who had been held by Hamas in Gaza for five years. After returning home, Tamimi declared that she did not regret what she had done: 'Absolutely not ... I would do it again today, and in the same manner.'[62]

Faced with such hostility, it can be hard for those studying extreme behaviour such as suicide terrorism to remain immune to moral or political sentiment, as they must if their research is to count for anything. It goes against the grain to accept that cultural and social forces can trump individual pathology in shaping behaviour this abhorrent. A good example is the popular tendency to label all suicide attackers as motivated primarily by the desire to kill themselves (suicidal in the clinical sense), as common among academics as the general public. Adam Lankford, a professor of criminal justice at the University of Alabama, argues in his 2013 book *The Myth of Martyrdom* that 'every act of suicide terrorism fits the definition of suicide'.[63]

Lankford's take is based partly on an extrapolation from Merari's latest study (mentioned above), in which Merari found suicidal traits in six out of the fifteen would-be suicide terrorists he interviewed; and partly on Lankford's own review of news and video reports on one hundred and thirty suicide terrorists that he claims reveals suicide risk factors in every one. Given that he counted hypothetical motivators such as 'brother killed' and 'sick with tuberculosis' among his risk factors,[64] and that Merari himself describes Lankford's thesis as 'speculative' and advises that 'there is no good alternative to psychological interviews and tests for assessing suicidality and other psychological traits',[65] we must treat such claims with caution. Surprisingly, *The Myth of Martyrdom* has been endorsed by such footsoldiers of empiricism as the Harvard professor and author Stephen Pinker, who applauded it for de-romanticizing 'this loathsome practice'.[66]

It would be convenient if we could dismiss suicide terrorists and other evil-doers as ill, aberrant or freakish. Alas, the evidence does not let us off the hook, and we must get used to the idea that they are not so different. As we saw from the work of Asch, Milgram,

Zimbardo and other psychologists, sane, rational people can easily 'break bad' and be coerced into doing things they would usually abhor, corrupted by group pressures or other situational forces beyond their control. Herbert Kelman, pioneer of the use of social psychology in international conflict mediation, has found that 'many, perhaps most, torturers are not sadists but ordinary people, doing what they understand to be their jobs'.[67] Most abominations arise from ordinary minds distorted by exceptional circumstances.

Yet this is not the whole story, for not everyone obeys, not everyone conforms, not everyone stands by. Always there are dissenters, people who resist the social forces that consume others. Who are they, and how does heroic behaviour arise – both in times of conflict and in everyday life?

4

Ordinary Heroes

In ancient Greece, to be recognized as a hero required exceptional effort. For a start, you had to be dead, preferably killed by spectacular means. Prior to this you needed to demonstrate abilities and behaviours far superior to those of other mortals. Take Hercules. To atone for the sin of killing his own family (not entirely his fault), he had to complete twelve labours, most of which involved slaying or capturing a fearsome beast. After a series of other adventures comparably heroic, he eventually lost all his skin to a corrosive poison and ended his life atop a funeral pyre that he himself had built.

The conception of heroes as anomalous, fearless and accomplished remains part of the culture, even if we expect a little less of our modern-day Hercules. Yet this view is out of step with reality. Research into heroic and altruistic behaviour shows that people who risk their own safety or the approbation of their peers to help others are often surprisingly ordinary, and that heroism is more commonplace than we tend to imagine.

Consider the classic psychology studies on conformity and evil that we visited in the last chapter. Their headline findings give the impression that whatever someone's moral convictions, situational forces will lead them astray. Often, this is not what happens. About a quarter of participants in Solomon Asch's line experiments were unmoved by the group's erroneous judgements. More than a third of volunteers in Stanley Milgram's first round of shock-machine studies disobeyed the experimenter at some point, and a few always dropped out at the first sign of the victim's distress. One or two of Philip Zimbardo's prison guards remained just and decent. It is not inevitable that people will be persuaded to do bad things.

What can science tell us about the nonconformists? Are they independent to the bone, or are their dissenting acts essentially random, never likely to be repeated? Are they special cases, or could all of us take a stand against evil, if only we knew how?

Examples of heroic dissenters are everywhere in history. Typical of the type were the residents of the French village of Le Chambon-sur-Lignon during the Second World War, who gave sanctuary to thousands of Jews and others fleeing the Nazi regime despite the explicit orders of Marshal Pétain and the Vichy government – in league with the Third Reich – to deport all refugees to concentration camps in Germany. The villagers resisted this policy from the outset. On 23 June 1940, the day after Pétain signed the armistice with Germany, Le Chambon's two Christian pastors, André Trocmé and Edouard Theis, called on their parishioners not to 'submit passively to a totalitarian ideology' and 'to use the weapons of the Spirit to oppose the violence that they will try to put on our consciences'.[1] Over the next four years, the community defied all attempts to terrorize and intimidate them into obedience. They thwarted frequent police raids to unearth refugees who had been cleverly hidden in the countryside. They obtained forged ID cards and shepherded hundreds across the border into neutral Switzerland. They even educated refugee children in a specially built school.

Why did this community rebel against the Vichy authorities when most of France co-operated? Several things stand out about their act of disobedience. First, it was an appeal to common morality, in this case Christian morality, that resonated with everyone in the community more strongly than Pétain's call for a 'new social order'. Second, Le Chambon's residents identified with the refugees because they themselves were descendants of Protestant Huguenots who had been persecuted as a religious minority in Catholic France in the seventeenth century. Third, it was immediate: Trocmé and Theis's rallying cry a day after armistice set a precedent for resistance. Finally, it was a collective act on many levels – social, religious and historical – and, as we learned from Milgram's and Asch's research, it is far easier to defy authority in partnership with others.

Much of this also tallies with observations that Milgram made about the dissenters in his shock-machine experiments. For instance, those who objected early on to administering the shocks were more likely to fold eventually. He also believed that previous experience of authoritarianism could open people's eyes to conformist pressures: Gretchen Brandt, a thirty-one-year-old female medical technician who refused to turn the switch beyond 210 volts, had grown up in Nazi Germany. 'Perhaps we have seen too much pain', she replied when asked if this influenced her decision.[2]

The village of Le Chambon is one of many examples of widespread communal dissent in Nazi-occupied Europe. Perhaps better known is the operation by the Danish resistance movement, in which many ordinary Danish citizens participated, to evacuate eight thousand Jews to Sweden by sea in October 1943 to prevent them being deported to Nazi concentration camps. People from all walks of life, from civil servants to taxi drivers to students, arranged for their Jewish friends and neighbours – and in some cases, total strangers – to be hidden in fishing boats, ferries, rowboats and even kayaks and transported across the Øresund Strait despite constant surveillance by German patrol boats. As a result of this and other Danish efforts, more than ninety-eight per cent of the country's Jews survived the Holocaust. Likewise, the people of Bulgaria managed to save the country's 48,000 Jews from deportation through a campaign that emphasized their Bulgarian identity above all else, so that to consent to the Nazis' demands would have seemed like a betrayal of national principles. 'Our sufferings are their sufferings, our joys their joys too', proclaimed the Bulgarian Communist parliamentarian Todor Polyakov.[3] Group identity is both powerful and malleable: for the Bulgarian Jews, being 'one of us' represented the difference between life and death.[4]

Heroic acts of dissent or altruism are often socially driven. Samuel Oliner, a professor of sociology at Humboldt State University in California, has spent much of his career trying to understand why people risk their lives to help others. In 1982 he founded the Altruistic Personality and Prosocial Behavior Institute in Arcata, California.[5] He has a strong personal motivation: a Jew, he owes his life to a non-Jewish peasant woman who helped hide him from the Nazis in Poland during the Second World War after his family had been carried off to a concentration camp and many of his neighbours machine-gunned into a mass grave. In the 1980s, Oliner and his wife Pearl, a fellow academic, interviewed more than four hundred 'rescuers' who had helped fellow Jews in Nazi-occupied Europe at great risk to themselves. They found that while fifty-six per cent of them were not members of a formal network such as a political party, religious group or resistance organization, almost all depended on such networks to sustain them 'materially and emotionally'.[6]

Still, there are plenty of stories of lone heroes. Consider Paul Grüninger, chief of police in the Swiss canton of St Gallen in the late 1930s, who defied official orders and allowed some three thousand refugees fleeing persecution under the Third Reich to cross the border and find sanctuary in Switzerland. Afterwards, he was stripped of his job and pension.[7] Or Sergeant Joseph M. Darby, a twenty-four-year-old US Army reservist who, in January 2004, blew the whistle on the Abu Ghraib prison abuses. He and his wife were forced into hiding for several years out of fear of retaliation from fellow soldiers. Or think of Irene Gut, a Polish nurse who hid twelve Jews in the basement of a German officer's house during the Second World War while she was working under duress as his housekeeper; Maria von Maltzan, the daughter of a German count who helped scores of Jews and political enemies of the Nazis to escape from Berlin; Aleksander Jevtic, a Serb who saved dozens of Croats at an internment camp from almost certain death during the Balkan Wars of the early 1990s by fooling his colleagues into thinking that the Croats were actually Serbian;[8] and hotel manager Paul Rusesabagina, who sheltered more than a thousand Hutus and Tutsis during the 1994 Rwandan genocide. All of these individuals seemed compelled to act outside any collective impulse – and often against the status quo.

In his book *An Ordinary Man*, Rusesabagina describes the psychology involved in these kinds of heroics:

> When your individuality is dissolved into the will of the pack you then become free to act in any way the pack directs. The thought of acting otherwise becomes as abhorrent as death … If nobody can find it within themselves to stand outside the group and find the inner strength to say no, then the mass of men will easily commit atrocities for the sake of keeping up personal appearances. The lone man is ridiculed and despised, but he is the only one who can stand between humanity and the abyss.[9]

In the 1960s, the American psychologist Perry London set out to investigate what distinguishes maverick rescuers from the conforming masses. It was the first study of its kind, and to begin he interviewed twenty-seven Christians who had persistently worked to save Jews from the Nazis. He noticed that many of them shared three characteristics: an enduring spirit of adventurousness that normalized risk-taking; a sense of being socially marginalized, for example due to a physical disability or being part of a religious minority themselves, which made it easier for them to defy the majority; and a strong identification with a moralizing parent.[10] Unfortunately, London never managed to raise the funding he needed to complete his study before he died in 1992. More recently, one of his collaborators, the human rights campaigner and rabbi Harold Schulweis, remarked that adventurous personalities did not appear to be the norm among the rescuers he and London had interviewed. 'He found people who were very ordinary, very passive, suddenly there is something that happens, I don't know. Do you know who is gonna save you? Can you guess right now? I'm sorry to disappoint you.'[11]

Schulweis called this 'the mystery of goodness'. Does it mean that goodness is as banal as evil, as Zimbardo has claimed – that ordinary people are capable of heroism in the same way they might be capable of cruelty, given the right circumstances? Not necessarily. In their study of rescuers who helped Jews during the war, the Oliners found that many of them shared basic values of compassion, fairness and personal responsibility. 'If you can save somebody's life, that's your duty', was how one of them rationalized their actions. 'When you see a need, you have to help', insisted another.[12] Milgram found something similar in his obedience studies among those who defied the experimenter's orders. The main difference between them and the rest, he noted, was that they saw themselves – rather than the experimenter – as primarily responsible for the suffering of the victim.[13] Moreover, the people interviewed by the Oliners – like those interviewed by London – said they had learned their values from their parents.

Another psychologist, Eva Fogelman, discovered something similar in her conversations with about three hundred wartime rescuers. Again, her interest was not just academic: Fogelman's father, who was Jewish, owed his survival to the generosity and compassion of Polish farmers. For this reason, though Fogelman studied social psychology and personality under Milgram at the City University of New York, she found herself more interested in dissenters than conformists. Her heroes, she noticed, shared a surprisingly consistent set of humanistic values instilled in them in childhood:

> I began after a while to wait for the recital of one or more of those well-known passages: a nurturing, loving home; an altruistic parent or beloved caretaker who served as a role model for altruistic behavior; a tolerance for people who were different; a childhood illness or personal loss that tested their resilience and exposed them to special care; and an upbringing that emphasized independence, competence, discipline with explanations (rather than physical punishment or withdrawal of love), and caring.[14]

One of the hardest questions facing those investigating the motivations of heroes and evil-doers is whether malevolence is more likely in some cultures than in others. Are the actions of people like Adolf Eichmann, or horrific events such as the Rwandan genocide, more conceivable in places where there is a high regard for authoritarian values? Ervin Staub, a professor of psychology at the University of Massachusetts, thinks the answer is yes. However, he believes that altruism derives from personal values, and that it can be learned.

Born in Hungary to Jewish parents, Staub's experiences as a child during the Second World War have led him to dig deep into the human psyche for the origins of both evil and altruism. He credits two people in particular for saving him and his family from the Nazis: Raoul Wallenberg, a Swedish diplomat who protected thousands of Jewish families like Staub's by issuing them with sham Swedish passports and sheltering them in safehouses; and Macs, a Christian woman who worked as their maid and whom Staub has described as his 'second mother'. 'When things were bad she could have left us, but she stayed', he says. 'She took my sister and me into hiding for a while with Christian families. Then we went to one of Wallenberg's protected houses. She would prepare dough and take it to a bakery to make into bread for us to eat. She was caught by Hungarian Nazis who threatened they would kill her, hands up against the wall. But she continued to do these things, not only for us but for other people in the house.'[15] Staub cites Macs as the inspiration for his interest in the psychology of maverick heroes. Long after the war, he continued to visit her in Hungary, to give his thanks. He says she introduced him to the possibilities of human kindness.

You might think a career studying evil would take the edge off anyone's faith in altruism, but Staub appears indelibly optimistic. He manages to look warm and friendly even when discussing genocidal atrocities, conducting his speech with palms upturned. On the bookshelf in his office in Amherst sits a snapshot of him with the Dalai Lama; beside it is an old, black-and-white photograph of a much younger man boasting Hollywood looks – 'an old friend of mine', he chuckles, 'a picture of me a long time ago'.

Like Fogelman, London and the Oliners, Staub is convinced that the key to altruistic behaviour and moral courage – sticking to one's values in the face of hostile peer pressure – lies in a person's upbringing. His message is that we can be socialized from a young age to bring those who are outside our immediate circle of kith and kin within our empathetic reach. Children whose parents are caring and affectionate, and who give them firm guidance, grow up feeling secure in their relationships with others, less threatened by outsiders and more inclined to take responsibility for the welfare of people outside their group.[16] That's the general rule. As it happened, the path to heroic action for Staub's saviour was rather more remarkable. Cruelly mistreated by a stepmother after her mother died when she was quite young, Macs was sent to work for other families as a nanny and found herself transformed by her loving connection to the children in her care. 'This is altruism born of suffering', says Staub. 'Rather than turn you against others, suffering can lead you to open your heart. If people reach out to you, it can give you a sense of power, it can make you realize that the past is not the present.'

If we do reach out, who, in particular, are we most inclined to help? The late American philosopher Richard Rorty believed people are more likely to favour those with whom they feel some solidarity, and that solidarity is strongest among groups that are 'smaller and more local than the human race': a fellow American, for example, or a fellow Catholic, or a comrade in a political movement.[17]

Yet group solidarity is not a necessary condition for altruistic behaviour. Most rescuers of the Jews appear to have been driven more by a universal morality than a local one. Their in-group consisted of the whole of humankind, all of whom they thought deserved to be free from persecution. 'They believed in humanity and were incredulous that people were being killed simply because of their Jewishness', recalled one Holocaust survivor interviewed by the Oliners.[18] A former Dutch army officer who ran an underground resistance group and saved many Jews from the Nazis expressed it like this: 'You should always be aware that every other person is basically you. You should always treat people as though it is you, and that goes for evil Nazis as well as for Jewish friends who are in trouble.'[19] This ethic is encapsulated in the famous lines by the poet John Donne, 'No man is an island, entire of itself ... any man's death diminishes me, because I am involved in mankind',[20] and in the humanist philosophy of the fourteenth Dalai Lama: 'To overcome our tendency to ignore others' needs and rights, we must continually remind ourselves of what is obvious: that basically we are all the same.'[21]

Recently, three psychologists at Western Kentucky University developed a measure to calculate how people differ in their propensity for a universal morality – how inclined we are to include all humanity in our in-group. They have named it the Identification With All Humanity scale.[22] Those who score lowest on the assessment tend to be authoritarian or individualistic in outlook; for example, they see their in-group as morally superior to other groups, or they view human relationships in terms of 'everyone for themselves'. Those who score highest also score high on personality traits such as agreeableness and openness to experience, and they tend to care a lot about issues such as global poverty, hunger and human rights. But they are also more neurotic – they worry overly about the little things in life – a finding that has baffled the researchers.

It would also have baffled the humanistic psychologist Abraham Maslow, who in the mid-twentieth century was one of the first to focus on his subjects' positive qualities and their capacity for growth rather than their pathologies. Maslow found human kinship to be a common characteristic among people he studied who had realized their full potential as human beings and were free of neurosis, psychosis and emotional instabilities. These self-actualizers 'have a deep feeling of identification, sympathy, and affection for human beings in general', he said. 'They feel kinship and connection, as if all people were members of a single family … [They] have a genuine desire to help the human race.'[23] Unfortunately, such people appear to be rare. Maslow thought that while everyone in theory is capable of reaching this state of fulfilment, less than two per cent do so (he counted Abraham Lincoln, Thomas Jefferson and Albert Einstein among them). If true, heroes are indeed exceptional.

That is not how Zimbardo sees it. In need of a respite after finding himself 'up to his neck' in evil, he has spent the last few years analysing the motivations of courageous people across all walks of life. He says the idea that heroes are always exceptional people is romantic, a fabrication of ancient myth as well as modern media. 'We want to believe that these individuals have an intrinsic moral fiber, have had a special upbringing, possess a unique constellation of personality traits, or are altruistic beyond what can be expected of the rest of humanity.'[24] But the evidence suggests otherwise, he says. Heroes, like evil-doers, are often quite ordinary. Furthermore, he believes an act of valour is no less special for being unpredictable, and its perpetrator no less worthy of acclaim. Better still, it means 'we are all potential heroes waiting for our moment'.[25] By this imagining, Umberto Eco's observation is close to the mark: 'The hero is always a hero by mistake. He dreams of being an honest coward like everyone else.'[26]

The presumption that courageous deeds spring from exceptional people applies particularly to war heroes. The popular view is that they are born extraordinary, that they possess some innate character trait that persuades them to step forward when most of us would shrink back. But it tends not to work like that. Acts of heroism on the battlefield, or anywhere else, are usually committed by those who are not known for their courage. It might be the first and the last brave thing they do. To paraphrase the explorer Ranulph Fiennes, even wimps might do something extraordinary when the circumstances are right.[27]

My maternal grandfather was awarded a Military Cross for leading his tank squadron on foot towards a heavily armed German garrison in the Netherlands in April 1945. He never spoke of his own bravery, nor of the fear he must have personally felt. But he would speak occasionally of the courage of those he fought with, and in particular how 'you never quite knew how an individual would behave under fire'.

His favourite example was Ian Liddell, a fellow Coldstream Guards officer best known for a very different leadership role in a jazz band, whom he described as 'anything but a smart regular officer although extremely nice and very popular'. Liddell's company was charged with capturing a bridge over the river Ems near Lingen, in north-west Germany, a tricky prospect since the bridge was clearly mined and defended by 150 German infantry with 88mm anti-tank artillery guns. To the astonishment of those watching, Liddell decided to deal with it himself, running onto the bridge under intense enemy fire and cutting the wires to the bombs. For his heroism, he was awarded the Victoria Cross (VC), though he never received it: he was killed by a sniper's bullet less than three weeks later.

Stories of unlikely war heroes abound. Noel Godfrey Chavasse twice earned the VC – one of only three soldiers to do so – after rescuing wounded men under heavy fire at the Somme and again at Passchendaele. Since he also received a Military Cross and was Mentioned in Dispatches, you might think him a candidate for a 'heroic personality'. Yet, on his arrival in France, at the beginning of the war, he wrote to his father: 'I do not intend to run any risk at all, unnecessarily; my blood is not heroic.'[28] More common among war heroes are those who act on the spur of the moment, with no time to think. Billy McFadzean, a twenty-year-old rifleman with the Royal Irish Rifles, had barely a second to consider the consequences before he threw himself onto a box of primed grenades when it slipped into a crowded Allied trench during the battle of the Somme. He was blown to pieces, as no doubt he knew he would be. Only one of his colleagues was injured. Or take Jack Randall, who was awarded the VC posthumously in 1944 for silencing a Japanese machine-gun bunker by throwing in a grenade and sealing the aperture with his body. Randall was described by a friend as 'disorganised ... almost a rubbish soldier, not a typical military man at all, and not someone you would expect such a great act of heroism from'.[29]

The protagonists of such stories appear driven not so much by the scent of glory as the impulse to protect their comrades from harm. 'I wasn't scared. I wasn't thinking about my safety. I was just thinking about the guys, you know, getting them out of the burning vehicle', said Johnson Beharry, who in 2005 become the first living recipient of the VC in thirty years after saving the lives of several comrades in Iraq, twice manoeuvring his armoured vehicle out of ambushes to safety. 'It's your friends that you live with, that you socialize with, that you work with, that you've known for a number of years, that are in trouble and need help.'[30]

In 2007 Matthew Croucher, a Royal Marine reservist, came close to emulating Billy McFadzean's heroic act while on night patrol in

Helmand Province, Afghanistan. Croucher's unit was investigating an abandoned Taliban compound when he felt something brush against his shin. Realizing he had triggered a tripwire grenade, he slipped off his daysack, jammed it against the device and lay on top of it to shield his comrades from the blast. He waited seven or eight seconds for it to go off, a long time when you're convinced you're going to die. When the explosion came, it threw him several feet into the air, perforated his eardrums, gave him a nosebleed and concussion and left him otherwise unscathed. The rest of his unit escaped with minor shrapnel wounds.[31]

Croucher's shredded daysack is on display in a large glass case in the Lord Ashcroft Gallery's Extraordinary Heroes exhibition at the Imperial War Museum in London, along with the George Cross (GC) he received for his act of valour.[32] Exhibited in this exalted way, it has taken on a life of its own, a metaphor for a soldier's self-sacrifice. You feel it deserves its own medal. The exhibition is full of artefacts of heroism: a pilot's goggles, a submariner's diving suit, a pistol belonging to an undercover agent, a holy bangle worn by an Indian Bren-gun carrier, medals aplenty. Confronted with a room full of heroes, it seems natural to look for common traits, but the owners of these paraphernalia all seem very different.

That has not dissuaded the exhibition's curator, the historian Nigel Steel, from trying to define bravery in terms of certain qualities shown by VC and GC holders. He has identified seven heroic attributes: boldness (act fast), aggression ('hot' courage), leadership (inspire others), skill (use what you have and use it well), sacrifice (your life for someone else's), initiative (stepping up) and endurance (no surrender). Still, Steel's list amounts to a description of the deed rather than the doer. Heroes are not bold, aggressive or altruistic in all that they do. They may only be moved once to an extraordinary feat. Of the 1,359 recipients of the VC, fewer than a third received additional decorations or awards of any other kind.

Steel says all heroes share one quality that he chose not to include on his checklist: they are all caring, in the sense that they are quick to take responsibility for those around them. This trait was also cited by Didy Grahame, who as secretary of the Victoria Cross and George Cross Association in London has probably known and conversed with more decorated men and women than anyone alive. Grahame notes that a disproportionate number of VC and GC holders are an older brother from a large family, the son of a widowed mother, or have had other early life experiences that have given them a habit of solicitude. By this reckoning, combat heroes are like the people who rescued Jews in Nazi-occupied Europe, and the individuals who refused to co-operate in Stanley Milgram's shock-machine experiment.

The understanding that heroes should be heroic in all that they do was enshrined in the founding warrant of the VC, which decreed that any recipient subsequently found guilty of treason, cowardice or a serious crime shall have their award erased in order to 'maintain pure this most honourable distinction'. Fortunately this was amended in 1931 after an intervention by George V, who reasoned that a VC-holder should be allowed to wear his medal even on the scaffold. The public perception of courage as an innate quality rather than an emergent behaviour will be harder to shift. This is problematic, because it leads us to expect too much of our heroes, especially those who have served in our armed forces. Johnson Beharry says he has noticed that people now disapprove of him doing things he used to do before his award, such as going to a nightclub.[33] They require from him a perpetual nobility. Such expectations are way off the mark. As the American humourist Will Rogers noted, being a hero is about the shortest-lived profession on earth. 'Everybody thinks

I'm a hero because I was awarded the VC', says Beharry. 'But I'm just a normal soldier who can't get away from his demons. I close my eyes, start sweating and seeing my dead friends.'[34]

———

Notwithstanding the role of childhood influences in altruistic behaviour, it is very difficult – perhaps impossible – to predict who will conform and who will resist in any given situation. Presumably there were plenty of people in occupied Europe with moralistic parents who chose not to help their Jewish neighbours. What can the psychology of heroism tell us about how *we* might behave?

Stephen Reicher, whose work on crowds we encountered in chapter 2, and his colleague Alexander Haslam have argued that instead of trying to understand this kind of behaviour exclusively in terms of situations or dispositions, it makes more sense to consider 'social identities' – in other words, to examine how people identify with the various other players in the game. Thus in Milgram's obedience studies, the issue becomes: why did most people identify more strongly with the authoritative experimenter than with the victim, and why did some people not? A lot depended on how the experiment was set up and how the different relationships were organized. Milgram's subjects were more likely to acquiesce to the experimenter's demands when they were in the same room as him and separated from the victim; likewise, since the study was advertised as a scientific experiment, participants tended to be more complicit when it took place at Yale, a prestigious university in keeping with an important study, than in the nearby city of Bridgeport.[35]

Reicher and Haslam's emphasis on group identity came out of their own twist on the Stanford Prison Experiment, conducted in

December 2001 in collaboration with the BBC, involving fifteen volunteers in a makeshift prison created in Elstree Film Studios in north London. (A four-part documentary was broadcast the following May.)[36] They introduced several changes to Zimbardo's set-up. For instance, the researchers themselves did not assume a role and did not direct the guards how to behave. The outcome was rather different. Instead of conforming blindly to the roles assigned them, the behaviour of both guards and prisoners depended on how much they bonded with each other and the extent to which they formed an 'in-group'. For instance, the guards immediately disagreed among themselves over how to behave, and as a result they never developed a shared sense of identity; by contrast the prisoners, instead of becoming passive and submissive, showed increasing unity and eventually staged a rebellion that led to the downfall of the prison regime. Haslam says this demonstrates that authoritarian regimes arise not simply because people obediently step into roles, but only when those roles allow them to connect with their accomplices.

This type of solidarity can be a basis for highly effective resistance against tyranny. Haslam mentions three well-known examples in real-world prisons: the hunger strikes and disobedience among republican inmates at the Maze prison outside Belfast during the Troubles, which forced the British government to rethink its strategy in Northern Ireland; the unity among political prisoners on Robben Island, many of whom went on to form the government of post-apartheid South Africa; and the dramatic revolt and escape of Jewish prisoners from the Nazi concentration camp at Sobibor in 1943, spearheaded by a tight-knit group of inmates who had served together in the Russian Red Army.[37] In all these cases, says Haslam, a strong sense of common purpose inspired prisoners to gang up against the authorities and overturn the status quo.

But what if there are no fellow dissenters? Is there anything we can do as individuals to ensure that we don't just conform to the norm, that would make it easier for us to take a stand, whether it's against dubious profiteering, the bullying of a work colleague or the mistreatment of a prisoner? Zimbardo has recently turned his attention to this question. He set up the Heroic Imagination Project, which aims to teach managers, employees, schoolchildren and others the psychological skills required to resist conformity, bullying and mindless obedience.[38] Advice includes: 1) be mindful of what you are saying or doing rather than just going with the flow ('don't hesitate to fire a wake-up shot to your cortex!'); 2) always maintain a sense of personal responsibility for your actions (following orders is never a justification); 3) distinguish between legitimate authority figures, whose wisdom or expertise justifies their position, and pseudo-leaders whose claims to power have no substance; and 4) develop a 'heroic imagination' by imagining physically or socially risky situations and how you might behave in them.

Ervin Staub has been on a similar mission for several decades, conducting experiments to test what he calls 'active bystandership' – people's capacity in the presence of others to help those in distress. Following the vicious beating of Rodney King by members of the Los Angeles Police Department in 1991, he worked with the California police to encourage officers to speak out against the use of unnecessary force. He has also set up a programme to teach schoolchildren in western Massachusetts how to oppose violence and bullying.

For more than a decade Staub and his wife, the clinical psychologist Laurie Anne Pearlman, have been working in Rwanda, which is still recovering from the politically fuelled slaughter of more than 500,000 Tutsis by the majority Hutu population in 1994. They hope to find effective ways to teach people to resist the strong cultural impulse in Rwanda's hierarchical society to obey authority and avoid dissent – an approach they believe could reduce the chances of a repeat of the genocide. Staub maintains that 'in difficult times people rely on authorities even more. It makes it hard for them to step aside, to look at what's going on and to oppose what the group is doing.'

During the genocide, popular radio stations incited Hutus to violence against their Tutsi neighbours. The broadcasts, some of them on state-controlled stations, trumpeted 'Hutu power' and the idea that Tutsis were the collective, common enemy. Staub and Pearlman decided that radio could also be a powerful vehicle for disseminating a message of reconciliation, one that talked about the common identity of Rwandans but also encouraged people to get involved and challenge authority figures about immoral acts. Since 2004, their educational radio drama *Musekeweya* ('New Dawn') has been teaching people about the roots of conflict and how to resolve it. More than ninety per cent of the population tunes in. And it appears to be working: the research team has noted more positive attitudes among listeners towards members of other social and ethnic groups, a greater enthusiasm for reconciliation and more willingness to air their grievances.[39] They have since begun similar projects in the Democratic Republic of Congo, which experienced ongoing violence after the events in Rwanda, and Burundi, where some 300,000 died in a civil war between 1993 and 2005.

Education is essential, says Staub, because people's response in violent or dramatic situations is nearly always subconscious and peer-driven. 'If you teach them to be more self-aware, they may be able to resist the influence of their environment.'

Situational passivity: the bystander effect

You're walking along the street on your way to work when you notice a man lying sprawled on the pavement, face down and unmoving. You are not the only one to have seen him: three or four others have gathered around, but they're doing nothing useful. What do you do?

In public emergency scenarios such as this, researchers have observed time and again that most of us do little or nothing if there are others standing watching. This finding has been a favourite of mine since my student days, when I was beaten up outside a nightclub while twenty of my friends – quite a few of whom happened to be rugby players – stood by, too goggle-eyed to intervene.

Psychologists believe that passivity among bystanders is largely a product of the situation. They point to several factors likely to be involved, including fear of appearing incompetent and hope that someone else will take responsibility. Unsurprisingly, people are more likely to get involved if they view the victim as part of their own social group (not that that helped me!).[40]

Despite years of study, no one has yet found a way of countering the bystander effect. The most successful strategy could be to encourage onlookers to focus on the things they have in common with the victim – as the philosopher Richard Rorty suggested, to use our imagination to 'see strange people as fellow sufferers'.[41]

Given how often cruelty and immorality seem to arise from our social conditions, with people slipping together and with breath-taking frequency into roles legitimized by higher authority, as the Polish sociologist Zygmunt Bauman said,[42] there is a strong case for making certain that people are aware of our tendency for impulsive collusion. We need to steel ourselves against what the political theorist Hannah Arendt called the 'sheer thoughtlessness'[43] that leads people to suspend their capacity for moral judgement and reflection. It is not enough to rely on a few righteous and morally strong people to steer society away from bad behaviour: no temperament is immune to the pull of social conditioning. Our notion of 'character' has proved too unpredictable a guide. As David DeSteno and Piercarlo Valdesolo argue in *Out of Character*, their 2011 book on moral decision-making, 'Hypocrisy and morality, love and lust, cruelty and compassion, honesty and deceit, modesty and hubris, bigotry and tolerance ... can coexist in each of us'.[44]

The pioneering social psychologists of the postwar years have proved one thing: it will be very difficult for us to prevent future genocides or murderous regimes without a greater awareness of our vulnerability to social forces.[45] This applies, too, to the conformist pressures that bear down on us in everyday life: in boardrooms, in committee meetings, in government administrations, in community groups and college fraternities. The psychologists would have us ask ourselves every time we make a decision: am I doing this because it is right, or because those around me are making it *feel* right? Thinking about what is going on can help make heroes out of any of us.

We turn next to an attribute of group psychology that has little to do with rational consideration. Many of the war heroes profiled in this chapter acted with no forethought when their moment came. Their bravery stemmed from loyalty to their colleagues, an unconscious impulse that drives behaviour on the battlefield. Group cohesion holds armies together, and its properties have been exploited by leaders for as long as men have been fighting wars.

5

Bands of Brothers

———

It is hard to travel far in Vermont's Green Mountains without encountering the state's most notorious hero of the American Revolutionary War, Ethan Allen. His image is commemorated on battle memorials, street signs, hotels, an Amtrak train and one of America's biggest furniture chains, even though no one knows for certain what he looked like. Drop his name into conversation at a bar or shop counter and you will be regaled with preposterous fables of his exploits passed on from schoolbooks and oral history. 'Those Allen boys – they sure liked to party', declared Maria, my hostess at the Ira Allen Inn, a chestnut-beamed house with comically undulating floorboards that Ethan had built with his brother Ira in 1779.[1] 'They'd hold a meeting then, whooa, party!'

Brought up in rural Connecticut, Allen established his reputation as an agitator after following several of his relatives north into an area west of the Connecticut River known as the New Hampshire Grants (what today is the state of Vermont). On arrival he found himself in the middle of a long-running disagreement. On the one side stood landowners such as himself who had bought the titles to their properties from the governor of New Hampshire, which bordered the grants to the east. On the other was the province of

New York, which bordered the grants to the west and also claimed dominion. The New York government declared the New Hampshire deeds fraudulent and threatened to evict the settlers if they failed to buy an additional title. This irked Allen and his neighbours. In the summer of 1770, they assembled in the Catamount Tavern in Bennington (now the historical centre of southern Vermont) and, fortified by the house tipple – cider cut with rum – founded a resistance group that would protect their interests from the meddling 'Yorkers'. They were known as the Green Mountain Boys.

As a 'band of brothers', the Green Mountain Boys were highly effective. They played a major role in the military defeat of Britain in the Revolutionary War, and in the brief flash of history, between 1777 and 1791, when Vermont was independent of both Great Britain and the newly founded United States. These were frontier men, and you might therefore expect them to be individualistic and self-sufficient, yet the Green Mountain Boys were also renowned

Fig. 6 The Green Mountain Boys in council.

for their loyalty. Many of them were literally brothers, or cousins or neighbours in a close-knit community. Such bonds, secured in blood and in the mutual dependency of day-to-day survival, can make for a formidable fighting force.

———

'The gods of the hills are not the gods of the valleys', bellowed Allen after the New York government warned him and his fellow settlers not to try any dirty tricks against their western landlords.[2] The Yorkers didn't have to wait long to discover what he meant. Soon after their inaugural meeting, Allen's freedom fighters, faces blackened and fir twigs fixed rakishly in hat-bands, set about strong-arming off the territory any New York surveyors and tenants they could find. Rather than wage war, they issued florid threats and staged humiliating punishments; until the outbreak of the Revolution in 1775 they managed to avoid killing anyone. Yorkers caught trying to enforce the New York edict might find the roofs of their houses removed, or be hauled off for a creative whipping known as 'chastisement with the twigs of the wilderness'. Occasionally, they would be subject to a more public shaming, as in the case of the unfortunate doctor Samuel Adams, who was hoisted in a swinging chair to the top of the Catamount Tavern's twenty-five-foot sign where he endured several hours of mockery from the patrons.[3] In 1774, the New York authorities bewailed this 'dangerous and destructive spirit of riot and licentiousness, subversive of all order and good government' and offered a reward for the capture of the Green Mountain Boys' leaders.[4] By then, however, few New York grant-owners had the stomach to cross into the New Hampshire Grants to take up their titles.

It is easy to imagine how Allen's insurgents might have had the upper hand in the mountains of western Vermont. The forest is so ubiquitous that when travelling on foot away from towns or roads it can be hard to catch your bearings, even on ridges and hilltops. One windless morning, I walked for seven or eight miles along the Long Trail, a wilderness footpath that runs unbroken through the Green Mountains from Massachusetts to the Canadian border. Not once did I glimpse a waymarking view though the aspen, birch, maple, oak and hemlock. It was an absorbing woodland climb nonetheless. There are endless distractions in the shadow of these trees – paper trails of shredded birch bark, grouse scuttling in the undergrowth, fungi fanning out of dead wood like Saturnian rings – and you need always to know where you are going. 'The Green Mountain Boys will not be frightened, and they shall ambush you', Allen counselled anyone seeking to enforce the law of the gods of the valleys. 'For they well understand the narrow passes of the mountains, and are lusty and strong, and are well skilled in the use of the bow.'[5]

The social fabric of this band of brothers is best demonstrated by looking at how they mustered for their most famous action, the capture of the British-held Fort Ticonderoga in the early days of the Revolution. When the discord between Britain and its colonies escalated into all-out war in April 1775, the Boys buried the hatchet with the Yorkers and joined the fight against the tyranny of Mad King George. Almost immediately they agreed to try to take Ticonderoga's huge star-shaped citadel, situated at a prime vantage point overlooking Lake Champlain on the western boundary of the New Hampshire Grants.

Allen collected a core group of renegades and set out from Bennington on the seventy-mile march north. Along the way he recruited volunteers from farms, homesteads and taverns, most of whom were related to him or knew him personally, or knew him by reputation as a protector of their land rights against the government of New York. By the time the group stood within a cannon ball's arc of the fort, Allen had gathered a 'kin army' numbering 230, including at least three of his brothers (Ira among them), three of his cousins and a fraternity of village and farming families, one of which contributed at least six members across two generations.

They were a motley crew, according to Willard Sterne Randall, Allen's latest and most thorough biographer. He counts among them hunters and trappers, a lawyer and a tavern owner, town clerks and shopkeepers, a poet, a recent Yale College graduate, immigrants fresh off the boat from Scotland, England and Ireland, and a future congressman. They arrived at their staging point, Hand's Cove, on the shore of Lake Champlain, 'in their work clothes or in buckskin hunting shirts made by their wives, sisters, or mothers ... in linsey-woolsey, fustian or plush, in wool stockings, moccasins or rude boots, in prized beaver hats or bearskin caps, in calico or silk waistcoats'.[6]

A ragtag bunch, but a cohesive one. In a comprehensive analysis of the men's social dynamics, one American historian noted how, on the eve of Revolution, Allen managed to fuse 'disparate groups of western Vermonters into a highly motivated, insurgent organization replete with all the features of a revolutionary political entity'.[7] They were bound together by their frontier spirit and their loyalty to one another, notwithstanding the differences between them. This unity of background and purpose appears to have been central to their victory at Ticonderoga. Even though there were thousands of British loyalists living in the New Hampshire Grants, and many others who wanted no part of the Revolution, the British soldiers manning the fort remained unaware they were the target of attack until dawn on 10 May 1775, when they woke to discover Allen and his party lined up on the parade ground. The British commander surrendered immediately, and thus the first American offensive of the war was won with no lives lost and barely a shot fired, to the 'agreeable disappointment' of Allen's men.[8]

In recognition of their achievement, the Green Mountain Boys were incorporated into the American army as an independent regiment, with Allen and his cousin Seth Warner in command and able to choose their own officers, an unusual concession. Five months after Ticonderoga, Allen was captured by the British in a hair-brained attempt to take Montreal and spent the next two and a half years in captivity. Warner took over command of the regiment, which went on to rout the British in August 1777 at the Battle of Bennington, a few miles from the Boys' old hangout, the Catamount Tavern. It was another decisive victory, one that cost the British nearly a thousand men. Like the Yorkers before them, the redcoats were ill-equipped for fighting in the woods.

The importance of social cohesion to military effectiveness has long been recognized by generals and strategists. Henry V appeared to make much of it before his victory at the battle of Agincourt in 1415 against French forces that were vastly superior in both numbers and nourishment. Shakespeare's rendering of his motivational address – 'We few, we happy few, we band of brothers; for he today that sheds his blood with me shall be my brother'[9] – thereafter became a rallying cry for generations of English troops facing daunting odds on the eve of battle.

In the American Civil War, in which both Union and Confederate soldiers suffered great hardships and high risk of death for little and irregular pay, group loyalty was the 'cement of the armies'.[10] It compensated for inadequate training and a pervasive lack of discipline among the troops. In the Union army this was largely by design. Volunteer companies consisted of men from the same town or valley who knew each other well. They joined up, fought and died together, and they were rarely replaced by outsiders.

The effectiveness of building an army out of homogenous groups that already existed in civilian life has been demonstrated recently by Dora Costa and Matthew Kahn, both economists at the University of California, Los Angeles (they happen to be married to each other). In *Heroes and Cowards*, a sociological study of the Civil War, they show that Union army soldiers who served alongside others who were recruited from the same area, were of about the same age and shared the same peacetime occupation (such as farmer or labourer) were far less likely to desert or go AWOL. These factors, which helped define a unit's group identity, were significantly more important than morale or ideological fervour in determining whether someone stuck with the fight.[11] In this most gruesome of conflicts, loyalty to the friends around you counted for everything.

Consider this depiction of the pull of brotherhood in a letter from a Civil War veteran, a volunteer with the 122nd New York infantry regiment. On 9 July 1864, he wrote to his sister:

You ask me if the thought of death does not alarm me. I will say I do not wish to die ... I myself am as big a coward as any could be, but give me the ball [bullet] before the coward when all my friends and companions are going forward. Once and once only was I behind when the regt was under fire, and I can't discribe [sic] my feelings at that time none can tell them only a soldier. I was not able to walk ... but as soon as the rattle of musketry was heard and I knew my Regt was engaged I hobbled on the field and went to them.[12]

Nearly a century later, during the Second World War, cohesion and camaraderie were just as crucial in persuading men to fight. The pioneering American sociologist Samuel Stouffer surveyed more than half a million US soldiers during the conflict as director of the Research Branch of the War Department's Education and Information Division. He asked them about their attitudes to war, what drove them during combat, how they felt about their role as a soldier and whether the things for which the US was fighting were worth risking their lives for. Stouffer's findings contradicted much of what the Army hierarchy believed about the psychology of conflict. The most important motivational factors governing combatants' will to fight were not idealism, leadership, survival or hatred of the enemy, as was commonly supposed, but group solidarity, along with the desire to finish the fight and get home to their loved ones.[13]

The Army took Stouffer's results seriously, translating them into policy and using them in propaganda films such as Frank Capra's series *Why We Fight*. For the first time, military leaders began to trust scientific analysis over conventional wisdom when considering how best to prepare soldiers for battle. Stouffer even helped them reduce desertion rates by recommending that soldiers be sent home on leave wearing their uniforms rather than civilian clothes. In uniform they were treated as heroes by their families, which boosted their self-esteem and made it more likely they would return to their units.

Among Stouffer's researchers during the latter stages of the war was Irving Janis, the father of 'groupthink' theory, who was drafted into the army in his early twenties and spent several months interviewing US troops fighting in Europe. Janis was astonished at how often soldiers would turn down a promotion if it meant being moved to another unit, and how often ill and injured men refused sick leave, or even discharged themselves from hospital against medical orders in order to return to their buddies. 'Time and again we encountered instances when a man failed to act in accordance with his own self-interests [for fear of] letting the other guys down', he recalled.[14] Second World War combat historian S. L. A. Marshall observed that taking a single soldier from a broken unit and assigning him to another was rarely effectual, but that a pair of soldiers re-assigned together would usually fight well.[15]

Lieutenant E. W. Stoneham, who fought with the Royal Artillery during the First World War, encapsulated the spirit of fellow-feeling:

> The comradeship among men was really most extraordinary and very difficult to describe. On one occasion I was offered a safe job behind the lines if I would care to join Brigade Headquarters. It was very tempting but I didn't want to go. There was something about the relationship with the men that one didn't want to break. One would somehow have felt rather a traitor to them, so I refused it and stayed with them.[16]

This kind of group loyalty in the face of enemy fire is by no means specific to men. The exclusively female volunteer nurses and ambulance drivers of the First Aid Nursing Yeomanry (FANY), who served on the western front from 1914 to 1918, were well known for their comradeship and devotion to duty at a time when the military establishment did its best to keep women out of military roles. FANY volunteers were in the thick of it, carrying mutilated men to hospital as shells exploded around them, often at night with their lights off in the freezing cold, the air full of the smell of burnt flesh. One volunteer described the experience as 'an awful hell of agony'.[17] A profile of the FANY camps in *Vogue* reported that they were 'up to their knees in blood, amputating, tying up, bandaging, without rest or relief', a degree of commitment that the author argued laid to rest 'the irritating masculine "gag" that women cannot work together'.[18]

Why does group cohesion in times of danger have such a dramatic effect on motivation? The obvious answer is that it is critical to survival. A soldier's chances of getting through a firefight are far greater when he is fighting among others whose characters and capabilities he knows well. 'You want them to support you when you are pinned down or in a bad spot and they need to feel that they can count on you', explained Lawrence Nickell, a mortar-man in the US 5th Infantry Division in the Second World War.[19]

Soon after the Allied invasion of Iraq in April 2003, Leonard Wong, a professor of military strategy at the US Army War College, took a research team to the country to try to understand what motivates soldiers in battle. After many interviews, he noted that US infantrymen felt a level of trust with their fellow soldiers that exceeded anything they had previously experienced, greater than between husband and wife, or father and son. '[Your comrade] means more to you than anybody', one soldier told him. 'You will die if he dies. That is why I think that we protect each other in any situation. I know that if he dies and it was my fault, it would be worse than death to me.'[20] Death before dishonour: a soldier's maxim, and the most common regimental motto.[21]

In investigating why camaraderie is essential for combat effectiveness, Wong has found it instructive to look at cases where relationships have broken down, when loyalty has disintegrated in the face of rivalry, mistrust or inadequate leadership. Very often this leads to a unit's failure in battle. During his research mission to Iraq in 2003, Wong interviewed Iraqi prisoners of war who told him of a spectacular lack of cohesion within the Iraqi Regular Army. Platoons had fragmented along tribal or regional lines, they said, and many soldiers had deserted. Wong described the disintegration of the Iraqi army as 'a good case study of what happens ... when social cohesion and leadership are absent'.[22] On an individual level, a fractious unit is a bad place to be. Facing the horrors of battle without the emotional security of a sympathetic leader and a community of pals can be highly destabilizing. It can also be a fast track to post-traumatic stress disorder (PTSD): one of the primary risk factors for PTSD is the lack of a strong support network.

By the same measure, an army can make up in cohesiveness what it lacks in numbers or armaments. During the Vietnam War, the North Vietnamese Army remained astonishingly resolute in the face of overwhelming US firepower and logistical support. Despite being inferior on every traditional measure of military strength, it had what its chief of staff, Van Tien Dung, called 'moral superiority': highly motivated, loyal soldiers fighting under a caring, well-organized leadership. It helped that, under the country's mobilization law, close-knit villages came together as 'self-defence forces', armed by the government. The British military fielded a similar advantage over Argentine forces during the Falklands War in 1982. The logistical challenge of fighting eight thousand miles from home, with limited air power and against superior numbers, mattered less on the ground, where it quickly became apparent that Argentina's conscript units were poorly organized. A condition of the Argentine surrender was that their officers could keep their pistols as protection against their own men, a testament to how badly trust in authority had broken down.[23]

One of the most illuminating analyses of bonding among soldiers is a study by University of Chicago sociologists Edward Shils and Morris Janowitz into the remarkable tenacity of the retreating Germany army during the final months of the Second World War. Received wisdom had it that the Wehrmacht continued to fight effectively and experience low desertion rates because its soldiers adhered to the ideology of National Socialism. But Shils and Janowitz discovered something different. The typical German soldier, they claimed, carried on throwing himself into battle because his immediate group met his basic, organic needs: '[It] offered him affection and esteem from both officers and comrades, supplied him with a sense of power and adequately regulated his relations with authority.' The high command manipulated these dynamics from the start. For example, it made sure that men fought side by side with others of similar age and ethnic background (the most effective units were largely made up of Germans, with few Austrians, Czechs or Poles). They moved entire divisions into and out of the front line to give new recruits a chance to integrate into their units before seeing any action.[24] When, twenty years later, US morale and battlefield success were suffering during the Vietnam War, Janowitz was one of several sociologists who argued that a policy of frequently rotating soldiers and officers into and out of units was to blame. Firepower counts for nothing without solidarity.[25] [26]

How do you get people to pull together who are not all cut from the same cloth – when you cannot rely on indigenous uniformity, as the Wehrmacht did, or the kind of social ties exploited by the Green Mountain Boys? Armies use all kinds of ruses. Close-order marching and other drills that encourage synchronous movement are customary in training despite being irrelevant for combat because they are a well-established way of breaking down boundaries and building trust and co-operation.[27] (Marching in step has also been shown to improve group economic decision-making, an idea that has yet to be fully exploited by business managers.)[28]

Initiation rites, which are common to fraternities, social clubs and other brotherhoods the world over, serve a similar psychological purpose, despite being often humiliating, sadistic, unsafe and nearly always officially unsanctioned. The aim is to encourage novices, through a painful sacrifice, to value membership of the group. Removing an apple from the buttocks of a fellow greenhorn before a bunch of jeering veterans or having your regimental badge imprinted on your flesh is actually going to make you feel good, since you will be admitted to that privileged club of those who have endured the same.

Rituals promote social stickiness. They bind people together. How so? Harvey Whitehouse at the University of Oxford has spent a good part of his career trying to answer this question. He is currently leading a $5 million project at Oxford's Institute of Cognitive and Evolutionary Anthropology examining the role of ritual in social behaviour, child development and political systems.[29] He believes one of the reasons rituals are so effective is that they are hard to forget. If you experience something frightening or painful it becomes part of your life story, and if you experience it with others then 'you extend your sense of self to them and to all intents and purposes they become part of who you are'. The more traumatic the ritual, the richer the experience, and the stronger the connections between those who took part, he says.

Being under fire together can have a similar effect. In 2011, Whitehouse and his doctoral student Brian McQuinn travelled to Libya to study group cohesion among the revolutionaries fighting Muammar Gaddafi's forces in Misrata. They discovered that the rebels who had been through the most intense firefights reported feeling closer to the men in their units than they did to their own families. As Whitehouse has found elsewhere, the more terrifying the shared experience, the closer the group. The researchers observed that some Libyan rebel groups used rituals to help them during battles. 'Even during the most intense house-to-house fighting, there would be one member of the brigade who carried no arms at all, whose job was simply to lead the chanting', says Whitehouse. 'They chanted *Allahu Akbar* as they fought. These kinds of things instil greater courage. They also serve in the long run to bind the group even more tightly together.'[30]

It can take weeks or months of living and training together for a bunch of comrades to build deep trust, but once established such bonds are hard to break. Veterans frequently talk about their squad or section as if they were family. 'We eat, drink, [go to the bathroom] – everything – together', one American soldier told Wong in Iraq. 'I think that it should be like that ... I really consider these guys my own family, because we fight together, we have fun together ... We are to the point where we even call the squad leader "Dad".'[31]

Irving Janis, reviewing his observations of combat soldiers during the Second World War, tried to understand such yearnings in terms of the Freudian concepts of separation anxiety and transference. In extremely fearful situations, he reasoned, people's primary childhood anxiety – separation from their mother or father – is reawakened, compelling them to seek reassurance in any available group. 'Thus, the company commander or the surgeon is likely to become a symbolic representative of the father, and a fellow soldier or fellow patient may become a substitute for an older or younger brother.'[32] Losing a cherished leader or any of this surrogate family, or even being separated from them, can be traumatic. One unnamed American soldier in Italy during the Second World War described being transferred to another unit as like becoming 'an orphan … you feel lost and lonesome'.[33] The death of a colleague on the battlefield is widely cited by military psychiatrists as the greatest source of anguish for soldiers, akin to a parent losing a child, because it so often triggers feelings of remorse, guilt and anger at having failed to do more to protect them.[34] Such sentiments have been expressed many times in art and literature, never so eloquently as by Erich Maria Remarque in *All Quiet on the Western Front*:

> These voices, these few quiet words, these footsteps in the trench behind me recall me at a bound from the terrible loneliness and fear of death by which I had been almost destroyed. They are more to me than life, these voices, they are more than motherliness and more than fear; they are the strongest, most comforting thing there is anywhere; they are the voices of my comrades.[35]

———

One rainy day towards the end of 2012, I drove to a house in a small cul-de-sac on the south coast of Britain to meet someone who knows a fair bit about how military units co-opt the small-group dynamics of a family. Alan Biffen, who is eighty-eight, piloted one of the Royal Air Force's seven-man Lancaster bombers during the war, a dangerous and intimate assignment. Crammed inside a metal fuselage, anti-aircraft shells exploding all about them, Lancaster crews survived or died together, and their chances of dying were extremely high. Out of 125,000 airmen who flew with Bomber Command, more than forty-four per cent were killed – worse survival odds than those of an infantry officer during the First World War.[36]

I was met at the door by Alan's amiable companion of four years, Ziggy, a twelve-year-old golden retriever who resembled an ornate rug. Halfway through our conversation Ziggy would make a series of retching sounds and deposit something indigestible on the carpet, an incident that stood out because Alan's home is immaculately kept. Paintings of aircraft dominate the walls, including one of the Lancasters he flew. He was neatly dressed in brown corduroys and a claret sweater, his grey hair swept back. He has a healthful air. He looks like a survivor. Indeed, he has survived two wives. There is resilience in his family. His brother Tony, a Spitfire pilot, died aged ninety-one three weeks before my visit. His father survived the Somme, though he was badly wounded.

Alan joined the RAF when he was seventeen, having lied about his age. After completing his training in the cloudless skies above Arizona, he spent a year as a staff pilot helping newbie navigators find their way through the capricious British weather. Then, in 1944, he was given his own crew. They were lucky: they flew some fourteen missions together, returning each time virtually unscathed. Despite knowing the odds, Alan says they never once discussed the possibility of getting hit:

> It was a foregone conclusion: if we go, we all go together. So let's stay close. Let's be sure that we all know what we're doing and make every effort to get there and back. I remember once seeing a bomber fire-balling in the sky, the whole thing going up, hit by an ack-ack shell. Not a word was said, because every one of us thought, there but for the grace of God go we. You didn't think it would happen to you. Ever. I don't know why people think like this. Perhaps it's the psychological effect of being with other people, getting through a difficult situation with them.

At one point during our conversation Alan adjusted his gold-rimmed spectacles and acknowledged some cognitive dissonance: 'I look back on it sometimes and think, I suppose we did do that, or have I read it all in a book somewhere?' Yet he was very clear on what it felt like, and when he spoke of his crew it was as if he had been with them yesterday. I asked him how he came to be with those particular six men, whose average age was twenty-two. It was strange, he said.

We were all put into a hall. Right-o chaps, they said, choose your crew. And that was it. You all mingled about. We'd all ask each other questions. Within ten minutes you would either move on to someone else or you'd say, fair enough, would you like to be my navigator, wireless operator, bomb aimer or whatever. That's how all air crews were formed.

At first glance this seems like a curiously random selection process, given how much time the men would be spending in each other's company in the most testing conditions. But such choices are often best left to intuition. Analyse too closely the multitudinous permutations of character and disposition and you can end up with nonsensical outcomes, as many a recruitment consultant will quietly attest. Group bonds are built not so much through the meshing of personalities as through interdependency born of shared experience. As Alan and his six crew members soon found out, to survive in a Lancaster bomber required teamwork.

It didn't take one long to realize that you couldn't fly the airplane by yourself. You had other people, and not only were you responsible for them but you depended on them. I depended on my navigator to tell me where to go, on my bomb aimer to line up correctly and set his bombsight, on the gunners to keep looking out for enemy fighters. The essence of the close friendship within the crew was that you instinctively knew your life might depend on one or other of them at any time. It was a feeling of complete trust.

In a study of psychological distress among US Air Force personnel in the war, military psychiatrists Roy Grinker and John Spiegel observed that group bonding served as a defence against trauma. Bomber crews quickly became inseparable, even though they were thrown together mostly by chance. 'Day after day, on mission after mission, this mutual dependence is made to pay dividends in safety and effectiveness of the combat crew', they noted. 'It is no wonder then that the emotional relationships between these fliers assume a special character. The men and their plane become identified with each other with an intensity that in civil life is found only within the family circle.'[37]

Even that may be understating it. Irving Janis maintained that the psychological processes found in combat units are like those shaping group behaviour in everyday life.[38] Yet it rarely feels that way to those who have experienced both worlds. 'The companionship and respect and general feeling that I had as a crew member of a Lancaster is something I've kept with me for all these years and I shall never forget it', said Alan. 'It's a feeling of gratitude and I'm glad I experienced it. I don't say it made me a better person, but it certainly gave me something which I haven't experienced at all in my civilian life.'

I left him feeling the way I used to feel after talking to my grandfather about the war: grateful that he had chosen to share his experiences, and aware that the only people who could truly understand them were the ones who were there with him. Later, I traced a connection between these two men. Alan had mentioned a rare daylight bombing raid he made on the French town of Caen soon after the D-Day landings. My grandfather, on the ground in Normandy with the Coldstream Guards at the head of a troop of tanks, evidently saw those bombs. His diary tells of 'a thousand bombers bombarding the Germans north of Caen … As dawn broke we saw the amazing sight of all these bombers … I thought nothing could survive this onslaught. I could not have been more wrong.'[39]

———————

War, or the training for war, provides all the ingredients for powerful group attachment, but it is not the only arena where such forces are at play. Combat units are not the only bands of brothers. Take New York City's Fire Department (FDNY), known as 'New York's bravest', which is famous for its culture of loyalty.

The FDNY is as intimate an organization as any in the military. Brothers, fathers, sons and uncles serve together, and the honour of being a member is passed down, generation to generation. Even those who are unrelated regard each other as family. That is hardly surprising, given the way the service is run. On duty in the firehouse, the crew don't just work, train and check equipment together. They live together, sleep at close quarters and share meals. Then, when the bell sounds, they go out and risk their lives together.

This partly explains what happened to the FDNY on 11 September 2001. At 8:46 that morning, Joe Pfeifer, a FDNY battalion chief, was checking a gas leak in a street in downtown Manhattan when the sound of a plane unusually close overhead caused him to look up in time to see it hit the north tower of the World Trade Center. He was the highest-ranked officer in the area and he knew this was his call. So he and his team loaded up and headed straight for the building, where they set up a command post in the lobby amid the wreckage and the broken glass and the dazed and injured people. By then, just about all the active fire crews in the city were making their way downtown and, as they arrived, Pfeifer ordered them up the stairs, towards the remains of the plane some ninety floors above them that was burning away the skeleton of the skyscraper.

Among them was Pfeifer's brother Kevin, a company lieutenant in the FDNY. Later Joe recalled: 'We spoke only a few words then gave each other a look as to worry if the other was going to be okay. But people needed to be evacuated and there were many people trapped. So my brother started walking up the stairs attempting to rescue those in need.'[40] He never saw him again. After the south tower collapsed, Joe gave the order for all firefighters to evacuate the north tower, recognizing it was only a matter of time before it, too, would fall. Kevin started to make his way down. He reached the tenth floor, then realized that some of his comrades were heading towards a blocked exit and paused to redirect them. Many of those he helped made it out, but Kevin ran out of time. He was one of 343 New York firefighters who died that day.

Joe Pfeifer was one of several FDNY firefighters to lose a close relative on 9/11. John Vigiano Sr, a highly respected retired fire engine driver whose father had been a firefighter, lost both his sons: Joe, a policeman, and John Jr, a third-generation fireman. In radio and TV interviews, Vigiano Sr said that the FDNY's sense of brotherhood was the main reason John Jr had signed up, having originally set his sights on being an entrepreneur. 'He wanted to be the next Donald Trump. He was going to make a million dollars and take care of his mother and father.' But then his father had become seriously ill. 'In 1984 I came down with throat cancer', said Vigiano Sr. 'He noticed then how my unit took care of us, and he says, "I'm going to become a fireman".' The FDNY issued him the same badge his grandfather had worn, no. 3436. Joe was thirty-four when he died, and John was thirty-six, a coincidence of numbers that Vigiano says gives him comfort.[41]

In a close-knit outfit, the sense of loss when things go wrong in the field can be hard to bear. Yet Pfeifer has said that many acts of bravery by FDNY firefighters, and even their fabled aggression against the toughest fires, are a result of the intimate working conditions. Consider the many men who were about to go off duty when the hijacked planes hit the Twin Towers on 9/11 but elected to carry on rather than leave their buddies to the biggest fire of their lives.

This culture of loyalty, which often plays out as competitiveness between units, stretches back more than a century and a half, to the era when New York City's fire service consisted of rival gangs who would battle for the honour of putting out a blaze by racing each other to the scene. Terry Golway, a historian at Kean University, whose father, father-in-law, godfather and uncles were all New York City firefighters, claims the competition was so intense that 'many companies, when confronted with crowded streets, jumped curbs and hauled their engines along sidewalks, to the dismay and occasional horror of the general public'.[42]

Rivalry between groups can spark extraordinary acts of devotion and altruism, but it is not always to the common good. On 9/11, the FDNY and the New York Police Department (NYPD), long-standing rivals in emergency response, failed to share information that could have saved lives. When the south tower collapsed, the NYPD's Emergency Service Unit, observing the events from a helicopter, noticed that part of the north tower was glowing red from the intense heat and radioed a rapid evacuation order to all the officers inside. It repeated this order some minutes later when it noticed that the tower was starting to buckle and leaning to the south. But it did not pass on any of this to the FDNY, whose commanders had no aerial view and were not aware of the dire state of the building's infrastructure. When the FDNY eventually issued an evacuation order, it came without the same heightened sense of urgency. So while police officers were jumping from landing to landing by sliding down the banisters to escape the building, many firefighters were walking down the stairs.[43] Around one hundred and fifty firefighters died in the north tower. An official investigation found that the lack of communication contributed to the high numbers of deaths.[44] There was no suggestion that the NYPD deliberately withheld information from the FDNY. Instead, it was a tragic example of how in-group bias can lead to organizational failure when there is no strategy for co-operation in place.

———

The effectiveness of the FDNY derives from relationships forged in adversity – the same ingredients that catalysed the Green Mountain Boys, RAF bomber crews and numerous combat units throughout history. The people in these groups shared salt together, as Aristotle put it: their friendships were built on experiences knowable only to themselves. It may seem self-evident that cohesion in groups is strongest in times of crisis, since it is in our interests to act altruistically towards those on whom our lives depend. But that doesn't fully explain why the bonds of brotherhood run so deep in these cases, nor why they endure. Nor does it answer the question raised in the next chapter: why, in other kinds of groups that operate in extreme environments, such as polar expeditions and space shuttle crews, it can be so hard to predict whether team members will get along and how they will behave in an emergency.

Nearly a century after the American Revolutionary War, descendants of the original Green Mountain Boys once again came down from the valleys to fight – this time for the Union army during the Civil War. As before, there was no questioning their loyalty: twice as many Vermont soldiers died during the conflict per head of population compared with any other Union state; the First Vermont Brigade lost more men in action than any other brigade in the history of the US Army.[45]

The roots of this sacrifice are not lost on the people of Vermont today. The Vermont National Guard is still known as the Green Mountain Boys, though women have served in it for over half a century. Its official banner is the same standard that was carried by the original Green Mountain Boys through the hills in pursuit of the British at the birth of America: thirteen white stars on blue, against a field – naturally – of green.

6

In It Together

It was early January 1993, and Mike Stroud and Ranulph Fiennes were halfway through an unsupported crossing of the Antarctic continent via the South Pole, a journey of such unrelenting hardship that nobody had previously attempted it. Both men were experienced adventurers; each had a high regard for the other. Three years earlier, the pair had trekked five hundred miles across the shifting, splintering ice of the Arctic Ocean, ending their journey one hundred miles short of the North Pole after being ground down by severe malnourishment, snow blindness and hypoglycaemia. 'We felt close', wrote Stroud in his book *Shadows on the Wasteland*, 'linked by a camaraderie that had grown through the hardships we had endured, a feeling of unified suffering and achievement, tainted only by our failure.'[1]

To those of us who have never travelled there, the Arctic and the Antarctic may seem interchangeable. They are not. Stroud and Fiennes found Antarctica, with its vast icefields and treacherous crevasses, another challenge entirely, and human behaviour grows capricious in the face of the unknown. Even great friends can surprise each other. And so it happened. On day fifty-four of their slog, when Stroud developed debilitating diarrhoea and had to stop to rest, Fiennes abruptly decided to ditch his companion, telling him he would radio for an aircraft to pick up the stricken explorer and carry on without him. It was the kind of hissy fit you might see in the school playground. This was Stroud's reaction:

> I started to feel the anger rising. From deep inside, it welled up to fill me with fury. I had been waiting for this man for the best part of two months as he did his stupid plod behind me. Now he had the bit between his teeth because I had part of his load on my sledge. How did he dare to threaten me for causing a brief delay?[2]

Almost immediately, Stroud later acknowledged, Fiennes expressed genuine remorse for what he had done. They went on to complete their expedition and they remain firm friends. But the stand-off changed something, at least for a while. 'I doubted that I would ever trust him not to do the same again', Stroud wrote.[3] Other explorers view their relationship with a mixture of amusement and wonder. Fellow polar adventurer Eric Larsen reckons that Stroud and Fiennes kept working together simply because 'they hated each other less than they hated everybody else'.

Nearly twenty years to the day since this incident took place, on the morning of 6 December 2012, I met Mike Stroud on the deck of the SA *Agulhas*, an ice-strengthened supply ship that he and Fiennes, along with others, had acquired for their latest improbable venture. The objective this time was to traverse a two-thousand-mile stretch of Antarctica through the polar winter, when perpetual darkness reigns and temperatures can dip to −80° Celsius. It was the last remaining polar exploration prize still up for grabs. Later that day, they would cast off from their mooring near Tower Bridge on the south bank of the Thames on what Fiennes had immodestly called

The Coldest Journey (the expedition's official name), which he said was sure to be 'without a doubt the greatest and most challenging polar expedition of all time'.[4]

The morning was fittingly chilly, below freezing and cloudless – unusual for London – and Stroud and I were awaiting the start of the press conference at which the expedition team would titillate the world's media with talk of battery-heated clothing, low-temperature metal failure and unfathomable crevasses. He was animated, professorial in his square-rimmed spectacles, and seemed unaffected by the cold: in his blue hooded parka he looked fit for temperatures far lower than this. I asked him about the diarrhoea incident on the 1993 Antarctic trip, and about a previous occasion in the Arctic when he confessed to hating Fiennes so much that he considered shooting him and pitching his body into the sea.[5] He appeared to have forgotten all about them. 'I'd have to re-read the passages in my book that you're referring to. My recollection is that although there were pressures on us and a few episodes of very brief blowing up, overall we did phenomenally well.' Then he added, mischievously: 'I have a very defective short-term memory, the only psychological trait that's important for getting involved repeatedly in things like this.'

This time, although the trek was his idea, Stroud wasn't going. Instead, he had agreed to serve as medical adviser and science director. Originally, he had imagined that he and Fiennes would make the traverse alone by ski, helped by strategically placed supply dumps. The plan now was for six people to travel in an 'ice train' consisting of two insulated metal cabooses pulled by specially adapted Caterpillar tractors run on aircraft fuel (they would require 70,000 litres). Even with all this technology, the journey would take a year to complete, too long for Stroud to be away from his day job as a consultant gastroenterologist at Southampton University

Hospital. His verdict on Fiennes's ostentatiously ambitious shot at polar glory? 'Close to insane. Trying to operate with complicated machinery in that environment is asking for trouble.'[6]

Fiennes is famous among explorers for his iron willpower and his single-mindedness, qualities which have carried him across both polar icecaps, up the north face of the Eiger and to the summit of Everest, often in extreme conditions and at considerable physical cost (severe frostbite, snow blindness and a heart attack). The actress Joanna Lumley, a trustee of *The Coldest Journey* expedition, has described him as 'quite simply one of the big beasts of the world today'. Stroud calls him 'extraordinarily resilient and utterly determined. His drive is unparalleled in anyone I've ever met.'

At the press conference, Fiennes sat eagle-like on the makeshift stage with members of his ice team, scrutinizing his audience. At six feet four he loomed a head higher than his five colleagues, and at sixty-eight he was three or four decades older than everyone except fifty-four-year-old traverse navigator Brian Newham. He looked patrician, paternalistic and slightly impatient. As a rule, he does not smile cheaply. His face is never still, his bushy grey eyebrows twitch constantly like antennae in search of a signal. His responses are deadpan and free of cliché. When questioned why he was crossing Antarctica in winter, he cited the age-old British rivalry with the Norwegians who, he said, 'consider the polar regions to be theirs and not for people like the Brits to muck around in'. I asked him whether he expected the members of the team to get along living in such close proximity for so long. He said: 'I believe everybody should be treated like your wife. As you know there are two rules for getting on with your wife. Number one, let her think she always has her own way. Number two, make sure she always does have her own way. Does that answer your question?'

Not exactly. But then I'd heard him answer variations of this question in intriguing ways, once telling an interviewer that there are two kinds of people he tends to avoid taking to Antarctica: those who wear spectacles because they can't see through them when they mist up, and 'Yorkshire people' because they tend to be dour and disinclined to forgive and forget.[7]

For students of behaviour, explorers are a compelling breed, specifically because they wrestle constantly with one of the great challenges of human nature. They are by necessity highly driven, obsessive and single-minded in quest of their goal, whether it be a pole or a summit, a world record or a personal best. They want to be the first, the fastest or the most outrageous. Yet they can rarely achieve these things on their own, such are the extremes in which they operate. They must play teammate as well as maverick, and know when to play which. It's a game we all play in daily life, though on the polar ice or in a mountain blizzard it is a game of life and death. Little surprise that tensions and disagreements are commonplace on expeditions, and that unity is often threatened by rivalry and infighting.

One of the best-known cases of team dynamics gone awry occurred in 1985 on the *In the Footsteps of Scott* expedition to the South Pole. That Antarctic winter, a group led by Robert Swan (and which included Mike Stroud) camped at Cape Evans, just down the beach from Robert Falcon Scott's wooden hut. Later, some of them followed Scott's route to the pole. The official diaries of the trip give distinctly different accounts of their experiences. Take these two entries, both recorded on 9 April 1985:[8]

Gareth Wood: 'I find it difficult living in the hut at times. It feels like I'm the only one with any cleanliness or organization. The clean tea-towel is used as an all-purpose rag, then screwed up in a ball and deposited on the shelf. Am I the only one who uses the towel rail?'

Roger Mear: 'I am closest by a large degree to Mike; he is the only one with whom I share any interest that is not centred on the expedition. Gareth with his conscientiousness I find the most irritating, more so even than Robert, whose relationship with me is one of mutual tolerance fostered by the inevitability of our involvement with each other in the journey to come.'

Hardly a marriage made in heaven. Things got worse when Stroud, Mear and Wood made a sixty-mile trek, in darkness and temperatures down to −40° Celsius, across the Ross Ice Shelf to Cape Crozier to collect penguin eggs. Their plan had been to re-enact a trip made in 1911 by three members of Scott's party, though they hoped the outcome would be less appalling: Scott's men had to be cut out of their frozen clothing when they returned to the hut.[9] One of them, the zoologist Apsley Cherry-Garrard, dubbed it 'the worst journey in the world … no words could express its horror', noting that the cold had cracked all the men's teeth and frozen the pus in their blistered skin. This did nothing to diminish Cherry-Garrard's admiration for his colleagues, however:

They were gold, pure, shining, unalloyed. Words cannot express how good their companionship was. Through all these days, and those which were to follow, the worst I suppose in their dark severity that men have ever come through alive, no single hasty or angry word passed their lips.[10]

Unfortunately the same could not be said for Stroud, Mear and Wood, whose constant bickering and animosity caused them to lose their way and nearly their lives. This prompted Stroud to predict an 'unmitigated disaster' for the polar march that was scheduled to follow.[11]

Because expedition members depend absolutely on each other's skills and motivation for their survival when the going gets tough, choosing who is on your team may be the most important decision you make. The adventurer Eric Larsen has thought a lot about this – he has even co-authored a scientific paper on coping in extreme environments.[12] The first time I talked to him, in December 2012, he was about to set off on a solo bicycle ride to the South Pole, and his main concern was how he would cope with only a bike as a companion.[13] But he recalled several experiences where he had been frustrated by colleagues who did not share his precise goals (they were more interested in doing science, say, than reaching the pole), whose motivation did not come from within ('you need to have this fire inside of you that makes you want to do it!'), or – most disruptive of all – whose personalities did not fit. 'For me, personality is the biggest thing of all', he maintains – to the extent that while putting together his team for his 2010 North Pole trip he sent a survey to every applicant with fifty questions that he hoped would sort the nervous from the confident, the friendly from the cold. 'I asked them what they liked to eat, whether they were a morning or an evening person, what they found funny.' How did it pan out? 'It wasn't a conclusive success, but it helped me understand who those people were once we started training and working together.'

One of Larsen's co-authors on his paper on extreme environments is the Norwegian psychologist Gro Sandal of the University of Bergen, who for the past two decades has been studying the behaviour of adventurers and astronauts who operate in isolated or confined places. Sandal has identified three characteristics that she says are needed to ensure group cohesion: emotional stability, strong social and communication skills and commitment to a common goal.[14] However, she acknowledges that it is very hard to predict from people's personalities how they will fit when confined together on the polar ice or in a capsule two hundred miles above the Earth, and how well they will cooperate. She has found that sixty per cent of the variation in people's behaviour cannot be foretold from standard psychometric testing. This suggests that while Larsen's survey might reveal what his prospective teammates are like as individuals, it will tell him little about how they might get on as a group.

You can get a better idea, Sandal says, of who will make a good team member by observing them interacting in a trial setting. For instance, if you're preparing for a polar march, take them somewhere cold and hostile. 'Behaviour depends very much on social context. You have to take the behaviour of others into account.' That is especially true in extreme environments. Medical anthropologist Lawrence Palinkas, who has carried out dozens of behavioural studies in isolated and unusual places, has found that research scientists and others who 'over-winter' in Antarctica are influenced primarily by the physical and social conditions in which they are living rather than their personality traits. Psychological coping mechanisms are 'situation-specific', he argues, and 'not generalizable from one social environmental context to another'.[15]

Few stories of extreme adventure better illustrate the unpredictable power of environment over character than what happened to the Atlantic Odyssey rowing team in January 2012. The British-Irish crew was attempting to cross the Atlantic from east to west in a record-breaking thirty days. Skipper Matthew Craughwell had selected three top-level rowers and three experienced adventurers, a combination that everyone believed would maximize their speed and endurance. They planned to row in a two-hours-on/two-hours-off shift pattern from start to finish, an energy expenditure that would require each man to consume 12,000 calories every twenty-four hours (nearly five times the normal recommended level).

Among the expedition members was Mark Beaumont, a twenty-nine-year-old Scotsman who, four years previously, had taken eighty-one days off the record for the quickest circumnavigation of the Earth by bicycle. On that quest, he had pedalled more than ninety miles a day, every day, for twenty-eight weeks. A few months before the Atlantic endeavour, he rowed through the Canadian Arctic with five others to the 1996 location of the magnetic North Pole, a journey previously possible only on foot. So he knows a thing or two about how to keep motivated when you're on your own. 'You don't have the luxury of giving up', he says. He'd also been in enough scrapes on group expeditions to make him very choosy about who he journeys with. 'When you're filling in a CV before an expedition, all of us can write the same thing in terms of our training, we can all tick the same boxes, we all have the same qualifications. But that doesn't at all account for how people react under stress.'

This hit home dramatically on day twenty-eight of the Atlantic Odyssey row when a freak wave capsized the team's eleven-metre boat and pitched them into the sea some five hundred miles from their destination in Barbados. Had they not managed to free the life raft, they would have certainly drowned. Beaumont and others in the group dived repeatedly under the upturned hull to retrieve an emergency beacon, GPS tracker, satellite phone, fresh water and food. Not everyone reacted the same way. 'A couple of the guys went into pretty deep shock', he recalls. 'One of them could barely get a word out. He just shut his eyes and shut down. It is not a rational choice when you lose control of your actions.' Later, he explained to Beaumont what had happened. 'He told me, "I was completely out of my league. I thought the best thing to do was take up as little room as possible in the liferaft, shut my eyes and wait for it to pass, whether that was to die or be rescued".'[16]

———

Mike Stroud is well aware of the dangers of disharmony in expedition teams. Yet as medical director of Fiennes's *Coldest Journey* expedition, he chose not to use psychological compatibility tests to screen candidates. He doesn't believe they tell you anything. Before spending the winter together in their small hut at Cape Evans, he and the four other members of the 'In the Footsteps of Scott' venture had volunteered to undergo the psychological profiling used by NASA and the US Antarctic Program. The evaluation proved 'so wide of the mark … it utterly failed to identify those of us who found interpersonal relations difficult, while suggesting potential problems' where none arose. 'It's extremely difficult if not impossible to predict how people will behave', he says.

Several nations with bases in Antarctica use a battery of psychometric tests when selecting personnel, even though none of them has been scientifically validated. By contrast, the British Antarctic Survey (BAS) eschews assessments in favour of a more intuitive approach, drawing on performance in interviews and the judgement of experienced staff. This seems to work well in terms of team harmony, though it is hard to quantify what exactly the selection panel is measuring. To try to find out, Palinkas and his colleagues subjected 177 successful BAS candidates to the psychological tests used by other Antarctic organizations to see how well the scores matched the judgements of the panel. They found little correlation. This suggests that the characteristics the BAS considers relevant to coping in an Antarctic winter cannot be measured by psychometrics – or, at least, that the right psychometrics have not yet been discovered.[17]

Stroud also favours intuition. He believed that the five men going with Fiennes were easy-going and adaptable, which made it reasonably likely they would get along. I imagined also that they fit Fiennes's general requirement for 'placid, docile people who aren't malevolent in any way and who don't get too excited when things are going very well or too dismal when they're going badly'.[18] Certainly none of the team wore spectacles or came from Yorkshire. Still, Stroud reckoned things could go 'wildly wrong. It is going to be a very pressurized environment. We know from the history of polar expeditions that there has been unbelievable dissent in small groups cooped up in small boxes.'

In its social dynamics and the otherworldliness of its physical environment – highly confined, hostile, a disrupted day–night cycle

Fig. 7 *The Coldest Journey* expedition in Antarctica.

and the impossibility of rescue – *The Coldest Journey* resembled less an earthly pilgrimage than a trip through space. The research possibilities of this were not lost on Stroud, who is conducting an ongoing side study, dubbed the 'White Mars project', into the effects of the extreme conditions on human physiology and psychology. NASA and other space agencies are watching closely. Mental well-being and team cohesion are considered the number one risk factors in space exploration, those most likely to disrupt or terminate a mission.

To try to shed light on some of these behavioural and psychological unknowns, Russia's Institute for Biomedical Problems and the European Space Agency launched a simulated mission to Mars on 3 June 2010, isolating six 'astronauts' inside a mock spaceship near Moscow for 520 days and observing how they coped. By the time the hatch was unsealed on 4 November 2011, the researchers monitoring the experiment had gathered plenty of data about the effects of long-term confinement on sleep–wake cycles, stress levels, mood stability, loneliness, alertness, cognitive performance and motivation.

They noticed, for example, that the crew became increasingly sedentary as the mission progressed, and that by the end they were sleeping and resting on average more than an hour longer than at the start. Two of the six astronauts suffered exceptionally disrupted sleep patterns, to the extent that one or other of them was asleep when the rest of the team were awake – or vice versa – for more than twenty per cent of the 'trip'. David Dinges, a University of Pennsylvania professor who specializes in the cognitive and behavioural impacts of sleep loss and who co-authored one of the Mars520 studies, warns that this kind of dissonance could disrupt the co-ordination of the crew during long space flights.[19]

More worrying was the discovery that the astronauts' feelings of loneliness, which on average increased over the first six months before subsiding gradually (though with considerable individual variation), appeared to have a marked impact on their cognitive abilities. The lonelier they became, the worse they performed on various numerical tasks set for them by a research team. The leader of this team, Bernadette van Baarsen at the Sapienza University of Rome, thinks that impaired cognition such as slower reaction times could be a problem on space missions, particularly during emergencies when astronauts might have only a few seconds to respond. But she adds that it is impossible to know for sure without testing performance on a real-life mission. 'Mars520 was sort of real but not real. The crew members knew they were in a tank in the middle of Moscow.' What is certain, says van Baarsen, is that crew members 'must be in good shape socially. They must be able to communicate well, both with each other and with the crew on the ground. Failure to communicate would really threaten the safety of the mission.'[20]

Despite the lengthy period of isolation, the tight confinement and the potential for conflict among a culturally diverse crew (three Russians, a French, an Italian and a Chinese), the Mars520 simulation produced no dramatic group rifts nor great antagonism among team members. Still, a real mission to Mars could bring psychological challenges of a different order that may be impossible to simulate, such as the need for the team to be fully autonomous and self-sufficient for up to three years, a half-hour lag on all communication with Earth, and the supremely isolating experience of seeing your view of your home planet diminish to an insignificant speck. Stroud is sceptical that the Mars520 experiment captured any of this because the crew, he says, were

> basically locked in a box in a car park. Psychologically that is not the same. If something had gone wrong they could have come out, they could have gone to hospital. In Antarctica

you can't do that. There are real threats from the hostile environment. The chances of getting hurt or suffering from the psychological pressures are higher. To my mind it is vastly more real.[21]

In his White Mars project, Stroud is using polar exploration as a proxy for space travel. This may be accurate in the case of *The Coldest Journey*, but not for most polar expeditions. Polar trekkers must be highly self-reliant, but they do not necessarily need to be communicative. They fraternize with colleagues only when eating, striking camp or discussing tactics – unlike astronauts, who tend to be around each other a lot of the time. It helps, too, if polar explorers are obsessively driven, which means they are unlikely to be archetypal team players. In these ways they are a self-selecting lot: people who crave constant attention from others, or who demand orderliness in them, are unlikely to apply for a two-month toil across the ice. The social restrictions of the task and the strong possibility of equipment failure would quickly make a handicap of such traits. On the other hand, they could be a virtue if you're cooped up with your colleagues in a metal fuselage for a year and a half.

―――

When the journalist Rebecca Stephens became the first British woman to climb Everest in 1993 at the age of thirty-five, she had to learn what it takes to achieve the seemingly unachievable. But she learned just as much about the advantages of being part of a team. Convinced she could never have climbed it by herself, she came down the mountain with a sense that her companions had psychologically 'cradled her' across the icefalls and crevasse zones, had given her breath in the hypoxic air.

This is how she described her final push for the summit with the two Sherpa guides who accompanied her, Ang Passang and Kami Tchering:

> Working together as a tightly knit team of three, we were to enjoy very real practical advantages. We could take it in turns to lead and kick bucket steps in the snow for those who followed, for example, thus sharing the load. But far, far more important and memorable, was the psychological influence each one of us exerted on the other. Because it was all of us or none of us, the other two people's progress was equally as important as one's own. We cared for the others as much as we did for ourselves … their presence was my inspiration. When I lagged behind, a quick glance at the two figures ahead would draw me along, because I didn't want to let the two of them down, and I didn't want to let myself down either. My memory of our climbing the higher reaches of the South East Ridge is of the three of us acting as a single entity, joined as if tethered by an invisible rope.[22]

In the ultra-competitive macho sport of contemporary mountaineering, such sentiments are as atypical as a windless day at 29,000 feet.

Reflecting on her accomplishment twenty years later, Stephens says her experiences on Everest and the intense feelings of togetherness she felt on the mountain completely changed her attitude towards human interdependence. 'Before, I would call myself rather forcefully independent. It was all a delusion. My life was interconnected with that of friends, family and colleagues. I couldn't have managed on my own.'

Her words are reminiscent of Apsley Cherry-Garrard's account of his experiences on the 'Worst Journey in the World' through the Antarctic winter of 1911. The difficulties faced by his group forged relationships with 'friends who are better than all the wives in Mahomet's paradise', he wrote. 'Give me ex-antarcticists, unsoured and with their ideals intact: they could sweep the world.'[23] This Edwardian inclination to bear affliction cheerfully with those around you was tested *in extremis* the following year, when two of Cherry-Garrard's travelling companions perished with Scott in a tent on the polar icecap.[24] Their camaraderie held even in death. In a letter written hours before he died, Scott told his friend, the author and playwright J. M. Barrie, of their 'desperate state – feet frozen, etc, no fuel, and a long way from food. But it would do your heart good to be in our tent, to hear our songs and our cheery conversation.'[25]

This was adventuring at its most pure and beautiful, when colleagues pulled together or died together, and individual ambition was just one of many motivating factors and not the overriding one, and certainly not the most salient. After the First World War, George Mallory and other stars of British climbing felt the expectations of the entire Empire resting on their shoulders as they threw themselves time and again up Everest's remorseless slopes, what Mallory called that 'infernal mountain, cold and treacherous'.[26] The anthropologist Wade Davis suggests in his beautifully cast history of the 1920s Everest climbers, *Into the Silence*, that these men were driven by the need to travel far from the horrors of the wartime trenches. 'A war that came out of nowhere to consume a generation left in its wake a wasteland of isolation. Every man had to come to terms with the experience on his own.'[27] Except that on the mountain, they were never on their own.

If those golden days of more noble causes ever really existed – clearly Mallory was as obsessed as anyone with getting to the top first – many climbers believe that such selfless ideals are less common today. Most modern Everest expeditions comprise a disparate group of people of varying backgrounds, motivations, abilities and fitness levels, many of whom have never met before, let alone practised climbing together. They might pay an experienced guide tens of thousands of dollars to shepherd them up the mountain and help them reach the summit (or at least prevent them from dying). 'That isn't to say bonds can't be made', says Stephens:

> I only met the Sherpas when on the mountain and felt a tremendous togetherness with them, and certainly could never have climbed the mountain without them. But it's easy to imagine that if you don't know someone so well there might not be the same emotional leap to help when things go wrong, and I've heard it viewed that when you're above eight thousand metres you're on your own – a view I don't share, by the way.

The potentially catastrophic consequences of the lack of cohesion within some modern mountaineering teams became apparent in May 1996, when eight people – three of them experienced guides – died on Everest within twenty-four hours. Later, the disaster was attributed to two factors: a snowstorm that blew in unexpectedly while many climbers were still on the peak, and the disproportionately high number of people (thirty-four) from several different expeditions who were attempting to reach the summit that day. In that individualized milieu, there was little room for teamwork, as survivor Jon Krakauer recalled in his account of the disaster:

> In this godforsaken place, I felt disconnected from the climbers around me – emotionally, spiritually, physically – to a degree I hadn't experienced on any previous expeditions. We were

a team in name only, I'd sadly come to realize. Although in a few hours we would leave camp as a group, we would ascend as individuals, linked to one another by neither rope nor any deep sense of loyalty. Each client was in it for himself or herself, pretty much. And I was no different; I sincerely hoped Doug got to the top, for instance, yet I would do everything in my power to keep pushing on if he turned around.[28]

———

Cohesion sounds like a conspicuously desirable quality, a gold standard for which all groups should strive. Sometimes, however, it can have highly undesirable consequences, encouraging a warped decision-making process known as *groupthink*. Because cohesion feels great – it increases self-esteem and gives people a sense of power – there is a strong incentive to maintain it at the expense of all else. As a result, individuals are often reluctant to voice opinions or share information that might threaten the consensus. They purposefully avoid dissent, which can be a very dangerous situation indeed.

Irving Janis, the Yale University psychologist who coined the term groupthink more than forty years ago, described it as 'a deterioration of mental efficiency, reality testing, and moral judgment' caused by the pressure to conform to group norms.[29] One of his first bizarre encounters with the phenomenon was as a research psychologist studying groups of heavy smokers at an American addiction clinic. He noticed that as the course progressed, group members would pressurize each other into *increasing* the number of cigarettes they smoked each day, apparently to strengthen solidarity and put off the day when the sessions would end and they would have to go their separate ways. In one group, a vocal faction even took the far-fetched position that heavy smoking was an almost incurable addiction, and that drastically reducing their daily tobacco intake was futile. Anyone who demurred was ostracized. When Janis tried to point out that they were missing the whole point of the course, which was to help them cut down their smoking as quickly as possible, they ignored him. Group solidarity had become more important to them than their own health.[30]

The dynamics of addiction therapy might seem a far cry from the extreme motivation required of explorers. Yet groupthink is a risk wherever groups strive for harmony, when fear of rocking the boat can cause you to miss a gaping hole in the hull. Recently, it has contributed to some spectacular falls in the business world. For example, former staff at Lehman Brothers, the fourth-largest investment bank in the United States before it declared bankruptcy in 2008, claimed that the culture of in-house loyalty encouraged by CEO Richard Fuld made it almost impossible to voice dissenting views. In his fourteen years at the helm, Fuld transformed a divisive workplace into a harmonious one, but it became too much of a good thing. Executives failed to spot the obvious signs of dysfunction, or to point them out to their colleagues, because they were so fixated on agreeing with each other, or with their superiors. This is the kind of situation that Eric Schmidt, executive chairman of Google, has said he goes out of his way to avoid. 'What I try to do in meetings is to find the people who have not spoken, who often are the ones who are afraid to speak out, but have a dissenting opinion. I get them to say what they really think and that promotes discussion, and the right thing happens.'[31]

The same forces of groupthink are at play in office meetings and town-hall committees, parish councils and school boards. They are conspicuous, too, on jury panels, which use structured decision-making procedures to try to ensure unbiased deliberation. Even judges are not immune: studies of three-strong judicial panels in

US federal appeals courts have shown that a judge appointed by a Democratic president is likely to vote more conservatively when accompanied by two Republicans.[32] Such conformist tendencies are similar in kind to those noted by Solomon Asch in his line experiments in the 1950s. They derive from a lack of open debate, and also of social sensibilities: criticizing ideas means criticizing the individuals behind them, a high-risk strategy for anyone who values their place in the group.

One of the most high-profile groupthink-fuelled disasters was the loss of the space shuttle Columbia, which exploded over Texas while re-entering the atmosphere on 1 February 2003, killing all seven crew members. The immediate cause was the damage done to the shuttle's heat shield by a piece of foam insulation that had come loose during take-off. NASA could have corrected the problem while the shuttle was still in orbit, yet transcripts of its flight management team meetings during those sixteen days show a fatal reluctance to consider the worst-case scenario. In NASA's success-orientated culture of the time, in which technological risks were weighed against political and economic consequences, no one wanted to play the dissenter and question the status quo by pushing the possibility that the foam could have ruptured the shuttle's wing. According to one report, the team 'made it almost impossible' for dissenting information to be discussed.[33] For example, managers knew that foam had hit the wing but they refused to arrange satellite images to investigate further and even cancelled requests for satellite pictures from outside experts.

Another group effect just as dangerous and ubiquitous as groupthink is the tendency of people striving for cohesion to end up more polarized in their thinking than when they started off. A group of Democrats who share a mildly critical view of the tax outlook of the Tea Party movement will end up after half an hour of friendly

How to avoid groupthink in your organization

The psychologist Irving Janis, originator of the term 'group-think', listed eight symptoms, any one of which might indicate that a group is in danger of conforming to its own norms and corrupting its decision-making process as a result. If your organization exhibits any of these, it may be time to reassess its working practices:

1. An illusion of invulnerability, shared by most or all members, which creates excessive optimism and encourages taking extreme risks.
2. An unquestioned belief in the group's inherent morality.
3. A collective effort to discount warnings or any information that might force members to reconsider their assumptions.
4. Stereotyped views of enemy leaders as too evil to warrant genuine attempts to negotiate.
5. An inclination among members to self-censor any doubts they have about the apparent group consensus.
6. A shared illusion of unanimity over judgements that conform to the majority view, either due to self-censorship or the false assumption that silence means consent.
7. Direct pressure on any member who expresses strong arguments against any of the group's commitments.
8. The emergence of self-appointed 'mindguards' who take it upon themselves to protect the group from adverse information.

Source: Adapted from Irving Janis, *Groupthink: Psychological Studies of Policy Decisions and Fiascoes* (Houghton Mifflin, 1982), pp. 174–5.

discussion convinced its policies are insane. Loyal supporters of a struggling football club need only hunker down in a corner of a pub to convince each other of their team's inevitable end-of-season dominance. People with racist views end up more prejudiced after talking to others of their ilk. Business executives meeting to chew over a marketing strategy they all favour may conclude by boosting its budget even further despite risks that would be obvious to an outsider.

Polarization happens for two reasons: first, when you're surrounded by like-minded people you hear only arguments that support your own viewpoint, which are bound to reinforce it; second, we are always comparing ourselves with others and will shift our position so as not to appear out of line. The same kind of thinking is behind the phenomenon known as 'risky shift' in which adolescents, already prone to risky behaviour, become even more inclined to throw caution to the wind when they are with their peers. Adolescents are especially vulnerable to this because they put a very high value on social rewards, such as the respect of their friends, and are often blind to the negative consequences. At a time when they are spending increasing time with others of their age, they are highly attuned to social judgements. This was nicely demonstrated in an experiment led by the psychologist Laurence Steinberg at Temple University in Philadelphia, in which he measured the brain activity of adults and teenagers while they played a simulated driving game in an fMRI scanner. The teenagers, but not the adults, drove more recklessly – for example, stepping on the throttle at a changing traffic light – and at the same time showed more activity in their neural reward systems if they thought their friends were monitoring their performance in a neighbouring room.[34][35]

The Harvard University legal expert Cass Sunstein, co-author of the best-selling book *Nudge*,[36] has done more than anyone to try to bring the dangers of group polarization to official attention. As an adviser to President Barack Obama, he has been well placed to do just that, heading the White House's Office of Information and Regulatory Affairs from 2009 to 2012, where he tried to inject an understanding of behavioural economics into corporate, social and environmental regulation. We all need to be aware of polarized thinking, he warns in his book *Going to Extremes*, since it is happening all around us. 'It involves our economic decisions, our evaluations of our neighbors, even our decisions about what to eat, what to drink, and where to live.'[37] Like groupthink, polarization is primarily a situational, not a dispositional, phenomenon: chief executives are as susceptible as office clerks. And in the most extreme situations, it can lead to anarchy and terror: many radical fundamentalist groups start out as enclaves of like-minded people who become socially or psychologically segregated from the mainstream.

One of Sunstein's favourite examples of how even the most astute thinkers can be vulnerable to group polarization involves the ideologically fraught decision-making of judges in US federal courts of appeal. We've already established (again thanks to Sunstein) that these judges are liable to groupthink when outnumbered on a judicial panel by colleagues of a different political persuasion. It turns out they show even more bias when sitting with colleagues of the same persuasion. All-Republican panels deliver markedly conservative opinions, all-Democrat panels markedly liberal ones. In gay rights cases, for instance, Sunstein has found that overall, Republican-appointed judges vote sympathetically sixteen per cent of the time, and Democrats fifty-seven per cent. But on ideologically homogenous panels, Republicans vote in favour only fourteen per cent of the time, while Democrats do so one hundred per cent.[38]

Polarized ideologies have become a worrisome feature of America's political landscape (and are increasingly evident in other Western-style democracies where few parties dominate). It resembles a social centrifuge: competing interest groups are flung far from the middle ground with little hope of coalescing. Since the Gallup Poll started measuring ideology in the US in 1992, the proportion of the population describing themselves as 'moderate' has steadily diminished from forty-three per cent to thirty-five per cent, with an increasing percentage veering towards either conservative or liberal.[39] The country is geographically polarized too: the proportion of Americans living in 'landslide' counties, where the winning presidential candidate received more than sixty per cent of votes, rose from 26.8 per cent in 1976 to 47.6 per cent in 2008 and to 52.2 per cent in 2012.[40] Meanwhile, in Britain and elsewhere in Europe there is growing acknowledgement that three decades of political support for multiculturalism – the notion that different cultures and ethnicities should be able to express themselves in any way they choose – has led not to the social cohesion that was hoped for, but to a kind of fractured diversity in which isolated groups regard each other with suspicion.

Why this trend towards extremes? It is hard to say, though societal changes such as improved transport infrastructure, communication technologies and opportunities for home ownership have made it easier for people to move to areas where they will find others who share their moral and political values. This is even more true in our virtual worlds. The Internet, long heralded as a social leveller, in reality helps us fraternize with people whose opinions and prejudices reflect our own. It allows us to hear, as Sunstein puts it, 'more and louder versions' of our own views,[41] which is bound to entrench us further in our ideological castles.[42] The same is true of cable television, which offers viewers a choice of increasingly partisan news channels.[43] None of this is good news for social harmony. Moderation requires interaction; a healthy democracy needs a permissive culture of dissension.[44]

We shouldn't be afraid to put the reins on groupishness, to fight the stultifying and inevitable effects of groupthink and polarization wherever we encounter them: on committees, school boards, working groups, sports teams and government commissions, in courtrooms, churches, fraternities, political parties, regulatory agencies and corporate boardrooms. In this age of social enclaves, we should be cagey of consensus and instead celebrate nonconformity. I favour this advice from the American political activist, writer and self-described myth-buster Barbara Ehrenreich: 'No matter that patriotism is too often the refuge of scoundrels. Dissent, rebellion, and all-around hell-raising remain the true duty of patriots.'[45]

Hive of ideas

Ever since the American advertising guru Alex Osborn coined the term 'brainstorm' in 1948 to describe his group approach to tackling creative problems, psychologists have argued over whether it actually works. Not that this has affected its popularity in advertising, media and other creative industries, where it is still considered indispensable for ideas generation. So how effective is it?

The aim of traditional brainstorming is to negate some of the common conformist effects of group deliberation, such as people's reluctance to break from the majority view. Team members are brought together and encouraged to volunteer all ideas that come to mind and to free-associate without any threat of evaluation, criticism or negative feedback. In terms of number and quality of ideas, brainstorming sessions have been shown to be more productive than formal or hierarchical discussion groups. The problem is that they tend to be less productive than individual members working alone and aggregating their output.

There are three main reasons for this. One, having to wait your turn while someone else presents their idea can take the fire out of whatever you were going to express. Two, many people are inhibited from contributing freely to group discussions even when they know they won't be criticized openly – social anxiety still gets the better of them. Three, hearing other people's thoughts can lead to a kind of cognitive fixation on what has just been said, interrupting one's own creative flow.

An alternative solution is to divide brainstorming sessions into two stages. First, have team members generate ideas on their own, after first stressing the usual ground rules of free association and no (self) criticism. Then bring all the ideas to the table – anonymously if necessary – and brainstorm them further as a group, taking short breaks every few minutes to prevent participants becoming entrenched in whatever is currently under discussion. You might then add a third stage in which the ground rules are abolished and debate and criticism – which can aid creativity – are encouraged. This might sound labour-intensive, but it should exploit each person's strengths when you have no way of knowing how individual team members will behave when they are with others.

There's another option: electronic brainstorming, in which everyone generates ideas and then shares them anonymously via interconnected computers or social media platforms. This way you get to feed off other people's inspiration without the inhibiting effects of being in their physical presence. Several studies have found this to be successful: sharing through a screen can be a lot easier and more appealing than doing it around a table.[46]

The deleterious effects of cohesion can be found in any group of people striving for a common goal, be they Arctic explorers or Wall Street executives. Yet the advantages of working as a team usually far outweigh the risks. This is demonstrably clear in sports, where the rules of the game, the role and ability of each team member and the team's objective are transparent and ensure a high level of co-operation. 'In a well designed team, cohesion has the potential to increase trust, communication and caring and helping behaviour among teammates, all of which can increase performance', says Anthony Pescosolido, a management expert at the University of New Hampshire.[47] The effect is greatest over the long term, he adds. 'The longer that team members work together, the greater their ability to develop clear, well rehearsed routines and special-ized roles. The movie cliché of several members of a sports team having a momentary epiphany, engaging in a group hug and then leaving the locker room to outperform all expectations is only a movie cliché.' This explains why all-star teams that come together for a single game so often perform below expectations, and why the beginning of the new football season can be so painful for fans of teams that have signed a lot of new players. The sum of individual talents tends not to compensate for a lack of unity.

Cohesion can give a team the edge even in pursuits such as cycling where, as with mountaineering, the personal pursuit of excellence appears to be the prime motivator. Competitive road cycling requires spectacular individual effort, but winning races such as the Tour de France requires teamwork, because of the huge physical advantages of sheltering in a teammate's wake. Power and velocity share a cubic relationship, which means that for a cyclist to double his or her velocity requires an eight-fold increase in power.

The faster you are going, the more effort you need to up your speed. But a rider who follows in the slipstream of another can exert around forty per cent less power yet still maintain the same speed. When top cyclists like Bradley Wiggins ride in a capsule, with teammates in front, behind and on either side, the wind drag on his body is minimal and his power advantage can reach sixty per cent. Thus when his moment comes to make his move for the front he should have energy in reserve. The most successful teams are those that co-ordinate their riders to make the most of this basic law of physics.

Such tactics require considerable sacrifice from teammates, who, by riding in front and protecting the strongest members from wind drag, exhaust themselves and blow their own chances of winning. Recall, for instance, Chris Froome's searing efforts in support of Wiggins in the 2012 Tour de France. Many cycling enthusiasts believed Froome had a lot more in the tank and could have taken the yellow jersey himself (he won the Tour the following year). The sports physiologist and former cycling competitor Richard Davison, who has spent twenty years investigating the factors that affect performance and is currently helping to train the next generation of British Cycling coaches, says knowing you have given everything to get a colleague a shot at the lead can make such sacrifices seem more than worthwhile. 'You're working at the front of the pack way beyond what you know you can sustain, but it's for the betterment of the team. You're either pulling the group back or you're making sure your leader is in a position where it's up to them to show their physical power and win the race. It allows you to play your part.'

This is not the only level on which social dynamics can affect performance in competitive cycling. In what is recognized as the first social psychology study of all time, published in 1898 in the

American Journal of Psychology,[48] the psychologist Norman Triplett showed that American cyclists who competed in races against others, or who rode in tandem with a pace group, recorded average times over a mile that were twenty-six per cent and twenty-three per cent faster respectively than those who simply rode by themselves unpaced, against the clock. The mere presence of others appeared to have a significant energizing effect.[49]

———

The *Coldest Journey* expedition reached Antarctica on 20 January 2013 and quickly began to fulfil Stroud's darkest expectations. A month in, Fiennes developed frostbite on the fingers of his left hand after removing a glove to mend a ski binding. Requiring surgery, he flew out on the last plane to leave the continent before the onset of winter. The five others carried on, but in the middle of June, after struggling through poor weather and extensive and unexpectedly hazardous crevasse fields that had never before been tested in twenty-five-tonne vehicles, they decided to abandon the journey to the pole and stay put on the ice for the next four months until spring returned and it was light enough to withdraw safely. Psychologically, now more than ever, the enterprise resembled a trip through space. 'With the permanent darkness and claustrophobic conditions, the stresses will be all too apparent', predicted Stroud.[50]

What happened next is not entirely clear, since the data from the White Mars project are not yet available. One thing is certain: in terms of cohesion, the next four months were close to disastrous. Personality clashes and unforeseen behavioural issues led to serious divisions within the team. In a phone interview a couple of weeks after their return to the United Kingdom in late

November, Rob Lambert, the expedition's doctor, gave a bleak assessment. 'I wouldn't describe us as a team at all', he said:

> We were a group of individuals who had very different motivations for being there, very different ideas about what should happen. It opened my eyes to how people can behave when they're taken out of their normal environment. I don't think I would have believed it if I hadn't seen it for myself. Part of it was the environment we were in, part of it was peer pressure. Reading through my diary, I used the word "playground" an awful lot because it was exactly like that, the big kids picking on the little kids. You don't expect that from people in their twenties and thirties. It was a nasty situation.

Antarctic experts often describe the place as a psychological magnifying glass, in the sense that time spent there exaggerates certain aspects of people's personalities. Introverts become more introverted, extroverts more extroverted. Lambert thinks this is partly what happened with *The Coldest Journey*. Both he and Brian Newham, who assumed the leadership role when Fiennes left, think the selection process was not rigorous enough. There were difficulties within the group even before the expedition started out. 'Some of the guys didn't get on with some of the other guys', Newham told me. 'While we had a common goal [to cross the continent], that didn't matter so much, because we were very focused, very determined, we each did what we had to do to try and achieve that goal. Once it was taken away, the social dynamic deteriorated. There was no longer that common purpose. It made it more difficult on a group level.'

It seems unfair to describe *The Coldest Journey* as a failure. Its scientific experiments should produce valuable insights into the physics and chemistry of snow, the biology of micro-organisms in extreme habitats and the movement of the coastal Antarctic ice sheet, in addition to the physiological and psychological findings from the White Mars project. It also raised more than $2 million for Seeing is Believing, a global charitable initiative to fight avoidable blindness (though the original target was $10 million). In the annals of Antarctic exploration, however, it will go down as another example of a team sent floundering by irreconcilable personalities, of the near-impossibility of predicting how people will react to an alien environment, and of the 'unbelievable dissent' that can befall 'small groups cooped up in small boxes', as Stroud forewarned.

There are lessons a-plenty, not least for the backers of Mars One, a Dutch non-profit foundation that hopes to send four astronauts on a mission to Mars in 2024 to establish a permanent settlement, with no chance of return. Unless psychologists learn a lot more about small-group compatibility in the next ten years than they have in the last hundred, the risks involved in that will make *The Coldest Journey* seem like a camping holiday in comparison.

7

The Fear That Binds

Group dynamics have a transforming effect on the way we live, spurring us to high endeavour, dragging us to the moral low-ground. It is time now to consider the bigger picture: how do our group-orientated inclinations affect those who are not part of our circle, and society as a whole? Loyalty, unity and cohesion are all very well when we're in on the act, but nothing is more likely to play havoc with social harmony than an over-wrought affection for the norms of our in-group. This is a particular danger during times of threat, when our in-group becomes like the comforting arms of a parent, and any out-group a scapegoat for our insecurities – as the following example attests.

Fifty years after the end of the Second World War, Germany and the Netherlands made military history by appropriating a unit from each of their armies and merging them into a single binational organization, 1 German/Netherlands Corps. The new hybrid was inaugurated with grand ceremony on 30 August 1995 in the presence of both prime ministers, who were quick to make the most of its symbolic potential. It marches under the motto 'Communitate Valemus' ('together we are strong'). It is based in Munster, site of the 1648 Peace of Westphalia that ended the Thirty Years War and established the principle of national sovereignty in Europe. Both nationalities are represented at all ranks, and the command is rotated every two or three years. It is working pretty well. Despite some discomfort at the cultural disconnects – the Dutch are occasionally criticized for being a little too informal, the Germans for giving the impression they are constantly giving orders[1] – almost everyone involved agrees that this has been a ground-breaking exercise in military co-operation. With one unforeseen and near-calamitous exception.

In February 2003, the corps was deployed for six months to Kabul as part of the international security force set up by the UN to secure the capital against attacks by the Taliban and other groups who opposed Hamid Karzai's transitional government. The city was highly volatile. Foreign troops were under constant threat of attack from rockets, grenades and other explosives. On 7 June, four German signalmen were killed and twenty-nine wounded when a suicide bomber in a taxi rammed the bus on which they were travelling.[2] Amid this chaos and against all expectations, co-operation between German and Dutch soldiers disintegrated. The Dutch, the more experienced peacekeepers, resented taking orders from German commanders, who because of superior numbers and their responsibility for logistics, were de facto in charge. Dutch soldiers complained about everything from the supply of ammunition to the amount of beer their compatriots drank. German officers, in turn, accused their Dutch counterparts of being disrespectful. Back at 1 (GE/NL) Corps HQ, the generals could not understand why cultural frictions that had been amiably tolerated in Munster were fast leading to a diplomatic crisis in Kabul.

To find out more about what happened, I travelled to a village in the south of Holland to meet a retired colonel with the Royal Netherlands Air Force who had been in Kabul with 1 (GE/

NL) Corps during those fateful months. Anne Tjepkema was the mission's official war diarist, following in what he says is a strong German tradition (though he is Dutch). I arrived at his house in time for morning coffee – or, as it turned out, milk. Despite a distinguished career in service, his only obvious military affectation is an impressive clothes-brush moustache, which resembles one of the neatly trimmed hedges in his garden.

Tjepkema is soft-spoken and economical with his words. When I asked him how dangerous it was in Kabul he replied: 'We had the flag flying at half-mast over HQ most of the time.' As an example of the kind of precautions they had to take, he described what it was like going out to eat. 'There was just one restaurant where we would go. Iranian. I went there a few times. We would arrive with two jeeps, one of them with security people. I always had my pistol with me, and the pistol was loaded. I would always take a seat at the back so that I could see the entrance and could find my way out at the back. That was the first consideration you made when entering a restaurant.' In this environment, he says, differences in thinking and culture that previously had never been an issue suddenly became protrusive. 'Slowly you discovered things you would never have thought of.'

The incongruity that Tjepkema describes is well known to psychologists who have studied how people behave when they feel threatened. There is no more reliable way to trigger our groupish instincts than to step into an environment where we fear for our lives. We immediately turn to the people we are most familiar with and whose values and moral code we share. Suddenly it is our tribe against the world. Thus primed, we find it harder to co-operate with those who differ from us; we get frustrated by asymmetries that previously seemed redundant. In our hankering for certainty, we cling to what we know and cast those who disagree as foe or demonic.

The social psychologist Ervin Staub says this tendency of people to turn inwards is a normal response in difficult circumstances, and especially when there is social chaos or war. '[At such times] they relinquish, to some degree, their own personal identity. Their need for their group becomes very great.' Could this explain the disharmony between Dutch and German troops in Kabul? Almost certainly, according to a team of researchers in the Netherlands who questioned several hundred Dutch soldiers serving in Afghanistan and Munster in 2003. They found that the more worried the soldiers felt about dying, the less willing they were to collaborate with their German colleagues.[3] Simply being in Kabul, one of the most dangerous cities in the world, changed everything.

One of the most celebrated proponents of the distorting effects of fear on behaviour was a celebrated American polymath called Ernest Becker, an anthropologist who crossed into psychiatry and then sociology, and whose mission, according to his friend and fellow academic Ronald Leifer, was to understand 'himself, the human condition and the meaning of life'.[4] Becker's central thesis, developed in the 1960s and early 1970s from his observations of psychiatric patients, was that our outlook on life, our personality, cultural worldview, belief systems, moral understanding, sense of self and belonging, our desires, hopes and dreams – all the stuff that characterizes our humanness – is shaped primarily by our attempt to deny the terrifying inevitability of our own death. Being human is essentially perverse, he believed. On the one hand, we use our intellect and imagination to create identities and find meanings that set us apart from other animals and give us infinite worth. On the other, 'man is a worm and food for worms':

Man is literally split in two: he has an awareness of his own splendid uniqueness in that he sticks out of nature with a towering majesty, and yet he goes back into the ground a few feet in order blindly and dumbly to rot and disappear forever. It is a terrifying dilemma to be in and to have to live with.[5]

Becker believed that this existential contradiction lies behind many neuroses, which can be seen as over-zealous or misguided efforts to transcend our creatureliness, or to limit it (by obsessing over the importance of clean hands, for example). He also saw it as the root of evil: people will sometimes do whatever it takes to establish a sense of their own immortality, regardless of the cost to others.

In placing such philosophical questions about the human condition at the heart of intellectual enquiry, Becker rubbed up against the growing band of arch-empiricists who came to dominate social science and psychiatry faculties in the US and who considered matters of belief, ethics and values irrelevant to the pursuit of knowledge. His radical views – and his close association with Thomas Szasz, author of The Myth of Mental Illness and a strong critic of psychiatry – resulted in him getting fired from three American universities and resigning from another. In 1974, two months after his death from colon cancer aged forty-nine, he was awarded the Pulitzer Prize in non-fiction for his book The Denial of Death.[6] Today he is remembered, as Leifer put it, as 'an enigmatic, shadowy cult figure'.[7] Yet he has inspired many disciples. Three of them in particular have spent the past three decades cultivating his ideas into a theory of their own. Their insights provide a convincing explanation for why identifying with a group – whether a football club, a political party or an organized religion – comes so naturally to most of us, and why we cling to our groups (and scorn competing ones) all the more fiercely when we feel afraid.

———

If you think that dwelling for thirty years on the inevitability of one's death would make for a downbeat outlook, then you probably haven't met Jeff Greenberg, Tom Pyszczynski or Sheldon Solomon. These three graduate school buddies, who together have defied many sceptics in managing to turn Becker's ideas into testable scientific propositions, are among the most colourful and dynamic social psychologists around. They are notable, at first sight, for their hair. Greenberg has his pulled back in a ponytail; Pyszczynski, bald on top, sports a curtain of grey to his shoulders; Solomon's is a jaunty mullet. Their work, and their hair, found a new non-academic audience with the release of the 2003 documentary *Flight from Death: The Quest for Immortality*, narrated by actor Gabriel Byrne.[8] In this film, a smiling Solomon, standing before San Francisco's Golden Gate Bridge in a tie-dye T-shirt of psychedelic blues, greens, oranges, purples and yellows, sums up the central dilemma of human existence thus: 'The explicit awareness that you're a breathing piece of defecating meat that is destined to die and ultimately no more significant than let's say a lizard or a potato is not especially uplifting.'

Surmising that he would be fun to talk to, I travelled to Skidmore College, the liberal arts college in Saratoga Springs, New York State, where Solomon teaches. On the train journey from New York City there were reminders of death at every stop. It was 13 September 2012, two days after the American ambassador to Libya had been killed in a terrorist attack on the US consulate in Benghazi, and all flags were at half-mast.

I found Solomon sitting in his small office on the tranquil Skidmore campus, the door half-open, at ease in blue shorts, builders' boots and one of his trademark technicolor T-shirts. Like his fellow Becker-philes, he is a maverick in the straight-laced academy. He crosses disciplines at will. The books on his shelves cover biology, philosophy, psychology. He is as likely to quote from George Eliot or Virginia Woolf as Sigmund Freud or Charles Darwin. In the early days, he said, when the three of them started to dabble in these 'grand theories', they were criticized by both English lecturers and experimental psychologists. It took them years to persuade journal editors to publish their papers. He has no trouble, however, persuading students to attend his lectures. He is one of the most popular teachers at the college. On the RateMyProfessors website,[9] former pupils have awarded him accolades such as 'a modest, slightly-crazed, genius with a wicked sense of humor' and 'the hottest coolest prof on campus!' One of them remarks, approvingly, that he 'dresses like a hobo'.

Solomon's passage towards a theory of human behaviour has involved plenty of self-reflection. When he first read Becker's *The Denial of Death* while in his late twenties, it so disorientated him that he quit his job at Skidmore and wandered around the US doing construction work. 'I was like, wow, if he's right what the hell am I doing? I became momentarily disillusioned with my scholarly pretensions.' He toyed with becoming a chef.[10] All this makes him entertaining to be around. He is a busy conversationalist, never still, jerking his head, shrugging his shoulders, tapping his heel, spinning in his chair. He cusses freely. The effect is somewhat theatrical, but the message is serious.

The message is this. As a foil against the realization that we will one day die, we buy into cultural norms and ideas about reality that help give our lives meaning and allow us a symbolic stab at immortality. We subscribe to ideologies, join institutions, pledge undying loyalty to sports teams, adopt faiths and moral codes, create art or commit ourselves to our families or our work. In these common endeavours we achieve a sense of self-worth that we never could alone. During moments of danger, when we feel our mortality most keenly, we cling to our worldview – be it religious, scientific, cultural or philosophical – and to the people who share it with us as if our lives depended on it. This can get us into trouble: in reinforcing our own values and group loyalties, we are inclined to dismiss or disparage those who hold alternative views. Or as Solomon puts it, we make out that 'our god is better than your god and we will kick your arse to prove it'.

Greenberg, Pyszczynski, Solomon and others have so far conducted some five hundred experiments to test out this perspective on group conflict (which they have dubbed 'terror management theory').[11] In the first study, published in 1989, they asked twenty-two municipal court judges in Tucson to set bail for a defendant charged with prostitution, a crime all the judges considered immoral. Half of them also had to fill out a questionnaire asking them how they felt about the prospect that they would one day die. You can see where this is going. Those judges who were primed to think about death set bail terms on average nine times higher than their blissfully unconcerned colleagues ($455 compared with $50). Increasing their existential angst appeared to draw them closer to their deep-held values, making them more eager to punish the transgressor.[12]

Solomon and his colleagues have not tired of coming up with creative ways to measure this effect, which has held up across almost all the studies. In one – my personal favourite – they invited seventy-four psychology students to allocate a quantity of super-spicy hot sauce to someone whose political views differed substantially from their own, knowing that this person did not like spicy food and would have to eat the sauce. As suspected, those volunteers who were asked to 'jot down as specifically as you can what you think will happen to you as you physically die' were a lot more liberal with the chilli salsa picante.[13]

The suggestion that being reminded of our finitude – as opposed to anxiety in general, which does not have the same effect – makes us more aggressive towards those who are different from us has huge implications in the real world. It explains why, during periods of national insecurity – in the wake of a terrorist attack, for example, or during civil unrest or economic upheaval – people are prone to uncharacteristic feelings of solidarity towards members of their own 'tribe' (nation, neighbourhood or anything in between) and hostility towards outsiders.[14] Greenberg, Pyszczynski and Solomon and their collaborators have demonstrated such tendencies in dozens of settings across the world. For example, they have shown that, when forced to think about dying, Germans unconsciously sit closer to fellow Germans and further away from Turks; Dutch football fans make unrealistic predictions for how their national team will defeat Germany's; Italians overstate how they differ from other nationalities; Japanese are more derogatory towards those who criticize their country; Israelis are less receptive towards Russian Jews who have immigrated to Israel; Iranians favour suicide bomb attacks against the US over peace with the West (in the non-threat setting the opposite was true); and politically conservative Americans support pre-emptive attacks against certain Middle Eastern countries, including the use of nuclear or chemical weapons.

This is the psychology behind the theoretical principle known as the Hobbesian trap, which states that during rising tension between two groups fear will prompt one of them to strike first, making conflict highly likely. Yoda, the *Star Wars* Jedi master, had it about right in his caution to the young Anakin Skywalker in *The Phantom*

Menace: 'Fear is the path to the dark side. Fear leads to anger. Anger leads to hate. Hate leads to suffering.' In conflict, we share psychological space with our enemies: the same tendencies that make us want to kill them make them want to kill us.

———

On the morning of 10 September 2001, a warm unsettled Monday, Solomon took a train from his home in Newark, New Jersey, to New York City, on his way to Brooklyn College where he was teaching. He found the time to drop into his favourite bakery on the first floor of the World Trade Center to pick up his usual coffee and corn muffin, as he had done twice a week for the past two years. As he remarked later: 'What a difference a day makes.' The following morning, which was virtually cloudless in the eastern US, he drove straight to work since he needed to be there early, 'noting how the rising sun gave lower Manhattan, and especially the twin towers of the World Trade Center, a splendid glow'.[15] Within two hours of arriving at his classroom both towers were rubble, and Solomon found himself fuming and 'eager to witness (on CNN, of course) the utter obliteration of those responsible'.[16]

For most Americans, and for many around the world, the events of 9/11 triggered an existential crisis like none they had known. Their generally predictable and secure world suddenly seemed miragic. What does it say about the value of life if death can descend without warning out of the sky on a cloudless autumn day? It is hard to imagine a more visceral reminder of our mortality. Pyszczynski called 9/11 'an attack on Americans' psychological equanimity'.[17] The common response – heightened patriotic fervour, resolute national unity, hostility towards other cultures, intolerance of dissenting views, loud demands for retaliation, a resurgence in church attendance – is precisely what he, Solomon and Greenberg would have predicted.[18]

The political consequences were no less striking. A month after the attacks, George W. Bush achieved the highest approval rating of any president on record, over ninety per cent. It stayed that way for months afterwards and cut right across political boundaries. The vast majority of Americans also supported (at that time) his military campaigns in Afghanistan and Iraq. Becker would not have been surprised. In reinforcing America's traditional cultural values – 'in our grief and anger, we have found our mission and our moment ... the advance of human freedom now depends on us'[19] – Bush raised the sword on behalf of both Republicans and Democrats in a symbolic fight against all that threatened them. He was helping them, as Becker had it, to 'deny the terror of the world'.[20][21] In Americans' hour of crisis, the self-confident, crusading Bush was the perfect candidate to restore their faith both in their fundamental life-affirming ideals and their sense of well-being.

At first glance, the unified cross-political American response looks contradictory. Shouldn't liberals, who set great store by being progressive and open-minded, become *more* tolerant when they feel threatened by terrorism? This is usually what happens when people are made to think about death: liberals become more liberal, conservatives more conservative.[22] But 9/11 was different. The attacks posed such a fundamental threat to the American way of life that the rebound transcended partisan politics. 'All Americans took psychological refuge in a charismatic leader who declared that God had chosen him to rid the world of evil', says Solomon. And thus Solomon found himself momentarily condemning Islam and thinking that 'we should send a few warplanes over there – not that I knew where "there" was – and bomb them – not that I knew who "they" were'.

An indication of how the narrative of terrorism may have influenced voters in the 2004 US presidential election, which Bush won by a comfortable margin, comes from an experiment conducted by Solomon, Greenberg, Pyszczynski and others six months before election day. They approached 157 students in the cafeteria at Brooklyn College in New York and had half of them address appetizing statements such as 'briefly describe the emotions that the thought of your own death arouses in you'. The other half – the control group – were asked to think about being in pain. They then assessed their political orientation (overall they were moderately liberal) and asked them who they were more likely to vote for, Bush or Democratic presidential nominee John Kerry. The outcome was pretty astonishing. Those in the control group favoured Kerry over Bush by four to one, while those primed to contemplate dying favoured Bush over Kerry by almost three to one. Their choices seemed to have nothing to do with their political ideology: Bush appealed to existentially aroused conservatives and liberals alike, no doubt because his aggressive defence of American identity spoke to the deep-set fears they all shared.[23]

'The thing that astonishes us is that on the one hand our death reminders are very subtle. But the results of this subtle alteration of psychological conditions are staggering', remarks Solomon. This underlines psychologist Drew Westen's assertion that 'the political brain is an emotional brain', by which he meant that voting decisions are driven more by gut feeling than by rational argument.[24] This is why it can be extremely hard to change people's minds by presenting them with new information. Dan Kahan at Yale Law School has found people will find ways to dismiss evidence that carbon dioxide emissions cause global warming, for example, or that gun control has no effect on violent crime if it contradicts their core cultural values or the views of their social group.[25] In elections in particular, fear and empathy trump logic. 'No matter how bad Bush does on the war [in Iraq] and 9/11, just having voters think about it kills us', observed one Democratic strategist in May 2004.[26]

The Republicans made good use of 9/11 iconography and fear-inducing rhetoric to help them retain their standing with the electorate. 'Twin towers', 'terrorist threat', 'Al-Qaeda', 'national security' and related phrases became part of its campaign lexicon. More significantly, as far as the rest of the planet is concerned, this strategy helped them win the popular backing they needed for the war against Saddam Hussein despite no credible evidence that he had anything to do with Al-Qaeda's attacks on New York and Washington. Consider this from Bush's 2003 State of the Union address, delivered two months before the invasion:

> Evidence from intelligence sources, secret communications and statements by people now in custody reveal that Saddam Hussein aids and protects terrorists, including members of Al Qaeda. Secretly, and without fingerprints, he could provide one of his hidden weapons to terrorists, or help them develop their own ... It would take one vial, one canister, one crate slipped into this country to bring a day of horror like none we have ever known. We will do everything in our power to make sure that that day never comes.[27]

This is a psychological upper-cut, designed to bypass rational deliberation of the risks. Tony Blair followed a similar approach in the UK, comparing international prevarication over Iraq to the failure to rein in Hitler after the Nazi occupation of Czechoslovakia in 1939.[28] These are the tactics of leaders down the ages who have sought to drum up support for war by manipulating people's basic fears and reminding them of their vulnerabilities. It is one of the oldest tricks in the book, yet still it catches us out.[29]

———

9/11 was an outlier, unexpected and unprecedented. But it was not the first time in US history that dramatic events have led to an exaggeration of group differences on a national scale. And it doesn't require mass murder to trigger such an effect. Economic instability, if serious enough, can feel as destabilizing as a tangible mortal threat.

If you were living in the US in the year 1979, it is possible you'll remember it for the release of Michael Jackson's break-through, multi-million-selling album *Off the Wall*; or for the arrival of McDonald's child-friendly, parent-pleasing Happy Meal; or for President Jimmy Carter's altercation with a swamp rabbit while out fishing in Georgia. But not likely. More probably it will conjure up events more sobering: the nuclear meltdown at Three Mile Island; the Iranian hostage crisis; the Soviet invasion of Afghanistan. You may recall the pervasive sense of economic insecurity, which was well-placed: between 1979 and 1982, the unemployment rate in the US jumped from 5.8 per cent to 9.7 per cent,[30] and the price of basic household goods, as measured by the consumer price index, grew more quickly than in any equivalent period since the First World War.[31] This was the year Carter, in a televised address to the American people, warned of a fundamental threat to American democracy, and of a national 'crisis of confidence':

> It is a crisis that strikes at the very heart and soul and spirit of our national will. We can see this crisis in the growing doubt

about the meaning of our own lives and in the loss of a unity of purpose for our nation ... The symptoms of this crisis of the American spirit are all around us. For the first time in the history of our country a majority of our people believe that the next five years will be worse than the past five years.[32]

American society's response to this general air of uncertainty was similar in flavour to its response to 9/11. It developed what University of Michigan psychologists Richard Doty, Bill Peterson and David Winter called 'authoritarian syndrome'. Examining social trends from the era, they noted that between 1978 and 1982 Americans appeared more disciplinarian, more conservative and less tolerant of unconventional values and views compared with the five years that followed, when the economy had recovered and the air of crisis diminished. They observed, for example, higher levels of racial prejudice among high school students; more Klu Klux Klan activity; a dramatic rise in the number of anti-Semitic incidents, such as vandalism of synagogues; and a preference among television viewers for shows with powerful or dominating protagonists, and among pet owners for 'attack' dogs such as German shepherds over lapdogs such as Chihuahuas.[33] Inevitably, all this played into the hands of right-wing politicians: Ronald Reagan, tough on crime and aggressive towards the Soviet Union, won the 1980 presidential election by a landslide.

This goes to show that economic and social woes, when they threaten people's way of life, can be just as motivating as terrorist threats in sending them scuttling into the embrace of their in-group. In the late 1970s, as in the aftermath of 9/11, Americans felt vulnerable, and they resolved it by rallying to the central tenets of their culture, to feel more American, to feel more together. This, according to Becker, is what society is really for: a system that allows people to find meaning, to make life count, simply by taking part. When the system is threatened, the need to reinforce its symbols becomes paramount.

The idea that economic and social disquiet exaggerate our groupish leanings seems credible when you look at how often through history they have run hand-in-hand with persecution of out-groups. In one of the classic early studies in social psychology, Carl Hovland and Robert Sears at Yale University discovered that in the American Deep South, between 1882 and 1930, the level of mob violence against black people rose and fell in line with the price of cotton and the financial fortunes of the region's farmers (agriculture was the dominant industry at the time).[34] In a similar vein, support for the death penalty in the US is known to be higher in areas where there is greater inequality and where residents feel less safe (because of a high homicide rate, for example). Among conservative US states at least, the number of criminals sentenced to death and the number executed both go up at times of threat.[35]

The effect can play out across entire nations. Mass unemployment and high inflation in Germany in the 1920s and early 1930s helped fuel the rise of Nazism because the jobless and the lower middle class – particularly small traders who blamed large Jewish businesses for their marginalization – felt empowered by its strongly nationalistic ideology.[36] Sixty years later in east Germany, unemployment (on this occasion triggered by reunification with the West) was again the backdrop to a ballooning of xenophobic sentiment, resulting in a dramatic rise in the number of attacks against asylum seekers, refugees and other foreigners (from forty in January 1991 to around a thousand in each of the last four months of 1992).[37]

In the UK, opinion polls by the National Centre for Social Research show that public attitudes towards immigrants were markedly more negative in 2012 and 2013 than they were a decade previously.[38] This may reflect unease at the levels of immigration, exacerbated by one of the worst recessions in decades. Such conditions bring into focus what political analyst David Goodhart calls the 'awkward truth' about multicultural societies: 'that humans are group-based primates who favour their own and extend trust to outsiders with caution'.[39]

In 2001, the Harvard political scientist Robert Putnam found in a survey of 30,000 people across the US that more ethnically diverse communities show markedly less civic engagement: fewer people vote, volunteer and give to charity, because they trust each other less.[40] Putnam calls this 'turtling' – pulling in towards what is familiar. When resources and opportunities are limited, as in a recession, we tend to pull in further, our communities become more polarized and mistrust turns to hostility. Far easier to gain control over a chaotic environment by finding a scapegoat (immigrants? Jews? Muslims? benefit claimants? bankers?) than taking aim at the entire system. Hence Goodhart's wider point – for which he has drawn much flak – that it is insufficient in a representative democracy that administers a tax and spend welfare state for different ethnic groups merely to live side by side. Co-operation requires a level of solidarity. If diverse groups fail to integrate, you can bet that when the wheels come off the wagon the divisions between them will be exploited by all sides.

This invites a crucial question: how much social integration is required to immunize mixed communities against conflict? One answer comes from the political scientist Ashutosh Varshney, now at Brown University in Rhode Island, who wanted to know why violence between Muslims and Hindus in India was more prevalent in some places than in others. After conducting field research in six Indian cities – three peaceful (Calicut, Lucknow and Surat), three violent (Aligarh, Hyderabad and Ahmedabad) – he concluded that the key to ethnic harmony was intercommunal engagement at a deep level. It is not enough for two groups merely to know each other as neighbours or for their children to attend the same schools. They should be mixing in business associations, sports clubs, trade unions, political parties, community organizations, student unions, reading groups and so on. Integration at this level acts as a constraint on the polarizing strategies of political elites, explains Varshney. It gives communities an incentive to prevent sparks from turning into fires. That is what keeps the peace: in stable mixed communities, engagement is built into the civic structure.[41]

This is precisely what has not happened in the northern English city of Bradford, where in July 2001 ethnic tensions between whites and South Asians spilled over into widespread rioting. An independent review team set up by the government after the riots to assess community cohesion reported being 'struck by the depth of polarization' in Bradford and other northern towns and cities affected by ethnic violence. It reported segregation everywhere: in schools, voluntary groups, places of worship, in social and cultural networks, in the workplace: 'Many communities operate on the basis of a series of parallel lives. These lives often do not seem to touch at any point, let alone overlap and promote any meaningful interchanges.'[42] Bradford is still one of the most segregated places in Britain. More than a third of its primary and secondary schools are overwhelmingly Kashmiri Pakistani; forty-three per cent of its residents speak a language other than English at home.[43]

For an example of how difficult it can be to bring together communities that are culturally so far apart, look at Belfast. Here, around ninety per cent of housing estates remain either predominantly Catholic or predominantly Protestant despite the fact that in opinion surveys an overwhelming majority of residents say they would prefer to live in mixed-religion neighbourhoods.[44] Even when the will is there, the challenges of settling historically isolated communities into the same space are profound.

———

On my visits to Israel and the Palestinian Territories throughout the 2000s, while researching the psychology of conflict, I met few Israelis and Palestinians who in recent years had exchanged words with someone on the other side, let alone got to know them. Still today they see each other only through fences, on the television, at checkpoints, never to interact or ask questions. They cannot travel in each other's territories. They cannot get close enough even to argue. At an elementary school I visited in Gaza, the girls and boys pointed through the windows of their bullet-scarred classroom towards an Israeli residential settlement (since demolished) where Jewish children their own age were riding bicycles between the red-tiled houses. Yet Palestinian and Israeli children depict each other in their sketchbooks in almost identical ways: as animals, or monsters from some terrifying netherworld. Rarely as human. Since they cannot know each other, all they are left with is fear.

The necessity for members of different groups to become acquainted in the interests of social harmony is a central tenet of the 'contact hypothesis', proposed in 1954 by the American psychologist Gordon Allport as a way of reducing prejudice, negative stereotyping and enmity.[45] It is not hard to grasp the rationale: interacting and communicating properly with someone makes it more likely you will appreciate their point of view, recognize how they are similar to you and grow to trust them. It can be a lot harder than it sounds.

Allport concluded that for contact to be effective, various essential conditions should be in place. For example, the two parties should have equal status, a common goal and the support of their communities. The environment in Israel and Palestine meets none of these criteria, which makes it all the more remarkable that there are people on both sides who are willing to defy the mindset of their group and reach out. It is no coincidence that many of them have seen sons, daughters, brothers, sisters or parents killed in the violence. Confounded by their loss, they have sought another way of co-existing. Yitzhak Frankenthal, an Orthodox Jew whose son Arik was abducted and murdered by Hamas in 1994, has been a prime motivator, founding the Parents Circle for bereaved Israeli and Palestinian families[46] and more recently the Arik Institute for Reconciliation, Tolerance and Peace.[47] He also helped set up a telephone hotline service that allowed Israelis and Palestinians who had never met to talk to each other. It has fielded more than a million calls. 'I got the feeling I failed as a father. To lose my son. I needed to do everything to make sure that my other four kids should stay alive', he told me in his cluttered, cave-like office in Jerusalem in 2002.

Frankenthal's Palestinian partners appeared to think the same way. He sent me to Israeli-occupied East Jerusalem to meet Adel Misk, who today is the Palestinian vice-president of the Parents Circle. 'Most people ask me and Yitzhak how you can do this', said Misk. 'But we are the victims. We know the meaning of blood. If we succeed in talking and sitting together, we're sending a message. There is no other way. I believe in this.' Many others have believed in this – the heroic dismantling of group boundaries – none more so than the novelist John Steinbeck, who considered that every piece of honest prose that has ever been written is based on this principle: 'Try to understand men, if you understand each other you will be kind to each other. Knowing a man well never leads to hate and nearly always leads to love'.[48]

Fig. 8 In most West Bank towns, the only Israelis with whom Palestinians have contact are soldiers.

Search for Common Ground (SFCG) is the largest non-governmental organization dedicated to conflict resolution, and arguably the most successful. Since its inception in 1982, it has helped diffuse wars and reduce ethnic hatred in twenty-seven countries in Africa, Europe, the Middle East, Asia and North America. The philosophy is in the name: conflict arises from differences, and the most effective way to peace is to concentrate on similarities.

John Marks, SFCG's founder, who used to work as an analyst at the US State Department before becoming disillusioned with its policies in Vietnam, homed in on this 'commonalities' approach largely through on-the-ground experience and good sense. Recently, science has caught up. In 2009, Pyszczynski began a series of psychological experiments to see whether it is possible to soften people's instinctive prejudices against out-groups by reminding them of what they have in common with the rest of humanity. One of his first and most promising findings was that when American Christian fundamentalists, who had been primed to think about their own death, read Biblical passages highlighting the compassionate teachings of Jesus, they became less enthusiastic about the use of strong military force to defend US interests abroad. He got a similar result when he ran the experiment among Shi'ite Muslims in Iran: reading Qur'anic verses about compassionate values reduced Iranians' appetite for violence against the US and Europe.[49] He has also discovered that you can reverse people's innate bias towards supposedly threatening groups (in this case the attitudes of American university students towards Arabs) simply by making them look at photographs of family life in diverse cultures – parents and children sitting at dinner or playing together – or by having them read recollections of other people's favourite childhood memories.[50]

These results mirror SFCG's founding logic: there is something very powerful about reminding people of the things they share with others. In Solomon's view, the way to increase tolerance is to 'let go of our tribal mentality. Remind people that all humans have much more in common than we have that is different'. This might sound like wishful thinking, but it can happen of its own accord when people take part in an activity that transcends group boundaries. The most instructive manipulation in Muzafer Sherif's Robbers Cave experiment (described in the prologue) is when he brought his two warring bands of adolescent boys together to fix a problem with the camp's drinking water supply. This called for their urgent co-operation – by now all of them were thirsty – and as a result the fighting and name-calling that had prevailed over the previous week evolved into good-natured mingling. (Tellingly, simply bringing the two groups into contact – having them eat in the same building or watch a film together – was not enough to break down the barriers; hostility diminished only in situations that forced them to integrate and conspire on a common goal.)[51]

There are plenty of examples of this kind of deep association in action. From my own experience, one of the few areas in which Palestinians and Israelis have consistently worked together *in situ* in recent years is medical science, a discipline in which collaboration and sharing of knowledge are paramount, and in particular the cross-border monitoring of infectious disease. Another area, redolent of Sherif's experiment, is the preservation of water resources in the West Bank on which both populations depend. Such partnerships, while often beginning under a cloud of mutual suspicion, are ultimately sustained by knowing and above all by liking. Maintaining a bilateral academic relationship during a time of conflict is a lot easier if the two of you are also good friends.[52]

How should we use these insights? Keeping prejudice and inter-group hostility in check requires some understanding of the psychological dynamics at play, particularly among the media, politicians, religious and community leaders, so-called security experts and other figures who have special influence over public opinion. This shouldn't be too much to ask. We have lived with the ebb and flow of terrorism risks long enough to know that when a government raises its threat level (say from moderate to substantial in the case of the UK, or from orange to red under the old US system),[53] or a police chief warns that 'there can be no complacency',[54] it makes us all feel a little less secure, while having virtually no effect on our behaviour (what are we to do: take fewer flights, avoid public bins?). We also know that making us feel less secure has consequences of its own: a stirring of prejudices, and the acceptance of greater state powers. The result is the further alienation of the very communities on whom police depend most for information (Muslims, if the threat is from Islamic fundamentalism), since the way these out-groups are treated by the authorities and the public makes them understandably reluctant to come forward. Most leaders cannot resist the political advantages of putting fear of the enemy into the minds of the people, but it rarely makes us safer.[55][56]

The media's role is critical. While most journalists are aware that graphic reporting can aggravate social divisions, that does not seem to hold back proprietors and editors. In the months following the 9/11 attacks and on every anniversary since, the vivid images of death and destruction have been shown repeatedly on news channels, to the extent that most Americans and many Europeans live with a perpetual fear of terrorism completely out of proportion to the actual risk. It affects a lot more than our choice of home insurance or how we decide to travel. Psychologists at the University of Sussex have found in experimental research that being exposed to images of 9/11 increases racial prejudice,[57] a result that Greenberg, Pyszczynski and Solomon might have predicted. This has played out for real: successive surveys show that hate crimes and discrimination against Muslims in the US and Britain have been more frequent since 2001 than before.[58]

Fear sells newspapers, but it also distorts perceptions. The murder of the British soldier Lee Rigby on a street in Woolwich, southeast London, in broad daylight on 22 May 2013 was particularly traumatizing and terror-inducing because pictures and video of one of the killers ranting with bloodied hands about how the people of Britain would never be safe quickly did the rounds on social media and were re-circulated with little restraint (though to considerable public disapproval) by mainstream media. The damage inflicted by this 'if it bleeds it leads' media mentality is immediate and almost impossible to correct. Vivid imagery triggers a visceral response that overrides any rational assessment of the risks.[59] Telling someone who watched the Woolwich footage that they are five times more likely to be struck by lightning than killed by an Islamic extremist wielding a machete may help them sleep better at night. But it will not soften any instinctual death-denying biases they may have acquired towards Muslims as an out-group. (Over the month following the attack, the frequency of reported anti-Islamic incidents in England and Wales remained at four times what it had been previously.)[60]

———

Given how dramatically fear distorts our view of the world, how vividly it accentuates the differences between in-group and out-group and how easily it provokes our existential insecurities, how are we supposed to live with it? Short of turning off the television, disabling our news feeds and living off-grid, the best strategy is probably to be as sensitive as we can to our group identities and the many ways in which they can be manipulated. In other words, to see the dramatic headlines and the scaremongering of politicians for what they are: reality distorters. It is also worth invoking the effect reported by many astronauts of seeing Earth from space – a profound sense of awe at the fragility of this 'pale blue dot' and the interconnectedness of all the life on it. Step back far enough and group differences can seem inconsequential.

Roland Emmerich's *The Day After Tomorrow*, a disaster movie in which much of civilization is annihilated by the sudden arrival of a new ice age, is not recognized for its scientific accuracy. Andrew

Weaver, Canada's leading climate modeller, remarked that it 'creatively violates every known law of thermodynamics'.[61] But on the subject of behaviour in times of crisis, Emmerich might have a point. When hailstones the size of fists pummel Tokyo, a vortex of freezing air paralyses Scotland, snow starts falling on Delhi and a super-tsunami engulfs New York, there's a sense that everyone's in it together. Global disputes are forgotten, the US writes off all Latin American debt and developing countries open their borders to millions of displaced Americans and Europeans.

While most analysts predict that the effects of climate change – drought, famine and the flooding of heavily populated coastal areas – will lead to more conflict throughout the world as people compete for dwindling resources, an intriguing recent experiment led by Pyszczynski suggests this is not inevitable. When he asked people who had been primed with the usual anxiety-inducing imaginings of their own demise to think about the potentially catastrophic effects of global warming – melting ice caps, rising sea-levels, forced migrations, severe storms and long droughts – they expressed a lot more enthusiasm for peace-building and diplomacy than others who had been told to think only about a local catastrophe such as an earthquake. He also found that support for military action against Iran among American students at a Midwestern university completely evaporated when they were made to imagine this kind of climate-induced destruction.[62]

This is the best-case scenario: if and when climate change kicks in and it becomes clear we are all going to share the same fate, many of us will prefer to co-operate than fight, since we'll all be part of the in-group.[63] Even Sigmund Freud, rarely upbeat about the prospects for human civilization, saw a potential for global solidarity in calamity, noting in *The Future of an Illusion*: 'One of the few gratifying and exalting impressions which mankind can offer is when, in the face of an elemental catastrophe, it forgets the discordancies of its civilization and all its internal difficulties and animosities, and recalls the great common task of preserving itself against the superior power of nature.'[64]

For a worst-case scenario, you could always contemplate Cormac McCarthy's novel *The Road*, in which the survivors of an unknown apocalypse compete in a cauterized world for the last remaining nutritional resource: each other.[65] No manipulation of group psychology will save you when there is nothing to eat. Up to that point, however, anything is possible.

8

Together Alone

———

The unconscious influence of others is hard to ignore when you examine the multiple idiosyncrasies of our group behaviours. But this is not the only way to approach the subject. We can learn as much by looking at what happens to us when others are not there, when we are forced to get by on our own. Social isolation is often debilitating, but it is not always so. Some people manage it better than others, and the reasons for this tell us much about the human condition. The following story of a young British explorer who lived through a lonesome Arctic winter is an example of how being alone, physically, is not the same as being alone psychologically, and that whether you endure or wilt is largely to do with what or who you carry with you in your head.

August Courtauld was twenty-five and not long out of Cambridge University when he set sail for Greenland in July 1930 with the British Arctic Air Route Expedition, one of fourteen men of similar age, background and unrestrained enthusiasm for the unknown. Led by Courtauld's good friend Gino Watkins, their objective was to establish a weather station high up on the continental ice cap and collect data for a proposed new air corridor between Europe and North America. They set up base camp on the south-east Greenland coast and picked a spot for the station 130 miles to the north-west and 8,500 feet above sea level where they were confident of capturing the vagaries of the Arctic climate. It is hard to imagine anywhere more remote. Around it in every direction snow stretched to the horizon, a polar desert devoid of visible life.

Watkins had planned to run the weather station using a two-man crew rotated every four to six weeks. When the time came for Courtauld to take over, at the beginning of December, the extreme winds and drifting snow had taken such a toll on the expedition's supply arrangements that there was not enough food and fuel to sustain two men through the winter. Rather than abandon the place, Courtauld volunteered to stay and keep it going by himself. There was food to last one person five months, and he had no wish to travel back to base camp as the temperature had dropped to minus 44° Celsius and he already had frostbite in his toes. Reluctantly, his companions agreed. They held a farewell Christmas dinner, three weeks premature but sumptuous given the circumstances: game soup, sardines fried in olive oil, basted ptarmigan, plum pudding with rum sauce, angels on sledges, date and raisin dessert, mince-meat, jam and hot grog, washed down with tea.[1] Two days later, Courtauld watched them trudge across the ice towards the coast until they were a fleck on the south-eastern horizon. 'Now I am quite alone. Not a dog or even a mosquito for company', he wrote.[2]

But if he felt lonely he did not confess it in his diary. He expected his friends to return in a few weeks and there was plenty for him to do in the meantime. He took meteorological readings every four hours and did his best to keep the station walls clear of snow. He minded his kit, checked his supplies, prepared his food on the paraffin stove, treated his frostbitten toes. In idle moments he read books left by the previous occupants – *Vanity Fair*, *Jane Eyre*, *Martin Chuzzlewit*, *The Compleat Angler*. He played himself at chess, sung

Gilbert and Sullivan songs ('an awful row but there was no one to hear it'),[3] designed his dream yacht and planned a cruise around the west coast of Scotland with his fiancée. But life became progressively more difficult, as his diary illustrates:

December 21 – Went out to do some digging about noon and saw the old sun or half of it for the first time for a fortnight. Aurora wonderful tonight; like purple smoke wreaths twisting and writhing all over the sky. At ten o'clock it was completely still. The silence outside was almost terrible. Nothing to hear but one's heart beating and the blood ticking in one's veins.[4]

February 26 – At last the gales have died down and given way to cold clear weather though still the NW wind blows … Am down to the last four gallons of paraffin now. If the others don't turn up in three or four weeks, I shall be reduced to cold and darkness. If ever I get back to base nothing will induce me to go on the ice cap again. When the others will come God knows.[5]

March 1 – I am quite contented with my lot except for the bore of crawling out through the tunnel every three hours. The relieving party should have started during this last week of fine weather in which case with decent luck they should be here by the end of the month. Could certainly do with some fresh food although it is wonderful how well one keeps on these tinned rations.[6]

By now snow had begun to drift so heavily against the walls that he had trouble digging himself out. By the middle of March, the entrance was completely blocked. He cut a hole in the roof of one of the adjoining igloos, but within hours this too was sealed. Suddenly he was entombed in the perpetual dark, a narrow ventilator pipe his only link with the outside world, his supplies dwindling, his muscles atrophying.

> April 5, Easter Day – Now been here alone 4 months. No sign of relief. Only about a cupful of paraffin left and one or two candles. Have to lie in darkness almost all the time. Chocolate finished and tobacco almost (half a pouch left). What a change from last Easter at Falmouth or the one before at Abbotsbury! What wouldn't I give to be living either the one or the other again or to be with you my dearest.[7] But if it were not for having you to think about as I lie in the dark and cannot sleep life would be intolerable.[8]

> April 20 – Only one candle left. Hardly any paraffin. Lie in dark all day designing the ideal cruiser and the ideal meal. Left foot swelling up hope it isn't scurvy.[9]

He had no idea when his companions would rescue him – or if they were still alive.

———

Psychological experiments on the effects of social isolation and sensory deprivation indicate that being trapped alone for weeks in a freezing dark cave should have grave consequences for anyone's state of mind. Such research, being ethically dubious, is difficult to carry out today. Not so in the 1950s and 1960s, when China was rumoured to be using solitary confinement to 'brainwash' American prisoners captured during the Korean war, and the US and Canadian governments were all too keen to try it out.

Their defence departments funded a series of research programmes at Harvard and McGill university medical centres in which paid volunteers – mainly college students – were confined to sound-proof rooms, blindfolded and deprived of meaningful human contact. The idea was to see how they coped over days or weeks, but in most cases the trials were cut short because the students became too distressed to carry on. Few lasted beyond two days; many pulled out within twenty-four hours. They reported an astonishing array of symptoms, including prolonged anxiety, disorientation, emotional imbalance, panic attacks, impaired or irrational thinking, inability to concentrate, extreme restlessness and distorted audio and visual perception. They spoke of vivid hallucinations: squirrels bearing sacks marching across a field, prehistoric animals walking in a forest, a procession of eyeglasses filing down a street.[10] Some of the students slipped into delusory states, catatonic stupors or full-blown psychosis.[11] Donald Hebb, the psychologist who headed the McGill studies, wrote that the results were 'very unsettling to us … It is one thing to hear that the Chinese are brainwashing their prisoners on the other side of the world; it is another to find, in your own laboratory, that merely taking away the usual sights, sounds, and bodily contacts from a healthy university student for a few days can shake him, right down to the base.'[12]

It is not surprising that isolation should shrink us so (though it shrinks some more than others) when you consider that we derive meaning from our emotional states largely through contact with others. Biologists believe that human emotions evolved because they aided co-operation among our early ancestors who benefited from living in groups. Their primary function is social. With no one to mediate our feelings of fear, anger, anxiety and sadness and help us determine their appropriateness, before long they deliver us a distorted sense of self, a perceptual fracturing or a profound irrationality. It seems that left too much to ourselves, the very system that regulates our social living can overwhelm us.

How did Courtauld fare? His companions eventually reached the station after several failed attempts on 5 May, almost exactly five months since they had left him and forty-five days since the start of his incarceration. As they approached, it seemed likely he was dead. The area was almost completely drifted over. There were no signs of recent habitation, only the tattered remains of a Union Jack, the handle of a spade and the tops of various meteorological instruments showing through the snow. 'The whole place had a most extraordinary air of desolation', recalled the expedition's ornithologist Freddie Spencer Chapman.[13] Then Watkins spotted the end of the ventilator pipe. In trepidation he knelt beside it and shouted down. There came a faint, tremulous reply. He cut through the snow and through the canvas roof and soon he was shaking Courtauld by the hand and chatting to him about the capricious weather that had kept them at bay. Then he furnished him with snow goggles and pulled him up into the sunshine.

This is how Courtauld experienced his emancipation:

Suddenly there was an appalling noise like a bus going by followed by a confused yelling noise. I nearly jumped out of my skin. Was it the house falling in at last? A second later I realised the truth. It was somebody, some real human voice, calling down the ventilator. It was a very wonderful moment. I could not think what to do or say. I yelled back some stuttering remarks that seemed quite futile for the occasion.[14]

He emerged looking like some Old Testament eremite sent to fore-tell the apocalypse; or as Chapman remarked, 'as if he had stepped straight from Ober-Ammergau', in reference to a Bavarian town that isolated itself in the 1630s to protect itself from bubonic plague. 'His hair and beard were unkempt and long, and his face stained with smoke and grime.'[15] Courtauld complained only of 'a slight feeling of weakness due to the lack of exercise' but otherwise claimed to be 'perfectly fit'.[16] This may have been stoicism typical of the age. In photographs he looks sapling thin and somewhat ravaged. Remarkably, he appeared sane. His diary gives little away about his psychological health before or after his rescue, but nothing in what Watkins or Chapman or his other companions wrote suggests he suffered unduly. Within a week he was hunting ptarmigan in the mountains on Greenland's east coast with his friend J. M. Scott.

Fig. 9
August Courtauld emerging from the ice cap after five months in isolation.

Thereafter, Courtauld lived a fulfilling life. He married his fiancée Mollie – 'my dearest' in his diary entries – fathered six children, led his own expedition to Greenland, worked for naval intelligence during the Second World War, was appointed High Sheriff of Essex, served as honorary secretary of the Royal Geographical Society and spent many happy days at sea on his beloved yacht *Duet* before succumbing to multiple sclerosis and dying in 1959, aged fifty-four.

In 2009, August's grand-niece Chloe Courtauld retraced some of his journey in the Arctic, the first person to do so.[17] She has spent much time pondering why he emerged from the ice cap so little affected, which does seem astonishing. She thinks it had much to do with the daily routine he set himself, the regular collection of meteorological data, his disciplined house-keeping. It is possible that he was singularly robust in temperament, a psychological outlier. Perhaps his natural detachment helped, or his famed eccentricity, described by his fiancée Mollie as 'an almost total lack of regard for the orthodoxy of ordinary behaviour'.[18]

There is another hypothesis: that he owed his sanity to the solidarity he felt with his companions, his ability to transcend his imprisonment by reaching out to them, and his faith that they would find him. 'I knew that, even if Gino was having to wait for better weather, he wouldn't let me down', he noted in his autobiography.[19] In the official account of the expedition he writes of his certainty as the weeks passed that relief would come, and that 'some outer Force was in action on my side, and that I was not fated to leave my bones on the Greenland Ice Cap'.[20] It is clear from his writings that he thought often of his would-be rescuers, as if, as his biographer Nicholas Wollaston puts it, 'a thin connection ran back like a vein down the line of half-mile flags from the ice-cap station to the coast'.[21]

This is the power of community across the miles, a kind of spooky action at a distance. Courtauld's friend J. M. Scott, evoking Apsley Cherry-Garrard's thoughts towards his 1911 Antarctic colleagues, supposed that of all the bonds forged between men 'none is stronger than that forged on an Arctic expedition'.[22] To paraphrase theologian Paul Tillich, herein lies the difference between loneliness, which expresses the pain of being alone, and solitude, which expresses the glory of it.[23] The trajectory of loneliness is inward, towards a deep anguish, the arc of depression; that of solitude outward, towards a cosmic awareness, a larger sense of self. Courtauld cultivated the latter by carrying his colleagues with him in his head. He took Milton at his word: 'The mind is its own place, and in itself / Can make a Heav'n of Hell, a Hell of Heav'n.'[24]

Courtauld is one of many adventurers to have borne their isolation by casting their gaze out beyond themselves to distant companions, to God, or even into the landscape that surrounds them. Three years after him, the American naval officer and aviator Richard Byrd completed an almost identical feat in Antarctica, volunteering to occupy a meteorological station alone in the middle of the Ross Ice Shelf, 123 miles from the expedition's coastal base through the winter darkness and temperatures as low as −82° Celsius. His living quarters – a rough wooden shack – were luxurious compared with Courtauld's. He had primitive radio contact with the men at base camp who remained officially under his command. He had use of a gramophone.

Still he had to contend with the 'brain-cracking loneliness' of solitary confinement, waking to find himself 'groping in cold reaches of interstellar space, lost and bewildered ... Where am I? What am I doing here?'[25] And he had to endure the near-fatal effects of carbon monoxide fumes from a faulty stove and generator that rendered him so weak and delirious that he could do little but lie in his sleeping bag and contemplate the fact that if he turned off the devices which he knew were killing him, he would undoubtedly freeze to death. Yet he refused to radio for help because he didn't want his colleagues to risk their lives on a journey through the Antarctic winter, a feat undertaken only once before.[26] At the same time, he judged that if he succumbed to his torpor, 'with me would vanish the ephemeral tensions that held a hundred men to a single cause'.[27] Attuned to his responsibilities as a leader, he held out in his wretched state for four and a half months, until some of his men became suspicious of his increasingly disoriented radio transmissions and came anyway. They found a physical wreck, a 'wild-eyed wraith' with 'scarecrow body and long disheveled hair'[28] – but a psychologically stable one.

When real-time companions prove difficult to conjure up, imagined ones can do just as well. The climber Joe Simpson, who famously managed to drag himself off a mountain with a broken leg in the Peruvian Andes after his friend Simon Yates was forced to cut their rope and leave him for dead, hallucinated in his desperation that Yates and another colleague were walking with him, following just out of sight:

> I smiled, happy at the thought of company and help if I needed it. They would come if I called, but I wasn't going to call. They hung back out of sight, but I knew they weren't far behind.[29]

During Reinhold Messner's solo ascent of Everest's north face in 1980, so convinced was he that he was climbing with an invisible companion that he divided his food into two and worried about how both of them would fit into his tiny tent. It wasn't the first time he had felt a ghostly presence on a mountain, an experience he rationalizes as a survival mechanism: 'The body is inventing ways to provide company.'[30] Norwegian psychologist Gro Sandal, who has interviewed many adventurers about how they cope in extreme environments, agrees that transcending the reality of your situation in this way is a common coping behaviour. It allows people to endure danger. 'It makes them feel safer. It makes them feel less alone.'

A similar psychological mechanism may explain why ship-wrecked mariners marooned on distant islands have been known to anthropomorphize inanimate objects, in some cases creating a virtual cabal of imaginary companions with whom to share the solitude; and why solo sailors build emotional relationships with their boats. It sounds like madness but is likely a foil against it. In 2005, Ellen MacArthur broke the record for the fastest single-handed non-stop circumnavigation of the globe in a trimaran she nicknamed Mobi.[31] During the voyage, she signed emails to her support team 'love e and mobi', and in her published account uses 'we' rather than 'I' throughout, recalling how after crossing the finish line off north-west France she silently thanked her companion of the last seventy-one days for all they had endured together:

> There were no words, just an exchange in the language in which she'd talked to me out there, a language through which she'd wake me from my sleep to let me know she was in need of a little help … She was always watching out for me, as I was for her. If a boat could ever have a soul, then she did.[32]

Tom McClean, the former Parachute Regiment and SAS soldier who in 1969 became the first person to row across the North

Atlantic solo east to west, would no doubt sooner pitch himself overboard than indulge in this kind of sentimentality. This tough, easy-going man lives on a sea loch in the Scottish Highlands, in an area I know well. Many times I have boated past his place and spied on the various improbable craft ranged across his beachfront in which he has crossed that ocean (they include the world's smallest yacht,[33] and a vessel shaped like a bottle). His approach is to be resolutely goal-orientated and utterly determined, a quality he says he learned growing up in an orphanage. 'I tend to get on and just do it', he says. 'It's a hundred per cent tunnel vision when I'm out there. It's either eat, sleep or row, and if you're not doing one of those you're not making way.' Yet even he acknowledges an implicit relationship with his boat and all the things in it. 'Everything about you is one: the food, the clothes, the equipment. You're like a team in a way. It's just you and the gear. It's all you've got in the world.'

For many explorers deprived of human company, the landscape itself can serve as an effective surrogate, drawing them out of themselves into the beauty or grandeur of their surroundings. 'How little the worries of the World seem to one in such a situation as this', exclaimed Courtauld three months into his ice-cap hibernation. 'How grand and awful that are here, the things that grip the heart with fear, the forces that spin the Universe through Space.'[34] In Antarctica, Byrd found himself overwhelmed by 'the imponderable processes and forces of the cosmos, harmonious and soundless ... In that instant I could feel no doubt of man's oneness with the universe.'[35] For astronauts, gazing out of a porthole in wonderment at their home planet – 'that tiny pea, pretty and blue', as Neil Armstrong saw it – can serve a similar purpose.[36] This ability to absorb oneself in mental imagery may be one of the more useful personality traits for solo adventurers, allowing for meditative experiences or altered modes of consciousness that diminish the monotony and toil of travel.[37]

Solitude can be a blissful state, and explorers who adapt to it successfully may be better off alone than with a colleague. Stuart Grassian, a forensic psychiatrist who specializes in the effects of solitary confinement, believes that groups of two may be the most pathogenic of all, liable to sink into mutual paranoia and violent hostility.[38] Byrd in Antarctica wouldn't countenance leaving two men together, reasoning they would inevitably 'find each other out ... if only because once the simple tasks of the day are finished there is little else to do but take each other's measure'.[39] But for those who go it alone and fail to rise above their isolation – or at least find some kind of meaning in it – dissolution awaits. Loneliness falls heavy on them.

There is no more poignant illustration of the power of solitude to sink one person while lifting another up than the stories of Bernard Moitessier and Donald Crowhurst, two of the competitors in the 1968 *Sunday Times* Golden Globe round-the-world yacht race. The trophy, offered to the first sailor to complete a solo non-stop circumnavigation of the globe, was won in 313 days by Robin Knox-Johnston, the only one out of nine to finish. He seemed to relish being alone with his boat, but not as much as Moitessier, an ascetic Frenchman who practised yoga on deck and fed cheese to the shearwaters that shadowed him. Moitessier found the experience so fulfilling, and the idea of returning to civilization so distasteful, that he abandoned the race despite a good chance of victory and just kept on sailing, eventually landing in Tahiti, after travelling more than halfway round the world again. 'I continue non-stop because I am happy at sea', he declared, 'and perhaps because I want to save my soul'.[40] Crowhurst, meanwhile, was in trouble from the start. He left England ill-prepared and sent fake reports about his supposed progress through the southern seas while never actually leaving the Atlantic. Drifting aimlessly for months off the coast of South America, he became ever more depressed and lonely, eventually retreating to his cabin and consolidating his fantasies in a rambling 25,000-word philosophical treatise before jumping overboard. His body was never found.

———

In Jerusalem, one late evening during October 2004, while walking back to my hotel through the east of the city, I crossed paths with a man who is considered an arch-traitor by many in Israel, and a whistleblower-hero worthy of a Nobel peace prize in other countries. Mordechai Vanunu is famous for leaking highly sensitive material about Israel's clandestine nuclear weapons programme, for which he used to work, to *Sunday Times* journalist Peter Hounam in 1986, after becoming convinced that the country's nuclear ambitions were destabilizing the Middle East. Days before the *Sunday Times* ran Hounam's article, Vanunu was kidnapped by Israeli intelligence agents. He spent the next eighteen years in prison. When I ran into him, he had been out only six months, under highly restrictive terms. I recognized him because I had taken an interest in his story and had written to him in prison. He had written back, saying he was 'totally isolated' with little access to the media, and that he wanted his future life to be very far from Israel (he has still not been allowed to leave). In that Jerusalem street he looked smaller than I had imagined, hunched in his walk as if recoiling from the night. I was struck by his substantial eyebrows, the golden cross around his neck (he had converted from Judaism to Christianity two decades earlier), and most of all by how nervous he looked.

It is easy to understand why, once you know his story. The following day I sat with him in the garden of St George's Cathedral, the cloistered retreat in east Jerusalem where he had been staying, while he told me of his incarceration, eleven and a half years of which were in solitary confinement. He had moved between tiny windowless cells, his head in a sack, with no idea where he was, no sense of his surroundings and no view. His interrogators refused him access to a lawyer, his family, a phone. After a year, they gave him a TV and then disrupted the transmission of his favourite programmes. They tried to destroy his sleep by keeping the lights on in his cell day and night: no darkness for two years. They put a video camera in his cell, always on. They suggested he commit suicide. They held back his mail. They subjected him to constant noise and removed every sense of autonomy. They controlled every part of his waking and sleeping. 'Have you seen *The Truman Show*?'[41] he exclaimed. 'That is what I was living in.'

The day he left prison he announced to the world's press that the security services had tried to rob him of his sanity but failed. His former lawyer, Avigdor Feldman, has described Vanunu as 'the most stubborn, principled, and tough person I have ever met'. He seems to have coped a lot better with his isolation than many people would have done. Yet it became clear during our conversation that he had been profoundly affected. He was paranoid that the security services were still monitoring his behaviour minute by minute, fretting that they were interfering with his television. He was worried my tape recorder might somehow be transmitting our conversation. He propounded bizarre conspiracy theories: John F. Kennedy was killed by the French and other pro-nuclear governments because he tried to stop Israel obtaining nuclear weapons; British Labour leader John Smith was murdered rather than dying from a heart attack to allow Tony Blair to lead the party into the next election.

He believed in the existence of a secret world government that controlled the way people behave, what they think.

His delusional thinking is apparent in the letters he wrote to Hounam during his time in prison, some of which Hounam agreed to show me. By 1997, after more than ten years of solitary confinement, Vanunu had convinced himself that the British government had conspired to bring about the Second World War 'to convince [the] US to produce and use NWs [nuclear weapons]', which would then allow Britain covertly to test its own nuclear technologies on humans; that British spies were behind the Wall Street crash of 1929, the growth of Nazism in Germany in the 1930s, the Russian revolution and the rise of Mao Zedong; and that British Airways and other airlines were being paid by governments to carry spies around the world and this was the only reason they remained solvent.[42] Caught in a fantasy of his own making, he was anchored only by the limits of his imagination, which in the absence of company is no anchor at all.

Vanunu's condition is typical of those who, unlike Courtauld, Byrd and others, are shut away against their will, unprepared and without the psychological crutch of an organized support network to temper their isolation. The 25,000 inmates held in super-maximum security prisons in the US are testament to that. Several decades of research into the psychology of supermax prisoners has found that the majority suffer serious trauma as a result of being shut away, in their cells for up to twenty-three hours a day. This includes panic attacks, anxiety, loss of control, irrational anger, paranoia, hallucinations, excessive rumination, depression, insomnia, hypersensitivity to external stimuli, obsessive thoughts, cognitive dysfunction, self-mutilation and a host of social pathologies that would make it hard for them to function in normal society.[43] Between twenty-two and forty-five per cent have full-blown mental illnesses or brain damage.[44] A disproportionately high number kill themselves: in 2005, seventy per cent of prison suicides in California occurred in solitary confinement.[45] The longer the confinement, the more damaged the prisoner and the longer they take to recover – if at all.

Here is an example of the kind of pathology commonly found among supermax inmates, as witnessed by psychiatrist Stuart Grassian:

> [They] easily become preoccupied with some thought, some perceived slight or irritation, some sound or smell coming from a neighboring cell, or, perhaps most commonly, by some bodily sensation. Tortured by it, [they] are unable to stop dwelling on it. In solitary confinement ordinary stimuli become intensely unpleasant and small irritations become maddening ... I have examined countless individuals in solitary confinement who have become obsessively preoccupied with some minor, almost imperceptible bodily sensation, a sensation which grows over time into a worry, and finally into an all-consuming, life-threatening illness.[46]

One of the main causes of this institutionalized horror, psychologists agree, is the lack of social interaction. Without it, inmates find it very hard to maintain a sense of their own identity, the appropriateness of their emotions and how they relate to a wider social world. '[They] have no way to test the reality of their fantasies, and there is a tendency towards paranoia and an inability to control the rage that mounts with each perceived insult',[47] explains Terry Kupers, a forensic psychiatrist who has interviewed and evaluated thousands of supermax prisoners in the US, Europe and Africa over the past three decades. Compare that, he says, with an example from everyday life:

> I walk into a room. Two people are talking and lower their voices as I enter. I have the momentary fantasy they were talking about me and that's why they lowered their voices when I walked in. I approach them and their friendly greetings disabuse me of what I now can judge to be an erroneous and paranoid fantasy on my part. This kind of reality testing goes on in everyone's daily life. Prisoners in isolated confinement have no opportunity to check out their possibly paranoid projections with a sympathetic friend.

Craig Haney, the leading authority on the mental health of inmates in the US, has found that some of them purposefully initiate brutal confrontations with prison staff just to reaffirm their own existence, to remind themselves that they are human. To remember who they are.[48]

Many prisoners endure years of solitary confinement, but the ill effects can manifest themselves after only a few days. Shafiq Rasul, a British citizen who was detained for over two years by the US military in Afghanistan and Guantanamo Bay, said he felt he was going out of his mind after just a week in isolation. After five or six weeks, he confessed to American interrogators' (false) accusation that he had met Osama Bin Laden, because 'I was desperate for it to end and therefore eventually I just gave in'.[49] (This is a good illustration of why torture, which is what solitary confinement amounts to in many cases, is a highly unreliable procurer of the truth.)[50] Sarah Shourd, arrested in 2009 while hiking on the border with Iraqi Kurdistan and locked up in a ten-foot by fourteen-foot cell in Iran's Evin Prison for thirteen and a half months, suffered similar anguish:

After two months with next to no human contact, my mind began to slip. Some days, I heard phantom footsteps coming down the hall. I spent large portions of my days crouched down on all fours by a small slit in the door, listening. In the periphery of my vision, I began to see flashing lights, only to jerk my head around to find that nothing was there. More than once, I beat at the walls until my knuckles bled and cried myself into a state of exhaustion. At one point, I heard someone screaming, and it wasn't until I felt the hands of one of the friendlier guards on my face, trying to revive me, that I realized the screams were my own.[51]

Civilian victims like Shourd are among the most vulnerable because their incarceration comes out of the blue. Their world is suddenly inverted, and there is nothing in the manner of their taking – no narrative of sacrifice, or enduring for a greater good – to help them derive some meaning from it. They must construct a detached view unaided, a monumental task when alone.

Hussain al-Shahristani managed it. He was Saddam Hussein's chief nuclear adviser before he was tortured after refusing on moral grounds to co-operate on the development of an atomic weapon. He kept his sanity during ten years of solitary confinement by taking refuge in a world of abstractions, making up mathematical problems that he then tried to solve.[52] He is now deputy energy minister of Iraq. Edith Bone, a medical academic and translator, followed a similar strategy during the seven years she spent imprisoned by the Hungarian communist government after the Second World War, constructing an abacus out of stale bread and counting out an inventory of her vocabulary in the six languages she spoke fluently.[53] Ahmed Errachidi, wrongly held for five and a half years in Guantanamo, took refuge in a world of his imagination, flying

Fig. 10 Cell block in Guantanamo Bay detention camp.

'beyond a make-believe horizon, looking up at the sun, seeing its bright rays ... In my mind I could go anywhere.'[54]

Terry Waite managed it too during his five years – four of them in solitary – as a hostage of Hezbollah in Lebanon. But he was negotiating the release of other hostages as the Archbishop of Canterbury's envoy when he was kidnapped in January 1987, so he was very aware of the risks and had mentally prepared himself for the worst. He was also grounded by his faith, by which he resolved to 'hold fast to love': a compassionate man who in his autobiography expresses as much concern for his guards as himself.[55] Frank Reed, an American held in Lebanon at the same time as Waite, fared less well. The isolation and abuse he suffered left him deeply withdrawn, almost catatonic, according to Brian Keenan and Terry Anderson, fellow hostages who for a while shared a cell with him.[56] He refused

224

to exercise and sat for hours with a blanket over his head or with his blindfold down. He was lost in another reality. He appeared to recover, though after his release developed a drinking problem and was admitted to a psychiatric hospital.

Such experiences may be easier to take if you belong to a military organization, even though in wartime your captors will try to exploit you as a source of information. Keron Fletcher, a consultant psychiatrist who helped debrief and treat some of the western hostages held in Lebanon in the 1980s and early 1990s, says mock detention and interrogation exercises of the kind he himself underwent while serving with the Royal Air Force are a good preparation for the shock of capture. 'They teach you the basics of coping. Also, you know your buddies will be busting a gut to get you back in one piece. I think the military are less likely to feel helpless or hopeless. Hopelessness and helplessness are horrible things to live with and they erode morale and coping ability.'

US senator John McCain is a good example of how a military mindset bestows psychological advantages. His five and a half years as a prisoner of war in Vietnam, during which he stubbornly refused to yield to his interrogators and even revelled in antagonizing them despite being severely tortured, actually seemed to strengthen him. But note what he had to say about the two years he spent in isolation: 'It's an awful thing, solitary. It crushes your spirit and weakens your resistance more effectively than any other form of mistreatment ... The onset of despair is immediate, and it is a formidable foe.'[57]

———

Group loyalty can help soldiers endure interrogation and imprisonment, but they may find that their captors use it against them. Intelligence officers understand that while group bonds can inspire stubborn resistance, once they unravel and it becomes clear to a prisoner that his brothers-in-arms have betrayed the cause, even the most committed will lose the resolve to carry on. If no one capitulates, interrogators will try to trick them into believing that they have. The US Army Field Manual for intelligence gathering recommends exploiting a detainee's love for his comrades,[58] for example by convincing him that he could save their lives by providing information, or endanger them by withholding it.[59] A more devious approach is to play on his love for his family, a tactic Saddam Hussein took to extremes. Al-Shahristani, who was interrogated and tortured for three weeks before he was placed in solitary confinement, told me: 'The most painful thing in those torture chambers was to hear the screams of children being tortured to extract confessions from their fathers.'[60]

One afternoon, I drove from Jerusalem to a quiet neighbourhood in the Neolithic seaport of Ashkelon to meet a man who knows a great deal about how to get prisoners to talk, a man with as many enemies as admirers. For twenty-one years, Michael Koubi worked for Shin Bet, Israel's security agency, six of them as its chief interrogator. Between 1987 and 1993, he questioned hundreds of Palestinians, including many terrorists. He has a formidable reputation among his peers, and also among his victims. I use that word knowingly: even without physical pressure, which Koubi claims he has never needed to exercise, the intimidation, coercion and psychological bullying that interrogators typically use can leave long-lasting scars. I later met several former Palestinian prisoners who remain deeply traumatized a decade after their experience at the hands of Koubi's officers.

Koubi is about six feet tall and skeletal with an angular, bony face. He has few soft edges even when he smiles. He is how you'd expect a chief interrogator to look in, say, a Quentin Tarantino film. He is like a caricature of himself. He sat down and beckoned me into a chair so close to his that I could trace the capillaries in his oft-broken nose. He wore a red shirt. His eyes hardly flinched when he talked. I will not easily forget how he looked at me. I imagine there are many Palestinians who have not forgotten how he looked at them.

The question I most wanted to ask Koubi, the one most relevant to this chapter, was how he 'broke' Sheikh Ahmed Yassin. Yassin was the spiritual leader of the Palestinian group Hamas before he was assassinated by Israel in 2004. He was responsible for planning dozens of lethal terrorist attacks on Israeli soldiers and civilians. Koubi called him 'the most ruthless, cruel and evil person I have ever met'. He interrogated him at length in 1989. At first, he said, Yassin refused to co-operate, remained completely silent. So Koubi tried to lure him into conversation by discussing the Qur'an, a subject Yassin felt supremely confident about:

> I said to him, let's have a competition. I'll ask you a question about the Qur'an, and if I win I can ask you another about any subject and you have to answer. He was sure he would know it better than me. But I started asking complicated questions, and he didn't know the answers. When you are in prison, you forget things. For example, I asked him to tell me the name of the only sura out of the one hundred and fourteen in the Qur'an that did not contain the letter mim. He didn't know. I asked him how many verses there were in the Baqarah sura, the longest in the Qur'an. He had forgotten. So I won, and I started asking questions on other things.[61]

Still Yassin resisted, so Koubi played his ace. He brought into his cell Saleh Shade, Yassin's deputy in Hamas, who had already started to co-operate. With his head in a hood, Shade didn't know Yassin was there, and he spoke without inhibition about Hamas's military wing. 'At this point Yassin was convinced', said Koubi. 'It was a very dramatic change. I then sat with him for hundreds of hours while he talked about the ideology of Hamas. He even told other detainees to co-operate with me. If he could he would have killed me, but he respected me.'

I have not been able to corroborate Koubi's account, though the trap he sprang on Yassin has long been favoured by interrogators dealing with members of tightly bound groups. In an environment as stressful as an interrogation cell, almost everyone is vulnerable to the pull of their comrades. Yassin, a revered leader devoted to his cause, proved no exception. Nasra Hassan, who researches suicide terrorism in the Islamic world and met with him many times in his house in Gaza, once asked him about his time in prison in Israel and how he had coped. He told her he had not missed freedom and that the experience had not damaged him or disturbed him, partly because he had had more time to pray, partly because he had been surrounded by other Palestinians including many from his own group Hamas. (In her meetings with Yassin, Hassan found him 'very open, relaxed, very witty, with a great sense of humour, very sharp, very intelligent'. Recall Koubi's assessment of him as the most ruthless, cruel and evil person he had met. This sounds like a contradiction but it isn't – though our understanding of human nature rarely allows for such discomforting complexities.)

———

Just as physical isolation need not lead to the despair of loneliness, neither does social interaction preclude it. 'I never felt so lonely as in that particular hour when I was surrounded by people but suddenly realized my ultimate isolation', muses Paul Tillich in his meditation on loneliness and solitude.[62] Everyone experiences the pain of social rejection from time to time in everyday life,[63] and at first blush it is a healthy response, an evolved state that motivates us to interact with others and build the social connections that we need to survive. Stay lonely for long, however, and the effect is deeply negative. Social isolation unleashes an immune response – a cascade of stress hormones and inflammation – that can have a serious impact on health. Chronically lonely people have higher blood pressure and are more vulnerable to infection and disease. They sleep less well. They are more likely to abuse drugs or alcohol. They find it harder to maintain attention. Their logical and verbal reasoning diminishes. They are more likely to develop Alzheimer's disease and dementia. The precise biological mechanisms underlying these changes are still unclear, though researchers suspect it relates to the recent discovery that genes express proteins differently under different socio-environmental conditions. The outcome, however, is unambiguous.[64]

John Cacioppo, a University of Chicago professor and one of the foremost experts on how social behaviour affects the brain, considers loneliness as serious a risk factor for ill health as smoking, lack of exercise, hypertension and obesity. But what really counts, he says, is your subjective experience – how alone you perceive yourself to be:

Whether you are at home with your family, working in an office crowded with bright and attractive young people, touring Disneyland, or sitting alone in a fleabag hotel on the wrong side of town, chronic *feelings* of isolation can drive a cascade of physiological events that actually accelerates the aging process ... Over time, these changes in physiology are compounded in ways that may be hastening millions of people to an early grave.[65]

What matters, then, is not how many people you know but the quality of your friendships. You can have five hundred friends on Facebook and still feel lost. As social animals, the need for deep interaction is written in our DNA; starved of it we wither, we are half ourselves. The children rescued from Romanian orphanages in the early 1990s, who had been almost entirely deprived of one-on-one social contact since birth, grew up with serious behavioural and attachment issues that persist despite their integration into loving foster homes.[66] [67] The effects of loneliness in adulthood are generally reversible. But it requires meaningful connection, reaching out beyond ourselves, what Tillich described as 'self-transcendence'. Cacioppo says this has much to do with overcoming the sense of threat that comes with loneliness, the isolate's fear of the world. He recommends starting slow, playing with the idea of 'trying to get small doses of the positive sensations that come from positive social interactions'. The road to healthy connections, he says, paraphrasing an Alcoholics Anonymous motto, 'is always under construction'.[68]

Social alienation can affect all of us, though perhaps none more profoundly than soldiers, sailors and airmen who 'demob' after returning home from active service. Recall how military units feel much like families, and that military buddies bond with each other at a level rarely found in civilian life. Their co-dependency is absolute. Losing this brotherhood and starting anew in an unfamiliar civilian world can be lonesome indeed. The experience was particularly acute for Vietnam veterans, who unlike their fêted Second World War compatriots, returned home to anti-war marches, a hostile media and a largely unsympathetic public. Instead of communal endorsement they got condemnation, which according to the military psychologist Dave Grossman amplified the trauma of their combat experiences to 'a staggering degree of horror'.[69] Given that social support – including reassurance that what they did on the battlefield was necessary – is now known to be crucial for veterans' mental health, it is little surprise that the Vietnam conflict arguably resulted in more psychiatric casualties than any previous war in US history.[70]

The most recent research into the psychological health of soldiers returning from Iraq and Afghanistan underlines the dangers of leaving service without an adequate social safety net. A 2013 study of serving and ex-members of the UK armed forces, carried out by a group at King's College London (KCL), revealed that those who had returned to civvy street were more likely to be suffering from both PTSD and common mental disorders, such as depression and anxiety. The main reason for this, the researchers concluded, was the 'loss of social embeddedness and group cohesion', a breaking of close-felt ties that is often very hard to bear.[71]

Deirdre MacManus, a KCL forensic psychiatrist, has separately found that ex-soldiers are fifty per cent more likely to commit a violent offence than their colleagues still serving.[72] The transition to civilian life can be hugely stressful, she says. 'If they joined the military at sixteen and most of their buddies are from the military, and all of a sudden they distance themselves from those buddies, then who do they have as a support network? These guys can find themselves in significant social isolation.'

Military psychiatrists have been aware of the perils of re-integration for decades. In *Men Under Stress*, their classic 1945 study of how US Air Force personnel adapted to combat during the Second World War, Roy Grinker and John Spiegel noted that veterans were often so completely assimilated into their units that on entering civilian society they had to re-invent themselves in order to establish a sense of their individuality, a distressing process that could result in mental illness. The problem was that to become effective in the first place, a soldier had to submit entirely to the undemocratic military environment to which he then became accustomed. The question then was:

> ... whether or not an American soldier, once conditioned to this regressed and dependent position, can be helped back to independence and good health, or whether he must remain continually unadjusted, physically or psychologically ill, or forever in search of a strong group to give him the illusion of the strength he lost as a member of the military group.[73]

These dynamics are not exclusive to soldiers. Many of the thirty-three Chilean miners who in 2010 survived sixty-nine days trapped deep underground together after part of their mine collapsed have had huge problems adjusting to normal life since their rescue. This is no doubt due to several factors, including the corrupting influence of the media circus that turned them all into global celebrities. But it also seems likely that the time they spent together in those stressful circumstances – longer than any other group of men trapped underground – changed their relationships with one another, and in turn their relationships with their wives, children and friends. The film-maker Angus Macqueen, who interviewed several of the miners for a BBC documentary the following year, commented: 'The bonds of friendship and solidarity they forged down the mine are now stronger than those with their own families.'[74]

———

Loneliness, isolation, rejection: these are potent triggers of physical and mental ill-health. For a few people, the effect is even more extreme. Unable to build relationships with the people around them, they channel their estrangement into self-aggrandizing acts of violence. This is the psychology of lone wolf terrorists.

When Anders Breivik shot dead sixty-nine teenagers at a youth camp in Norway on 22 July 2011 and killed eight others by exploding a car bomb in Oslo, a lot of people presumed he was mad. How else would such perverse behaviour be possible? But a year later a court declared him sane – excessively narcissistic and megalomaniac, but not schizophrenic and not psychotic. He was found guilty of the murders and given Norway's maximum sentence.

He did, however, share a psychological profile with other 'lone wolf' killers, including Ted Kaczynski, otherwise known as the Unabomber, the architect of a seventeen-year bombing campaign against the modern 'industrial-technological system', which he considered incompatible with human freedom;[75] Eric Rudolph, who ran a lethal crusade against American abortion clinics; Oklahoma City bomber Timothy McVeigh; and some perpetrators of school and college massacres. All of them seemingly found it difficult to make meaningful connections with others about the things that concerned them. They were socially isolated, even from groups whose extremist ideology they shared. Kaczynski bemoaned being a 'social cripple' while living for twenty-five years in an off-grid cabin in a remote Montana wilderness. McVeigh fell out with many of his gun club acquaintances. Breivik was cold-shouldered by the right-wing Norwegian Defence League, which considered his views too extremist. Tamerlan Tsarnaev, the elder of the Boston bomber brothers, reportedly complained that he felt alienated and had no American friends.

The clinical psychologist Kathleen Puckett knows a lot about the mindset of such people. For twenty-three years she was an FBI agent, and for much of that time specialized in the behaviour of lone domestic terrorists. Between 1994 and 1998, she was the primary behavioural analyst on the Unabomber investigation. She was one of the few on the investigative team who, before Kaczynski was arrested in his Montana cabin in April 1996, believed he was the culprit.

In 2001, the FBI asked Puckett to dig deeper into what makes the likes of Kaczynski and McVeigh tick. After spending months going through their files, analysing their writings and mapping out their social lives, she marked out alienation as the critical factor, not just as a common characteristic but as a driving force behind their behaviour. 'Being a lone terrorist is a very hard thing to be', she says. 'It's lonely. All these men desperately wanted and needed social connection. Their inability to successfully connect with others drove them to search for connection to something greater, an ideology, that would not reject them, and would in fact provide the driver for their ultimate recognition by society as lone terrorists.'[76]

The characteristics of lone-wolf terrorists – unable to fit in, rejected by their social group, embracing a hate-filled ideology – are common also to many so-called school or college killers. Eric Harris and Dylan Klebold were routinely ostracized at Columbine High School, which according to their journals appeared to be one of the factors that drove them to massacre twelve of their classmates and a teacher.[77] Seung-Hui Cho, who shot thirty-two people at Virginia Tech University, was socially avoidant and awkward in company, according to those who knew him. Adam Lanza, who killed twenty children and six staff at Sandy Hook Elementary School (after shooting his mother), was profoundly socially anxious. There is a clear pattern here. When social psychologist Clark

McCauley looked into the case histories of forty-one young men who had carried out attacks in US schools between 1974 and 2000, he concluded that all but one had showed signs of being isolated or socially disconnected.[78] Another study, which looked at fifteen school shootings between 1995 and 2001, found that in thirteen of them the perpetrators had been ostracized, bullied or rejected by their peers.[79]

Clearly isolation by itself cannot explain every act of non-group violence. Most people who feel alienated or cast out by society do not express their frustration through bullets or bombs. But we can say this: ostracism is a potent agitator. We are all super-sensitive to it, are hard-wired to push against it.[80] Nobody chooses loneliness. Being left out can lead to depression or despair, or it can lead to rage. William James, perhaps the first scientific psychologist, acknowledged as much more than a century and a quarter ago in his writings on the social self:

> No more fiendish punishment could be devised, were such a thing physically possible, than that one should be turned loose in society and remain absolutely unnoticed by all the members thereof. If no one turned round when we entered, answered when we spoke, or minded what we did, but if every person we met 'cut us dead', and acted as if we were non-existing things, a kind of rage and impotent despair would ere long well up in us, from which the cruellest bodily tortures would be a relief; for these would make us feel that, however bad might be our plight, we had not sunk to such a depth as to be unworthy of attention at all.[81]

We've seen how people respond to social isolation in multifarious and often unpredictable ways. We've pondered survivors like August Courtauld, who invoked his distant companions to see him through his five months under the ice cap, and those who fared less well, such as hostage Frank Reed, flung without warning into a Lebanese hell-hole. We've encountered others, like Edith Bone with her abacus made from bread, who faced down their predicament with psychological flair.

What message can we take from these stories of endurance and despair? The obvious one is that we are, as a rule, considerably diminished when we are disengaged from others. But a more upbeat assessment seems equally valid: it is possible to connect, to find solace beyond ourselves, even when we are alone. We shouldn't underestimate the power of others to knock over prison walls or penetrate icy caves. This may take imagination, but the important thing is to build those social connections when we can. We never know when we might need them.

Epilogue

Reflecting on our social behaviour can be sobering, for the forces that shape it are potent and often beyond our control. Yet our sociality is arguably the thing that makes us special, that defines us as a species. It is no accident that isolation is incapacitating. As the neuroscientist Matthew D. Lieberman puts it in his book *Social*, 'this is what our brains were wired for: reaching out to and interacting with others. These are design features, not flaws. These social adaptations are central to making us the most successful species on earth.'[1]

Group tendencies bring satisfaction, and also much strife. Still, they can be vulnerable to reason, and thus it is profitable to be aware of them, even when the conditions they create are hard to stomach. Consider three cases.

1. Much evil is committed by people who are not psychopathic but who conform unthinkingly to the norms of their group, or who obey authority without questioning. Knowing that humans are wired to conform and how easily this can lead anyone astray, would potential evildoers behave differently? Possibly.

2. Decades of research by social psychologists have demonstrated that fear drives us closer to our in-groups and inflames prejudices against out-groups. Would the world be a safer place if political leaders, public figures, pundits, commentators and the media took this on board and refrained from using fear to motivate voters and sell news? Unquestionably.

3. Our fondness for mixing with others of our ilk – those who share our political and cultural values – is pushing disparate communities further apart (multiculturalism is divisive unless the different cultures interact). Would society be more harmonious if the various groups engaged more with each other? Highly likely, though hard to achieve.

Some of these findings are immediately applicable. We can start talking to people who are different from us, wherever we encounter them: breaking down barriers starts and ends at the grassroots. Elsewhere, progress requires institutional change. For instance, the public exploitation of fear could be restricted by an extension of hate speech laws to cover language or images that directly or indirectly inflame prejudice towards particular communities; or by a voluntary agreement among the media to report terrorist violence proportionately, akin to the World Health Organization's guidelines on the reporting of suicides that are aimed at preventing copycat cases.[2]

These are grave considerations, but they are by no means the only nor necessarily the most important consequences of human groupishness. Cohesion, the psychological stickiness that holds groups together, can inspire acts of extreme loyalty, endurance and courage, and it can dramatically improve the productivity of office workers, and the performance of sports teams. It can also be too much of a good thing: anyone in business or on a committee should beware the perils of groupthink, when colleagues become so fixated on agreeing with each other that their decision-making goes to pieces.

Awareness of our social natures can transform our experience in crowds, temper our herding instincts in investment and other choices, and even save our lives in a public emergency. It can enrich us day-to-day. The co-ordinated body language and contagious mannerisms of group encounters are enthralling to behold, especially when you are the only one conscious of them. It is reassuring to know that you are susceptible to the bright moods of your exuberant friends and the dark moods of your depressed ones. And the idea that altruism can be learned, and that we can all be heroic if we keep our wits about us, is encouraging to say the least.

Perhaps the most profound aspect of our groupishness is that it helps determine our sense of self. Identity is built not only on memories, but also on how people interact with us, a notion the neuroscientist Antonio Damasio dubs 'the social me'.[3] You are a mother, a brother, a social worker, a financier, an American, a friend, an introvert, an athlete, an artist because that is how others see you. Thus conceptions of selfhood are to some extent culturally determined. In collectivist societies in East Asia, personal narratives dwell on the context and social significance of events, while Europeans and Americans are more concerned with personal achievement. The 'terrible twos', when children start to assert their independence, are less histrionic and sometimes completely absent in some non-Western cultures.

Group identity comes before self-identity, and co-operation before autonomy. We are pulled by many currents, but it is the people we swim with who make us who we are.

Notes

___

PROLOGUE

1. David Cannadine, *The Undivided Past: History Beyond Our Differences* (Allen Lane, 2013), p. 5.
2. For a full explanation of this phenomenon, known as stereotype threat, see Claude M. Steele, *Whistling Vivaldi* (Norton & Norton, 2010).

CHAPTER 1: EMOTIONAL CHAMELEONS

1. Quoted in 'People's princess – or just a fast-fading fairytale?', *Observer*, 11 August 2002, available at: http://observer.theguardian.com/focus/story/0,6903,772521,00.html.
2. James Thomas, 'From people power to mass hysteria: media and popular reactions to the death of Princess Diana', *International Journal of Cultural Studies* 11 (2008), 362–76, p. 371.
3. Details taken from archives of *The New York Times*, 11–12 December 1930.
4. See Milton Friedman and Anna Jacobson Schwartz, *A Monetary History of the United States 1867–1960* (Princeton University Press, 1963); Paul Trecott, 'The failure of the Bank of United States', *Journal of Money, Credit and Banking* 24 (1992), 384–99; Niall Ferguson, *The Ascent of Money: A Financial History of the World* (Allen Lane, 2008).
5. R.C.J. Hermans, A. Lichtwarck-Aschoff, K. E. Bevelander, C.P. Herman, J.K. Larsen, *et al.*, 'Mimicry of food intake: the dynamic interplay between

eating companions', *PLoS ONE* 7, 2 (2012), e31027. doi:10.1371/journal.pone.0031027.

6. K.A. Patel and D.G. Schlundt, 'Impact of moods and social context on eating behavior', *Appetite* 36 (2001), 111–18.

7. H. Larsen, R.C. Engels, P.M. Souren, I. Granic and G. Overbeek, 'Peer influence in a micro-perspective: imitation of alcoholic and non-alcoholic beverages', *Addictive Behaviors* 35 (2010), 49–52.

8. R. Koordeman, E. Kuntsche, D.J. Anschutz, R. van Baaren and R.C.M.E. Engels, 'Do we act upon what we see? Direct effects of alcohol cues in movies on young adults' alcohol drinking', *Alcohol and Alcoholism* 46 (2011), 393–8.

9. Joanne Lumsden, Lynden K. Miles, Michael J. Richardson, Carlene A. Smith and C. Neil Macrae, 'Who syncs? Social motives and interpersonal coordination', *Journal of Experimental Social Psychology* 48 (2012), 746–51.

10. W.S. Condon and W.D. Ogston, 'Sound film analysis of normal and pathological behavior patterns', *Journal of Nervous and Mental Disease* 143 (1966), 338–47.

11. P. Totterdell, 'Catching moods and hitting runs: mood linkage and subjective performance in professional sport teams', *Journal of Applied Psychology* 85 (2000), 848–59.

12. J.H. Fowler and N.A. Christakis, 'The dynamic spread of happiness in a large social network: longitudinal analysis over 20 years in the Framingham Heart Study', *British Medical Journal* 337 (2008), a2338.

13. *New Scientist*, 3 January 2009, p. 25. Christakis's research team claims to have shown that many other behaviours and traits pass through social networks in a similar pattern to happiness – largely through the spread of social norms rather than through emotional contagion – including obesity, drinking habits, the decision to quit smoking, a preference for online privacy and loneliness. While these claims have been published in respected, peer-reviewed journals, the statistical analysis has been the subject of some controversy, with several researchers arguing that it is impossible to infer the cause of the clustering from the data – for example, it could be due to people sharing similar traits flocking together. See R. Lyons, 'The spread of evidence-poor medicine via flawed social-network analysis', *Statistics, Politics, and Policy* 2 (2011), doi: 10.2202/2151-7509.1024.

14. H.S. Friedman and R.E. Riggio, 'Effect of individual differences in nonverbal expressiveness on transmission of emotion', *Journal of Nonverbal Behavior* 6 (1981), 96–104.

15. T.E. Joiner, 'Contagious depression: existence, specificity to depressed symptoms, and the role of reassurance seeking', *Journal of Personality and Social Psychology* 67 (1994), 287–96; Gerald J. Haeffel and Jennifer L. Hames, 'Cognitive vulnerability to depression can be contagious', *Clinical Psychological Science* 2, 1 (2013), 75–85.

16. S.D. Pugh, 'Service with a smile: emotional contagion in the service encounter', *Academy of Management Journal* 44 (2001), 1018–27; E. Kim and D.J. Yoon, 'Why does service with a smile make employees happy? A social interaction model', *Journal of Applied Psychology* 97 (2012), 1250–67.

17. Many of them by Christakis and Fowler: see their book *Connected* (Little, Brown, 2009).

18. S. Côté and I. Hideg, 'The ability to influence others via emotion displays: a new dimension of emotional intelligence', *Organizational Psychology Review* 1 (2011), 53–71.

19. See Antonio Damasio, *The Feeling of What Happens: Body and Emotion in the Making of Consciousness* (Houghton Mifflin Harcourt, 1999).

20. P. Ekman and W. Friesen, *Facial Action Coding System: A Technique for the Measurement of Facial Movement* (Consulting Psychologists Press, 1978).

21. Paul Ekman, *Emotions Revealed: Understanding Faces and Feelings* (Times Books, 2003), p. 36.

22. Kirk Douglas, *The Ragman's Son: An Autobiography* (Simon & Schuster, 1988), p. 266.

23. For a summary of research on emotional contagion see E. Hatfield, R.L. Rapson and Y. L. Le, 'Primitive emotional contagion: recent research', in J. Decety and W. Ickes (eds), *The Social Neuroscience of Empathy* (MIT Press, 2009). For a deeper analysis see Elaine Hatfield, John Cacioppo and Richard Rapson, *Emotional Contagion: Studies in Emotion and Social Interaction* (Cambridge University Press, 1993).

24. David A. Havas, Arthur M. Glenberg, Karol A. Gutowski, Mark J. Lucarelli and Richard J. Davidson, 'Cosmetic use of botulinum toxin-A affects processing of emotional language', *Psychological Science* 21 (2010), 895–900.

25. A. Hennenlotter, C. Dresel, F. Castrop, A. Ceballos Baumann, A. Wohlschlager and B. Haslinger, 'The link between facial feedback and neural activity within central circuitries of emotion – new insights from botulinum toxin-induced denervation of frown muscles', *Cerebral Cortex* 19 (2008), 537–42.

26. There are also potentially positive implications for emotional health: other studies have found that injecting Botox into the corrugator or frowning muscle in the forehead can relieve symptoms of depression. For more on this

see Eric Finzi, *The Face of Emotion: How Botox Affects Our Mood and Relationships* (Palgrave Macmillan, 2013).

27. In videocast, filmed by *Technology Review*, March/April 2008.

28. 'To signal is human', *American Scientist* 98 (2010), 204–11, p. 207.

29. This appears to support the theory – often advocated but only recently bolstered with persuasive data – that communities with the greatest diversity of social connections tend to be the most economically developed. See N. Eagle, M. Macy and R. Claxton, 'Network diversity and economic development', *Science* 328, 5981 (2010), 1029–31.

30. 'The new science of building great teams', *Harvard Business Review* 90 (April 2012), p. 65.

31. Nadav Aharony, Wei Pan, Cory Ip, Inas Khayal and Alex Pentland, 'Social fMRI: investigating and shaping social mechanisms in the real world', *Pervasive and Mobile Computing* 7 (2011), 643–59.

32. Stanley Milgram, Leonard Bickman and Lawrence Berkowitz, 'Note on the drawing power of crowds of different size', *Journal of Personality and Social Psychology* 13 (1969), 79–82.

33. From Hatfield *et al.*, *Emotional Contagion*, p. 190.

34. Frank J. Bernieri, J. Steven Reznick and Robert Rosenthal, 'Synchrony, pseudosynchrony, and dissynchrony: measuring the entrainment process in mother–infant interactions', *Journal of Personality and Social Psychology* 54 (1988), 243–53.

35. R.B. Zajonc, P.K. Adelmann, S.T. Murphy and P.M. Niedenthal, 'Convergence in the physical appearance of spouses', *Motivation and Emotion* 11 (1987), 335–46.

36. Jack Kerouac, *On the Road* (Penguin, 1991), p. 10.

37. See Daniel M. Rempala, 'Cognitive strategies for controlling emotional contagion', *Journal of Applied Social Psychology* 43 (2013), 1528–37.

38. For example see F. Bernieri, J. Davis, R. Rosenthal and C. Knee, 'Interactional synchrony and rapport: measuring synchrony in displays devoid of sound and facial affect', *Personality and Social Psychology Bulletin* 20 (1994), 303–11.

39. For more on the dynamics of sequential voting see S. Nageeb Ali and Navin Kartik, 'A theory of momentum in sequential voting' (2006), available at http://www.kellogg.northwestern.edu/research/math/seminars/200607/kartik032807.pdf.

40. That is, corrected for consumer price inflation. From Robert J. Shiller, *The Subprime Solution: How Today's Financial Crisis Happened, and What to Do About It* (Princeton University Press, 2008).

41. Quoted in several sources, including Patrick Bajari, Chenghuan Sean Chu and Minjung Park, 'An empirical model of subprime mortgage default from 2000 to 2007', National Bureau of Economic Research working paper no. 14625 (2008), available at www.nber.org/papers/w14625.

42. In Robert J. Shiller, *The Subprime Solution*, p. 45.

43. For more on the spread of vivid or easily available ideas see Timur Kuran and Cass R. Sunstein, 'Availability cascades and risk regulation', *Stanford Law Review* 51 (1999), 683–768.

44. Gerd Gigerenzer, 'Out of the frying pan into the fire: behavioral reactions to terrorist attacks', *Risk Analysis* 26 (2006), 347–51. A similar effect was observed after the 2005 terrorist bombings on the London transport network: psychologist Peter Ayton and his team at City University, London, found that in the six months following the attack, many people chose to travel by bicycle rather than use the Underground, resulting in an additional 214 casualties (injuries and fatalities). Ayton's study was presented at the American Psychological Society 24th Annual Convention, Chicago, May 2012.

45. C.S. Enright, '9/11 anniversary media coverage: anxiety and expectations of future terrorist attacks', poster presented at the American Psychological Society 18th Annual Convention, New York, May 2006.

46. First in 'Learning to expect the unexpected', *Edge: The Third Culture* (www.edge.org), 19 April 2004.

CHAPTER 2: CROWD SMARTS

1. Robert Schofield, *The Enlightened Joseph Priestley: A Study of His Life and Work from 1773 to 1804* (Pennsylvania State University Press, 2004), p. xii.

2. In 1774, Priestley founded Britain's first Unitarian congregation in London, which rejected the popular Christian notion that God was three persons in one (father, son and holy ghost) and that Jesus was the son of God.

3. Joseph Priestley, *An Appeal to the Public on the Subject of the Riots in Birmingham* (J. Thomson, 1791), p. 28.

4. Ibid., p. 30.

5. Edmund Burke, *Reflections on the Revolution in France* (J. Dodsley, 1790), p. 117.

6. Ibid., p. 106.

7. From Hippolyte Taine, *Les origines de la France contemporaine: la Revolution*, vol. I (Libraire Hachette, 1896), pp. 40, 51.

8. Gabriel Tarde, 'Les crimes des foules', *Archives de l'anthropologie criminelle* 7 (1892), 353–86; translation in Susanna Barrows, *Distorting Mirrors: Visions*

of the Crowd in Late Nineteenth-Century France (Yale University Press, 1981), p. 144.

9. Scipio Sighele, *La foule criminelle: essai de psychologie collective* (Felix Alcan, 1901), pp. 62–3.

10. Gustave Le Bon, *La psychologie des foules* (Felix Alcan, 1895), published in English as *The Crowd: A Study of the Popular Mind* (Macmillan, 1896), p. 19.

11. Will Self, 'When it comes to riots, it's all relative', *New Statesman*, 22 August 2011.

12. Le Bon, *La psychologie des foules*.

13. From Gustave Le Bon, *Les lois psychologiques de l'évolution des peuples* (Felix Alcan, 1894); Gustave Le Bon, 'La psychologie des femmes et les effets de leur éducation actuelle', *Revue Scientifique* 46, 15 (1890), 449–60; Gustave Le Bon, 'Recherches anatomiques et mathématiques sur les lois des variations du volume du cerveau et sur leurs relations avec l'intelligence', *Revue d'Anthropologie*, 2nd series, 2 (1879), 27–104, quotations pp. 60–1.

14. Sigmund Freud, *Massenpsychologie und Ich-Analyse* (Internationaler Psychoanalytischer Verlag, 1921).

15. Hilaire Belloc was a great-great-grandson of Joseph Priestley through his mother's line, and no doubt aware of his ancestor's hounding by the Birmingham mob.

16. Hilaire Belloc, 'A force in Gaul', essay in *On Something* (Methuen, 1910), p. 160.

17. Le Bon, *The Crowd*, p. 68.

18. Charles Dickens, *A Tale of Two Cities*, book 2, ch. 21.

19. Jack London, *The People of the Abyss*, ch. 1. Later in the chapter, as he assimilates into East End life and gets to know the people, London finds he is no longer haunted by his fear of the crowd. He has become part of it. 'The vast and malodorous sea had welled up and over me, or I had slipped gently into it, and there was nothing fearsome about it.'

20. Émile Zola, *Germinal*, book 4, ch. 7. Translation in Barrows, *Distorting Mirrors*, p. 101.

21. In *The Long Valley*, a collection of short stories (William Heinemann, 1939), p. 137.

22. P.G. Zimbardo, 'The human choice: individuation, reason, and order vs. deindividuation, impulse, and chaos', in W. J. Arnold and D. Levine (eds), *Nebraska Symposium on Motivation* (University of Nebraska Press, 1969), pp. 237–307.

23. Ann Coulter, *Demonic: How the Liberal Mob Is Endangering America* (Random House, 2011).

24. The Daily Caller blog, 15 August 2012, http://dailycaller.com/2012/08/15/why-liberals-behave-the-way-they-do/.

25. The modern notion of leaderless crowds really began with the Bulgarian writer Elias Canetti, who, in *Crowds and Power* (Claassen Verlag, 1960; in English, Victor Gollancz, 1962), suggested that leaders cannot command crowds in the way that traditional theorists suppose and that crowds are more likely to take advantage of leaders than the other way round. This has evolved into a fascinating debate about the nature of leadership, with social psychologists, such as Alex Haslam at the University of Queensland, arguing that the most successful leaders are not defined by their personality traits as is generally believed, but by how well they reflect and pander to the social identities of their followers. They are characteristic of their group. George W. Bush is often considered a failure as a leader, yet after 9/11 he was immensely popular because he publicly identified with Americans' deepest fears and insecurities at that time. To explore further see Alex Haslam, *The New Psychology of Leadership* (Psychology Press, 2010).

26. S.D. Reicher, 'The St Pauls' riot: an explanation of the limits of crowd action in terms of a social identity model', *European Journal of Social Psychology* 14 (1984), 1–21, p. 17. The study was based on extensive interviews with participants, both at the time and afterwards, as well as police, legal and other reports, media broadcasts, newspaper accounts and photographs.

27. For more details on the theory, known as the Elaborated Social Identity Model of crowd behaviour, see Stephen Reicher, 'The psychology of crowd dynamics', in Michael A. Hogg and R. Scott Tindale (eds), *Blackwell Handbook of Social Psychology: Group Processes* (Blackwell, 2001), ch. 8.

28. A summary of the Kerner Commission report is available at www.eisenhowerfoundation.org/docs/kerner.pdf.

29. Since the violent protests at the World Trade Organization ministerial conference in Seattle in 1999, known as the Battle of Seattle, and particularly in the security-conscious post-9/11 era, US agencies have largely abandoned negotiation-led approaches to public order policing in favour of containment, surveillance and pre-emptive arrests, a tactic known as 'strategic incapacitation'. See Patrick F. Gillham, 'Securitizing America: strategic incapacitation and the policing of protest since the 11 September 2001 terrorist attacks', *Sociology Compass* 5, 7 (2011), 636–52.

30. Clifford Stott and Geoff Pearson, *Football Hooliganism: Policing and the War on the English Disease* (Pennant Books, 2007), p. 218.

31. In March 2012, Stott left his job as a lecturer in social psychology at the

University of Liverpool, where he had taught for nearly twelve years, and set up his own crowd management consultancy (www.ccmconsultancy.info). A few months later he re-entered academia full-time as a criminologist, having been appointed research fellow to the Security and Justice Research Group at the University of Leeds.

32. Stott and Pearson, *Football Hooliganism*, p. 78.

33. Ibid., p. 127. For more on differences between Scottish and English fan behaviour at France98 see Clifford Stott, Paul Hutchison and John Drury, '"Hooligans" abroad? Inter-group dynamics, social identity and participation in collective "disorder" at the 1998 World Cup Finals', *British Journal of Social Psychology* 40, 3 (2001), 359–84.

34. For a detailed analysis of police tactics, crowd events and the social dynamics involved in Euro2004 see Clifford Stott, Otto Adang, Andrew Livingstone and Martina Schreiber, 'Tackling football hooliganism: a quantitative study of public order, policing and crowd psychology', *Psychology, Public Policy, and Law* 14, 2 (2008), 115–41; also Clifford Stott, Otto Adang, Andrew Livingstone and Martina Schreiber, 'Variability in the collective behaviour of England fans at Euro2004: "hooliganism", public order policing and social change', *European Journal of Social Psychology* 37, 1 (2007), 75–100.

35. Clifford Stott, 'Crowd psychology & public order policing: an overview of scientific theory and evidence'. Submission to the HMIC Policing of Public Protest Review Team, 2009.

36. Available at http://www.hmic.gov.uk/publication/adapting-to-protest/.

37. For a more detailed description of the role of police liaison officers and an early analysis of their performance see Clifford Stott, Martin Scothern and Hugo Gorringe, 'Advances in liaison based public order policing in England: human rights and negotiating the management of protest', *Policing* 7, 2 (2013), 212–26.

38. 'Sussex police unleash their new weapon: "crowd psychology"', Indymedia. co.uk, 8 June 2012.

39. Speech to Parliament, 11 August 2011.

40. 'Punish the feral rioters, but address our social deficit too', *Guardian*, 5 September 2011, http://www.theguardian.com/commentisfree/2011/sep/05/punishment-rioters-help.

41. 'Theresa May: the lessons I learned from the report on the summer riots', *Daily Mail*, 18 December 2011, http://www.dailymail.co.uk/news/article-2075540/Theresa-May-lessons-SHE-learnt-weeks-LSE-report-summer-riots.html.

42. BBC TV news, 7 August 2011.

43. Roger Ball and John Drury, 'Representing the riots: the (mis)use of figures to sustain ideological explanation', *Radical Statistics* 106 (2012), 4–21.

44. House of Commons Home Affairs Committee, *Policing Large Scale Disorder: Lessons from the Disturbances of August 2011*. Sixteenth Report of Session 2010–12, vol. II (Oral and written evidence), Q93.

45. In email correspondence with the Metropolitan Police, 15 March 2013.

46. There are regional disparities: in London nineteen per cent of those arrested belonged to a gang, outside London less than ten per cent. It is unclear how many arrested gang members were charged or convicted.

47. Home Office, 'An overview of recorded crimes and arrests resulting from disorder events in August 2011' (2011), p. 5.

48. 'Punish the feral rioters', *Guardian*, 5 September 2011.

49. Published as *Reading the Riots: Investigating England's Summer of Discontent* (Guardian Shorts e-book, 2011); also see http://www.guardian.co.uk/uk/series/reading-the-riots.

50. The final report of the Riots Communities and Victims Panel, published 28 March 2012, is available at http://riotspanel.independent.gov.uk/wp-content/uploads/2012/03/Riots-Panel-Final-Report1.pdf.

51. Stephen Reicher and Clifford Stott, *Mad Mobs and Englishmen: Myths and Realities of the 2011 Riots* (e-book, Constable & Robinson, 2011).

52. In 'Reading the riot actors', *New Scientist*, 17 September 2011, p. 30.

53. Quoted in 'Facebook riot calls earn men four-year jail terms amid sentencing outcry', *Guardian*, 16 August 2011, http://www.theguardian.com/uk/2011/aug/16/facebook-riot-calls-men-jailed.

54. Data taken from Ministry of Justice, Statistical Bulletin on the Public Disorder of 6th to 9th August 2011 – September 2012 update.

55. *Reading the Riots: Investigating England's summer of discontent* (Guardian Shorts, 2011), http://www.theguardian.com/uk/2012/jul/03/courtroom-profiles-reading-the-riots.

56. Sentencing remarks by the Hon. Mr Justice Saunders, Inner London Crown Court, R. v. Darrell Desuze, 17 April 2012.

57. Julian V. Roberts and Mike Hough, 'Sentencing riot-related offending: where do the public stand?', *British Journal of Criminology* 53, 2 (2012), 234–56.

58. Reicher cites one case of social identity theory being used successfully in court, when a defendant accused of throwing stones at the police during the 1990 poll tax riots argued he was acting in self-defence. Although he was not personally under attack, the defendant maintained that since the police

were being hostile towards the whole crowd it was legitimate for him to view all police action as aggressive.

59. In John Drury, Chris Cocking and Steve Reicher, 'The nature of collective resilience: survivor reactions to the 2005 London bombings', *International Journal of Mass Emergencies and Disasters* 27, 1 (2009), 66–95, p. 79.

60. Interview in 'Seven years since 7/7', *Economist* blog, 6 July 2012, http://www.economist.com/blogs/blighty/2012/07/london-bombings.

61. Drury *et al.*, 'Nature of collective resilience', p. 82.

62. Ibid.

63. John Drury, Chris Cocking and Stephen Reicher, 'Everyone for themselves? A comparative study of crowd solidarity among emergency survivors', *British Journal of Social Psychology* 48, 3 (2009), 487–506.

64. See John Drury, David Novelli and Clifford Stott, 'Psychological disaster myths in the perception and management of mass emergencies', *Journal of Applied Social Psychology* 43, 11 (2013), pp. 2259–70.

65. Drury *et al.*, 'Everyone for themselves?', p. 10.

66. As confirmed by the Hillsborough Independent Panel in September 2012. *Hillsborough: The Report of the Hillsborough Independent Panel* (House of Commons, September 2012) is available at http://hillsborough.independent.gov.uk/repository/report/HIP_report.pdf.

67. Information on 9/11 response behaviour is derived from two sources: *Federal Building and Fire Safety Investigation of the World Trade Center Disaster: Final Report of the National Construction Safety Team on the Collapses of the World Trade Center Towers* (NIST NCSTAR 1, 2005); and E.R. Galea, L. Hulse, R. Day, A. Siddiqui, G. Sharp, K. Boyce, L. Summerfield, D. Canter, M. Marselle and P.V. Greenall, 'The UK WTC 9/11 Evacuation Study: an overview of the methodologies employed and some preliminary analysis', in W.W.F. Kligsch *et al.* (eds), *Proceedings of the 4th Pedestrian and Evacuation Dynamics 2008* (Springer Verlag, 2010), pp. 3–24.

68. Some of this detail first appeared in 'What would you do?', *Engineering and Technology* 4, 7 (20 April 2009).

69. *AIR 8/88. Report on the Accident to Boeing 737–236, G-BGJL at Manchester International Airport on 22 August 1985* (United Kingdom Air Accidents Investigation Branch, 1988), p. 135.

70. See B.E. Aguirre, D. Wenger and G. Vigo, 'A test of the emergent norm theory of collective behavior', *Sociological Forum* 13, 2 (1988), 301–20.

71. Elias Canetti, *Crowds and Power* (Claassen Verlag, 1960; in English, Victor Gollancz, 1962), ch. 1.

72. Reicher, 'St Pauls' riot', p. 16.

73. Shruti Tewari, Sammyh Khan, Nick Hopkins, Narayanan Srinivasan and Stephen Reicher, 'Participation in mass gatherings can benefit well-being: longitudinal and control data from a North Indian Hindu pilgrimage event', *PLoS One* 7, 10 (2012), e47291. doi: 10.1371/journal.pone.0047291.

74. The researchers studied the 2011 Magh Mela. At the 2013 event, an auspicious once-every-twelve-years variation known as the Kumbh Mela, which is attended by some eighty million people, thirty-six pilgrims died in a stampede at an overcrowded railway station in Allahabad. This was caused by the last-minute re-scheduling of a train that sent hundreds of passengers rushing onto a narrow overhead footbridge between platforms, resulting in a fatal bottleneck. The Kumbh Mela festival is generally known for its efficient organization and well-orchestrated crowd management.

75. See http://improveverywhere.com/missions.

76. Ashraf Khalil, *Liberation Square: Inside the Egyptian Revolution and the Rebirth of a Nation* (St Martin's Press, 2011), p. 123.

77. Zeynep Tufekci and Christopher Wilson, 'Social media and the decision to participate in political protest: observations from Tahrir Square', *Journal of Communication* 62, 2 (2012), 363–79.

78. One pamphlet circulating in Cairo entitled 'How to Protest Intelligently', giving practical advice such as how to confront riot police, specifically warned those reading it not to distribute it via Facebook, Twitter or other internet sites because they were being monitored by the Ministry of Interior. Email it or make photocopies, it urged. That did not stop several western media sources (such as the *Atlantic*) from posting large sections of it on their websites even before the most critical phase of the revolt, the 28 January 'Friday of rage', had begun.

79. Khalil, *Liberation Square*, p. 164.

80. Duncan Watts, 'Can the flap of a butterfly's wings on Facebook stir a revolution in the Middle East', essay published 29 March 2011 on www.everythingisobvious.com.

CHAPTER 3: BREAKING BAD

1. 'Eichmann and the private conscience' by Martha Gellhorn, *The Atlantic Monthly*, February 1962, available at http://www.theatlantic.com/past/docs/issues/62feb/eichmann.htm.

2. William L. Hull, *The Struggle for a Soul* (Doubleday, 1963), p. 40.

3. From Avner Less's introduction to *Eichmann Interrogated: Transcripts from the Archives of the Israeli Police*, edited by Jochen von Lang in collaboration with Claus Sibyll (Bodley Head, 1983), p. xix. It's worth noting that Less also claimed he found Eichmann to be a cunning liar with no sense of remorse.

4. David Cesarani, *Eichmann: His Life and Crimes* (William Heinemann, 2004), pp. 16, 367.

5. Barry Ritzler, in Eric Zillmer, Molly Harrower, Barry Ritzler and Robert Archer, *The Quest for the Nazi Personality: A Psychological Investigation of Nazi War Criminals* (Lawrence Erlbaum, 1995), pp. 8–9.

6. Ibid.

7. Hannah Arendt, *Eichmann in Jerusalem: A Report on the Banality of Evil* (Faber and Faber, 1963), p. 253.

8. Cesarani, *Eichmann*, p. 16.

9. From 'On Hannah Arendt', in Melvyn A. Hill (ed.), *Hannah Arendt: The Recovery of the Public World* (St Martin's Press, 1979).

10. 'Personal Responsibility under Dictatorship'. Lecture 1964. The Hannah Arendt Papers at the Library of Congress. Series: Speeches and Writings File, 1923–75.

11. From a handwritten note in the personal collection of Alexandra Milgram, quoted in Thomas Blass, *The Man Who Shocked the World* (Basic Books, 2004), p. 8.

12. Stanley Milgram, *The Individual in a Social World: Essays and Experiments* (Addison-Wesley, 1977), p. 126.

13. Milgram's experiments on authority and obedience have been much written about elsewhere. However, it is worth summarizing them in light of the 'power of others', especially given the critical role the experiments have played in our current understanding of the human condition.

14. For further details see Stanley Milgram, *Obedience to Authority* (Tavistock, 1974).

15. Twenty-five out of forty subjects.

16. Milgram, *Obedience to Authority*, pp. 49, 54, 87–8.

17. See ibid. for further details of the full range of obedience experiments and references to the original journal papers that carried the results.

18. For example, see Jerry M. Burger, 'Replicating Milgram: would people still obey today?', *American Psychologist* 64, 1 (2004), 1–11. Also see Blass, *Man Who Shocked the World*, appendix C.

19. W. Kilham and L. Mann, 'Level of destructive obedience as a function of transmitter and executant roles in the Milgram obedience paradigm', *Journal of Personality and Social Psychology* 29, 5 (1974), 692–702.

20. Letter to Henry Riecken, head of social science at the US National Science Foundation, 21 September 1961, quoted in Blass, *Man Who Shocked the World*, p. 100.

21. Milgram, *Obedience to Authority*, p. 6.

22. S.E. Asch (1951), 'Effects of group pressure upon the modification and distortion of judgment', in H. Guetzkow (ed.), *Groups, Leadership and Men* (Carnegie Press, 1951). For a fuller account see Asch's book *Social Psychology* (Prentice-Hall, 1951).

23. S.E. Asch, 'Opinions and social pressure', *Scientific American* 193 (1955), 31–5, p. 35, available at www.panarchy.org/asch/social.pressure.1955.html.

24. Read D. Tuddenham, 'The influence of a distorted group norm upon individual judgment', *Journal of Psychology: Interdisciplinary and Applied* 46 (1958), 227–41. See also Read D. Tuddenham and Philip D. McBride, 'The yielding experiment from the subject's point of view', *Journal of Personality* 27, 2 (1959), 259–71.

25. Asch, 'Opinions and social pressure'.

26. Rod Bond and Peter B. Smith, 'Culture and conformity: a meta-analysis of studies using Asch's (1952b, 1956) line judgment task', *Psychological Bulletin* 119, 1 (1996), 111–37.

27. These cultural tendencies of collectivism and individualism are strongly enduring. Research by Stanford University psychologists published in 2013 shows that European Americans are de-motivated by public appeals calling on people to work together to achieve change, but are more likely to respond to appeals encouraging them to take charge, such as President Obama's 2008 campaign slogan (via Gandhi) 'be the change YOU want to see in the world'. Asian Americans, however, find appeals to the common good energizing. MarYam G. Hamedani, Hazel Rose Markus and Alyssa S. Fu, 'In the Land of the Free, interdependent action undermines motivation', *Psychological Science* 24 (2013), 189–96.

28. The school closed down in 1994.

29. From Philip Zimbardo's introduction to the 2009 paperback edition of Stanley Milgram's *Obedience to Authority* (Harper Perennial Modern Classics), adapted for The Project on Law and Mind Sciences at Harvard Law School website, available at http://thesituationist.wordpress.com/2009/04/16/zimbardo-on-milgram-and-obedience-part-ii/.

30. For more detail on the Stanford Prison Experiment see P.G. Zimbardo, *The Psychological Power and Pathology of Imprisonment*. A statement prepared for the US House of Representatives Committee on the Judiciary, Subcommittee

No. 3, Hearings on Prison Reform, San Francisco, California, 25 October 1971; Philip Zimbardo, *The Lucifer Effect* (Random House, 2007); and www.prisonexp.org.

31. Zimbardo, *Psychological Power*, p. 154.

32. Ibid., p. 154.

33. From post-experimental video on www.prisonexp.org.

34. In July 1973, the American Psychological Association declared that the Stanford Prison Experiment had followed all ethical guidelines, though it later tightened its guidelines to ensure such suffering would not be repeated.

35. Zimbardo, *Psychological Power*, p. 211.

36. The report is available at http://www.cbsnews.com/stories/2004/04/27/60ii/main614063.shtml.

37. Zimbardo, *Psychological Power*, p. 328.

38. This quotation first appeared in 'They made me do it', *New Scientist*, 14 April 2007, p. 42.

39. Irving L. Janis, 'Group identification under conditions of external danger', *British Journal of Medical Psychology* 36 (1963), 227–38.

40. This quotation first appeared in 'They made me do it', *New Scientist*, 14 April 2007, p. 42.

41. F.D. Richard, C.F. Bond and J.J. Stokes-Zoota, 'One hundred years of social psychology quantitatively described', *Review of General Psychology* 7 (2003), 331–63.

42. During the second intifada which lasted from October 2000 to February 2005, 1,010 Israelis and 3,179 Palestinians were killed. Statistics from the International Institute for Counter-Terrorism, Herzliya, Israel, www.ict.org.il.

43. Details in Ariel Merari, *Driven to Death: Psychological and Social Aspects of Suicide Terrorism* (Oxford University Press, 2010).

44. For example, see Claude Berrebi, 'Evidence about the link between education, poverty and terrorism among Palestinians', *Peace Economics, Peace Science and Public Policy* 13, 1 (2007), doi: 10.2202/1554-8597.1101; Alan Krueger, *What Makes a Terrorist: Economics and the Roots of Terrorism* (Princeton University Press, 2007).

45. Claude Berrebi and others point out that while being poor is not an incentive to becoming a suicide terrorist, communal poverty and economic deprivation can make it more likely that better educated people will volunteer to sacrifice themselves. See Ephraim Benmelech, Claude Berrebi and Esteban F. Klor, 'Economic conditions and the quality of suicide terrorism', NBER working paper no. 16320, August 2010.

46. See Bruce Hoffmann, *Inside Terrorism* (Columbia University Press, 2006).

47. Casualty figures from the Israeli Ministry of Foreign Affairs and B'tselem (the Israeli Information Center for Human Rights in the Occupied Territories).

48. In 2003 Al-Zahar was himself targeted in a failed assassination attempt in which his eldest son and a bodyguard were killed.

49. Some of this detail first appeared in 'This is how we live', *New Scientist*, 11 May 2002, p. 40.

50. Scott Atran, *Talking to the Enemy: Faith, Brotherhood, and the (Un)making of Terrorists* (Ecco, 2010), p. 7.

51. Another occasion was in Pakistan-controlled Kashmir, when he had to hide in an abandoned mosque to evade agents of Pakistan's feared intelligence agency.

52. Merari, *Driven to Death*, pp. 174–5.

53. From surveys carried out by the Center for Palestine Research and Studies (available at www.pcpsr.org) and the Jerusalem Media and Communication Center (www.jmcc.org).

54. For further analysis of group processes in terrorism see Marc Sageman, *Leaderless Jihad* (University of Pennsylvania Press, 2008); and Ariel Merari, 'Social, organizational, and psychological factors in suicide terrorism', in Tore Bjorgo (ed.), *Root Causes of Terrorism* (Routledge, 2005), pp. 70–86.

55. While suicide bombers are not always religious, religion can help garner support for altruistic acts – including suicide bombing – carried out on behalf of the community. However, a 2009 study of attitudes among Palestinian Muslims, Israeli Jews and other religious groups found such support depended not on religious devotion (such as frequency of prayer) but on collective religious ritual (frequency of mosque or synagogue attendance). In other words, the key is not belief per se but the sense of community that derives from sharing it. See Jeremy Ginges, Ian Hansen and Ara Norenzayan, 'Religion and support for suicide attacks', *Psychological Science* 20, 2 (2009), 224–30.

56. See Peng Wang, 'Women in the LTTE: birds of freedom or cogs in the wheel?', *Journal of Politics and Law* 4, 1 (2011), 100–8.

57. Notwithstanding this programme, the Sri Lankan government has been accused of widespread human rights abuses against Tamil civilians, both towards the end of the war and during the peace that followed.

58. Some analysts, such as Peng Wang, claim the women were also motivated by the desire to overturn conventional Tamil gender roles. See Wang, 'Women in the LTTE'.

59. One former LTTE recruit I interviewed in London spoke of how she had joined up with six friends from school, and when her six friends were killed alongside her during an attack by the Sri Lankan army she took a cyanide pill to avoid being taken alive, because this is what they had been taught to do during training (she recovered after three months in hospital).

60. Since there are no available comparative data on the incidence of these psychological traits among the general Palestinian population, it is impossible to assess how critical the traits are to a person's decision to volunteer for a suicide mission.

61. For more on this study, see Merari, *Driven to Death*; Ariel Merari *et al.*, 'Personality characteristics of suicide bombers and organizers of suicide attacks', *Terrorism and Political Violence* 22, 1 (2009), 87–101; 'A psychologist inside the mind of suicide bombers', *New Scientist*, 17 July 2010, p. 45.

62. From the transcript of a video interview translated by the Middle East Media Research Institute, Washington DC, available at http://www.memritv.org/clip_transcript/en/3157.htm.

63. Adam Lankford, *The Myth of Martyrdom* (Palgrave Macmillan, 2013), p. 10.

64. Ibid., appendix A.

65. In email to the author, 15 January 2013.

66. See http://adamlankford.com/mythofmartyrdom_reviews.htm.

67. Herbert C. Kelman, 'The social context of torture: policy process and authority structure', in Ronald D. Crelinsten and Alex P. Schmid (eds), *The Politics of Pain: Torturers and Their Masters*. Series on State Violence, State Terrorism, and Human Rights (Westview Press, 1995), pp. 21–38, quotation p. 23.

CHAPTER 4: ORDINARY HEROES

1. Quoted in Francois Rochat and Andre Modigliani, 'The ordinary quality of resistance: from Milgram's laboratory to the milage of Le Chambon', *Journal of Social Issues* 51, 3 (1995), 195–210, p. 199.

2. Milgram, *Obedience to Authority*, p. 85.

3. Quoted in Tzvetan Todorov, *The Fragility of Goodness* (Weidenfeld and Nicolson, 2001), p. 66.

4. For a deeper discussion of social identity in wartime Bulgaria see S. Reicher, C. Cassidy, I. Wolpert, N. Hopkins and M. Levine, 'Saving Bulgaria's Jews: an analysis of social identity and the mobilisation of social solidarity', *European Journal of Social Psychology*, 36 (2006), 49–72.

5. See http://www.humboldt.edu/altruism/index.html.

6. See Samuel P. Oliner and Pearl M. Oliner, *The Altruistic Personality: Rescuers of Jews in Nazi Europe* (Free Press, 1988), p. 96.

7. For more on Grüninger's story see Francois Rochat and Andre Modigliani in Thomas Blass (ed.), *Obedience to Authority: Current Perspectives on the Milgram Paradigm* (Psychology Press, 1999), p. 91.

8. For Jevtic's story see Eyal Press, *Beautiful Souls* (Farrar, Straus and Giroux, 2012).

9. Paul Rusesabagina, *An Ordinary Man* (Bloomsbury, 2009), p. 248.

10. Perry London, 'The rescuers: motivational hypotheses about Christians who saved Jews from the Nazis', in J. Macaulay and L. Berkowitz (eds), *Altruism and Helping Behavior* (Academic Press, 1970), pp. 241–50.

11. Speaking at a conference on genocide and religion at Pepperdine University School of Law, Malibu, 11–13 February 2007.

12. Oliner and Oliner, *Altruistic Personality*, p. 169.

13. Milgram, *Obedience to Authority*, appendix II.

14. Eva Fogelman, *Conscience and Courage: Rescuers of Jews during the Holocaust* (Cassell, 1995), p. 254.

15. Staub explores the links between his childhood experiences and his academic work in greater depth in an essay in Samuel Totten and Steven Leonard Jacobs (eds), *Pioneers of Genocide Studies* (Transaction, 2002), pp. 479–504.

16. For more on the importance of childhood socialization see Ervin Staub, *The Roots of Goodness: Inclusive Caring, Moral Courage, Altruism Born of Suffering and Active Bystanders* (Oxford University Press, forthcoming) and *Overcoming Evil: Genocide, Violent Conflict, and Terrorism* (Oxford University Press, 2011), ch. 22.

17. Richard Rorty, *Contingency, Irony and Solidarity* (Cambridge University Press, 1989), p. 191.

18. Oliner and Oliner, *Altruistic Personality*, p. 167.

19. Interviewed in summer 1989 by the political scientist Kristen Renwick Monroe and quoted in her book *The Heart of Altruism: Perceptions of a Common Humanity* (Princeton University Press, 1998), p. 205.

20. In John Donne, *Devotions upon Emergent Occasions*, Meditation XVII, 1624.

21. Tenzin Gyatson, the Dalai Lama, *Ancient Wisdom, Modern World: Ethics for the New Millennium* (Little, Brown, 1999), p. 170.

22. Sam McFarland, Matthew Webb and Derek Brown, 'All humanity is my ingroup: a measure and studies of identification with all humanity', *Journal of Personality and Social Psychology* 103, 5 (2012), 830–53. The

Identification with All Humanity Scale is available at http://www.ravansanji.ir/?Escale7003IWAHS.

23. Abraham H. Maslow, *Motivation and Personality* (Harper and Row, 1954), p. 138.

24. Unpublished version of *The Banality of Heroism: Taxonomy, Types and Theory*, by Zeno Franco and Philip Zimbardo, supplied by the authors; later reproduced in various sources, for example, *Greater Good*, Fall/Winter 2006–7, pp. 30–5.

25. Ibid.

26. Umberto Eco, 'Why are they laughing in those cages?', in *Travels in Hyperreality: Essays* (Harcourt Brace Jovanovich, 1986), p. 122.

27. From video display at Lord Ashcroft Gallery exhibition: Extraordinary Heroes, Imperial War Museum, London.

28. Correspondence of Noel Chavasse, Bodleian Library, Oxford.

29. In an interview with Jack's grandson Frankie Randle for *Victoria Cross Heroes*, a documentary commissioned to mark the 150th anniversary of the VC, screened on Channel 5 in November and December 2006.

30. From written testimony at Lord Ashcroft Gallery exhibition: Extraordinary Heroes, Imperial War Museum, London.

31. Against the run of this argument, Croucher appears as close to a military archetype as you're likely to get: he had set his sights on being a Royal Marine Commando by the time he was thirteen years old.

32. The George Cross is awarded for acts of the highest valour that are not carried out in the face of the enemy.

33. *Victoria Cross Heroes* documentary.

34. Presentation at Lord Ashcroft Gallery exhibition: Extraordinary Heroes, Imperial War Museum, London.

35. For further discussion see Stephen D. Reicher and S. Alexander Haslam, 'After shock? Towards a social identity explanation of the Milgram "obedience" studies', *British Journal of Social Psychology* 50 (2011), 163–9; Stephen D. Reicher, S. Alexander Haslam and Joanne R. Smith, 'Working toward the experimenter: reconceptualizing obedience within the Milgram paradigm as identification-based followership', *Perspectives on Psychological Science* 7, 4 (2012), 315–24; S.A. Haslam and S.D. Reicher, 'Contesting the "nature" of conformity: what Milgram and Zimbardo's studies really show', *PLoS Biol* 10, 11 (2012), e1001426, doi:10.1371/journal.pbio.1001426.

36. Stephen Reicher and S. Alexander Haslam, 'Rethinking the psychology of tyranny: the BBC prison study', *British Journal of Social Psychology*, 45 (2006), 1–40.

37. See S. Alexander Haslam and Stephen Reicher, 'When prisoners take over the prison: a social psychology of resistance', *Personality and Social Psychology Review* 16, 2 (2012), 154–79.

38. See http://heroicimagination.org.

39. For further details see Staub, *Overcoming Evil*, pp. 369–86.

40. The bystander effect has been shown to be less pronounced under certain conditions, for instance when the spectators and the victim are all female, or for a man if he is the only male in the bystander group, or if the bystanders all know each other. For a study that tested these variations see S. Levine and S. Crowther, 'The responsive bystander: how social group membership and group size can encourage as well as inhibit bystander intervention', *Journal of Personality and Social Psychology* 95, 6 (2008), 1429–39. For a recent review of the bystander literature see P. Fischer, J.I. Krueger, T. Greitemeyer, C. Vogrincic, A. Kastenmüller, D. Frey, M. Heene, M. Wicher and M. Kainbacher, 'The bystander-effect: a meta-analytic review on bystander intervention in dangerous and non-dangerous emergencies', *Psychological Bulletin* 137, 4 (2011), 517–37.

41. Rorty, *Contingency, Irony and Solidarity*, p. xvi.

42. Zygmunt Bauman, *Modernity and the Holocaust* (Polity Press, 1989), pp. 166–8.

43. Hannah Arendt, *Eichmann in Jerusalem: A Report on the Banality of Evil* (Faber and Faber, 1963), p. 288.

44. David DeSteno and Piercarlo Valdesolo, *Out of Character* (Crown, 2011), p. 9.

45. For a detailed and illuminating study of the role and inner conflicts of a Nazi functionary in wartime Poland see Mary Fulbrook, *A Small Town Near Auschwitz: Ordinary Nazis and the Holocaust* (Oxford University Press, 2012).

CHAPTER 5: BANDS OF BROTHERS

1. Here he lived for a while with his second wife Fanny, who appropriately in this theatre of intrigue was the twenty-four-year-old widow of a British officer killed by Allen's compatriots.

2. Originally quoted in Ira Allen, *The Natural and Political History of the State of Vermont, One of the United States of America* (J.W. Myers, 1798).

3. From lecture notes by John Williams, former editor of the Vermont state papers, 2 December 1968, consulted in Vermont State Archives, Middlesex, Vermont.

4. The papers of Henry Stevens, 1739–1775 collection, Vermont State Archives:

Narrative of Proceedings of the Government of New York on New Hampshire Grants, September 1774.

5. J. Kevin Graffagnino, Samuel B. Hand and Gene Sessions (eds), *Vermont Voices, 1609 through the 1990s: A Documentary History of the Green Mountain State* (Vermont Historical Society, 1999), p. 40.

6. Willard Sterne Randall, *Ethan Allen: His Life and Times* (Norton, 2011), p. 38.

7. Donald A. Smith, 'Green Mountain Insurgency: transformation of New York's forty-year land war', *Proceedings of the Vermont Historical Society* 64 (1996), 197–235, p. 223.

8. In a letter from Ethan Allen to the Massachusetts Congress, 11 May 1875, Ethan Allen papers of Henry Stevens, 1770–1786 collection, Vermont State Archives.

9. *Henry V*, Act IV, scene iii.

10. Gerald F. Linderman, *Embattled Courage: The Experience of Combat in the American Civil War* (The Free Press, 1987), p. 34.

11. Dora L. Costa and Matthew E. Kahn, *Heroes and Cowards: The Social Face of War* (Princeton University Press, 2008); also this 2003 paper by the same authors: 'Cowards and heroes: group loyalty in the American Civil War', *Quarterly Journal of Economics* 118, 2 (2003), 519–48.

12. Saxton Collection, Henry E. Huntington Library, San Marino, California. Quoted in James M. McPherson, *For Cause and Comrades: Why Men Fought in the Civil War* (Oxford University Press, 1997), p. 87.

13. Samuel A. Stouffer, Edward A. Suchman, Leland C. DeVinney, Shirley A. Star and Robin M. Williams, Jr., *Studies in Social Psychology in World War II: The American Soldier* (Princeton University Press, 1949).

14. Irving L. Janis, 'Group identification under conditions of external danger', *British Journal of Medical Psychology* 36 (1963), 227–38, p. 227.

15. S.L.A. Marshall, *Men Against Fire: The Problem of Battle Command* (William Morrow, 1947).

16. From a taped interview held in the sound archives of the Imperial War Museum, London. Transcribed in Max Arthur, *Forgotten Voices of the Great War*, in association with the Imperial War Museum (Ebury Press, 2002), p. 200.

17. Grace McDougall, *A Nurse at the War: Nursing Adventures in Belgium and France* (Robert McBride, 1917), p. 55. Quoted in Janet Lee, 'Sisterhood at the front: friendship, comradeship, and the feminine appropriation of military heroism among World War I First Aid Nursing Yeomanry (FANY)', *Women's Studies International Forum* 31 (2008), 16–29.

18. F.T. Jesse, 'The first Aid Nursing Yeomanry: a personal impression of the

FANY camps in France – girls who are doing yeoman service', *Vogue*, May 1916, pp. 54–5. Quoted in Lee, 'Sisterhood at the front'.

19. Unpublished memoir, World War II Veterans Project, Special Collections, University of Tennessee, Knoxville, quoted in John C. McManus, *The Deadly Brotherhood: The American Combat Soldier in World War II* (Presidio Press, 1998), p. 324.

20. Leonard Wong, Thomas A. Kolditz, Raymond A. Millen and Terrence M. Potter, *Why They Fight: Combat Motivation in the Iraq War* (Strategic Studies Institute, US Army War College, 2003), p. 10.

21. The debate on whether group cohesion is crucial to performance in battle is by no means closed. Robert MacCoun at the University of California-Berkeley and others claim there is little evidence supporting a causal link between social cohesion and effectiveness, and that the key is *task* cohesion: 'All of the evidence indicates that military performance depends on whether service members are committed to the same professional goals, not on whether they like one another.' See Robert J. MacCoun, Elizabeth Kier and Aaron Belkin, 'Does social cohesion determine motivation in combat? An old question with an old answer', *Armed Forces & Society* 32, 4 (2006), 646–54.

22. Wong *et al.*, *Why They Fight*, p. 9.

23. For an excellent discussion of the dynamics of cohesion in modern armies see Darryl Henderson, *Cohesion: The Human Element in Combat. Leadership and Societal Influence in the Armies of the Soviet Union, the United States, North Vietnam, and Israel* (National Defense University Press, 1985).

24. Edward A. Shils and Morris Janowitz, 'Cohesion and disintegration in the Wehrmacht in World War II', *Public Opinion Quarterly* 12, 2 (1948), 280–315, p. 281.

25. The sociologist Robert B. Smith argues that a crucial variable in the relationship between cohesion, leadership and 'fighter spirit' is whether or not the military authority under whom soldiers are fighting is seen as legitimate. During the later stages of the Vietnam War, the US Army's legitimacy was questionable since it lacked political and popular support at home and was already winding down its campaign. See R. Smith (1983) 'Why soldiers fight', *Quality and Quantity* 18 (1983), 1–58.

26. Critics of the US Army's current organizational structure, which champions promotion as the foremost measure of success, claim that cohesion is being sacrificed because, as in Vietnam, officers are rotated too quickly. One of the critics is Scott Halter, a lieutenant colonel with seventeen years of service who is currently a strategic planner at the Pentagon. He claims that on an

assignment to Afghanistan several years ago, his brigade was sent into the field even though eight of its twelve battalion executive and operations officers had still not completed any training with their units. Over the next fourteen months, while the brigade was deployed, forty-six per cent of the officers were moved on, a situation that Halter says 'decreases cohesion, continuity and combat effectiveness' (Scott M. Halter, 'What is an Army but the soldiers? A critical assessment of the Army's human capital management system', *Military Review* (Jan–Feb 2012), 16–23). For further analysis of how personnel management is affecting unit cohesion in the US Army see Donald Vandergriff, *Raising the Bar: Creating and Nurturing Adaptability to Deal with the Changing Face of War* (Center for Defense Information, 2006).

27. For more on the psychological benefits of marching, dancing and other synchronous rituals see William H. McNeill, *Keeping Together in Time: Dance and Drill in Human History* (Harvard University Press, 1995); also Barbara Ehrenreich, *Dancing in the Streets: A History of Collective Joy* (Metropolitan, 2006).

28. See S.S. Wiltermuth and C. Heath, 'Synchrony and cooperation', *Psychological Science* 20 (2009), 1–5.

29. Details are available at http://www.icea.ox.ac.uk/research/ritual.

30. The Danish researcher Dimitris Xygalatas found a correlation between ritual intensity and strength of group identity – in this case measured as prosociality – in a quite different setting. At an annual Hindu festival in Mauritius, participants who pierced themselves with multiple needles, hooks and skewers, a painful exercise, gave significantly more to the local temple than those who simply came to sing and pray. D. Xygalatas, P. Mitkidis, R. Fischer, P. Reddish, J. Skewes, A.W. Geertz, A. Roepstorff and J. Bulbulia, 'Extreme rituals promote prosociality', *Psychological Science* 24, 8 (2013), 1602–5.

31. Wong *et al.*, *Why They Fight*, p. 13.

32. Janis, 'Group identification', p. 229.

33. Cited in Alfred O. Ludwig, 'Neuroses occurring in soldiers after prolonged combat exposure', *Bulletin of the Menninger Clinic* 11, 1 (1947), 15–23, p. 18, taken here from Joanna Bourke, *An Intimate History of Killing* (Granta, 1999), pp. 145–6.

34. This is known by psychiatrists as 'moral injury', defined as trauma arising from doing something that conflicts with deeply held moral beliefs, such as killing someone, or failing to do something you think you should have done, such as preventing the death of a fellow soldier. Moral injury can result in a range of pathological behaviours, including alcohol and drug abuse, severe recklessness, suicidal tendencies, running away from success

or positive feelings, bewilderment, hopelessness and self-loathing. Sufferers may also start to view themselves as immoral, irredeemable or irreparably damaged, or believe that they live in an immoral world. See Brett T. Litz, Nathan Stein, Eileen Delaney, Leslie Lebowitz, William P. Nash, Caroline Silva and Shira Maguen, 'Moral injury and moral repair in war veterans: a preliminary model and intervention strategy', *Clinical Psychology Review* 29, 8 (2009), 695–706.

35. Erich M. Remarque, *All Quiet on the Western Front* (Putnam, 1929), p. 232.

36. Thanks to the Royal Air Force Benevolent Fund for putting me in touch with Alan.

37. Roy R. Grinker and John P. Spiegel, *Men Under Stress* (Blackiston, 1945), pp. 23–4.

38. Janis, 'Group identification'.

39. Most of the German troops survived the bombardment by hiding in their bunkers and tanks. My grandfather's diary reports how they 'then with their armour-piercing shells more or less obliterated the 7th Armoured [Division] who never really fought again'. It would be another month before the Allies fully took Caen on 6 August 1944.

40. Memorial to Lt. Kevin J. Pfeifer written by Joe Pfeifer for the funeral mass held on Saturday 9 February 2002, New York City.

41. Details from an audio interview recorded in Baldwin, NY, by the StoryCorps oral history project (see http://storycorps.org/listen/stories/john-vigiano-and-his-wife-jan); and from the CBS television documentary *9/11: The Fireman's Story*.

42. Terry Golway, *So Others Might Live: A History of New York's Bravest – The FDNY from 1700 to the Present* (Basic Books, 2002), p. 70. The nineteenth-century rivalry between fire crews, which occasionally spilled out into mass street brawls, is colourfully depicted in Martin Scorsese's film *Gangs of New York*, though its scenes of brutal street massacres stretch the point a little.

43. Joseph W. Pfeifer, 'Understanding how organizational bias influenced first responders at the World Trade Center', in Bruce Bongar *et al.* (eds), *Psychology of Terrorism* (Oxford University Press, 2007), pp. 207–15.

44. *Federal Building and Fire Safety Investigation of the World Trade Center Disaster: Final Report of the National Construction Safety Team on the Collapses of the World Trade Center Towers* (National Institute of Standards and Technology, 2005).

45. Brigades in the Union army were as a rule made up of regiments from different states, to ensure that casualties were spread geographically and would not affect civilian support for the war. The First Vermont Brigade was an

exception: it was made up entirely of Vermonters, which helps explain the high number of casualties. More than 1,200 were killed at the Battle of the Wilderness alone, in May 1864.

CHAPTER 6: IN IT TOGETHER

1. Mike Stroud, *Shadows on the Wasteland* (Jonathan Cape, 1993), p. 24.
2. Ibid., pp. 106–7.
3. Ibid., p. 107.
4. From press material provided by *The Coldest Journey* media team.
5. Stroud, *Shadows on the Wasteland*, pp. 102–3.
6. Part of this quotation first appeared in my interview with Mike Stroud in *New Scientist*, 22 December 2012, p. 35.
7. From the BBC 4 Timeshift series documentary *Antarctica: Of Ice and Men*, broadcast 24 January 2014.
8. Roger Mear and Robert Swan, *In the Footsteps of Scott* (Jonathan Cape, 1987), p. 78.
9. The three Emperor penguin eggs collected by the 1911 expedition are preserved in the zoological collection of the Natural History Museum in London.
10. Apsley Cherry-Garrard, *The Worst Journey in the World* (Constable, 1922), ch. 7, p. 246.
11. Diary entry in Mear and Swan, *In the Footsteps of Scott*. Swan, Mear and Wood eventually reached the pole on 11 January 1986, personal grievances notwithstanding. At the time it was the longest unsupported polar march.
12. Gloria R. Leon, Gro Mjeldheim Sandal and Eric Larsen, 'Human performance in polar environments', *Journal of Environmental Psychology* 31, 4 (2011), 353–60.
13. He was forced to turn back after high winds and snowdrifts slowed his progress and made it inevitable he would run out of food before reaching the pole. See www.ericlarsenexplore.com.
14. See her study on another North Pole expedition, a 475-mile, 55-day unsupported march from the Canadian landmass to the pole by the Americans John Huston and Tyler Fish: G. Leon, G. Sandal, B. Fink and P. Ciofani, 'Positive experiences and personal growth in a two-man North Pole expedition team', *Environment and Behavior* 43, 5 (2011), 710–31. For an overview of research in this area see G.M. Sandal, G.R. Leon and L. Palinkas, 'Human challenges in polar and space environments', *Reviews in Environmental Science and Biotechnology* 5 (2006), 281–96.
15. Quoted in L.A. Palinkas, 'On the ICE: individual and group adaptation in

Antarctica' (2003), available at http://www.sscnet.ucla.edu/anthro/bec/papers/Palinkas_On_The_Ice.pdf, with reference to L.A. Palinkas and D. Browner, 'Effects of prolonged isolation in extreme environments on stress, coping, and depression', *Journal of Applied Social Psychology* 25 (1995), 557–76.

16. For more information about all Mark's endeavours see www.markbeaumontonline.com.

17. The Selection of Antarctic Personnel (SOAP) battery tests a range of psychological factors including emotional responses, anxiety levels, susceptibility to depression, interpersonal skills and personality type. See I. Grant, H.R. Eriksen, P. Marquis, I.J. Orre, L.A. Palinkas, P. Suedfeld, E. Svensen and H. Ursin, 'Psychological selection of Antarctic personnel: the "SOAP" instrument', *Aviation, Space, and Environmental Medicine* 78 (2007), 793–800.

18. From the BBC 4 Timeshift series documentary *Antarctica: Of Ice and Men*, broadcast 24 January 2013.

19. For further details of the findings see M. Basner, D.F. Dinges, *et al.*, 'Mars 520-d mission simulation reveals protracted crew hypokinesis and alterations of sleep duration and timing', *PNAS* 110 (2013), 2635–40.

20. For additional information see B. Van Baarsen, F. Ferlazzo, D. Ferravante, J.H. Smit, J. Van der Pligt and M.A.J. Van Duijn, 'Emotional and cognitive adaptation during 520 days of isolation: results from the LODGEAD Mars500 study', presented at the 63th International Astronautical Congress, Naples, 3–7 October 2012.

21. This quotation first appeared in Michael Bond, '"Insane" Antarctic winter crossing like space flight', *New Scientist*, 22 December 2012, p. 35.

22. Robert Heller and Rebecca Stephens, *The Seven Summits of Success* (Capstone, 2005), pp. 72–3.

23. Cherry-Garrard, *Worst Journey in the World*, Preface, p. vii.

24. Edward Wilson and Henry Bowers. The two other members of Scott's polar party, Edgar Evans and Lawrence Oates, died before reaching this point.

25. In J.M. Barrie, *Courage*, rectoral address to undergraduates of St Andrews University, 3 May 1922 (Hodder and Stoughton, 1922), p. 32.

26. Quoted in Wade Davis, *Into the Silence: The Great War, Mallory, and the Conquest of Everest* (Bodley Head, 2011), p. 441.

27. Ibid., p. 381.

28. Jon Krakauer, *Into Thin Air* (Macmillan, 1997), p. 163.

29. Irving Janis, *Groupthink: Psychological Studies of Policy Decisions and Fiascoes* (Houghton Mifflin, 1982), p. 9.

30. Ibid., p. 8.

31. Quoted in interview with James Manyika, 'Google's view on the future of business: an interview with CEO Eric Schmidt', *McKinsey Quarterly*, November 2008.

32. Cass R. Sunstein, David Schkade and Lisa Michelle Ellman, 'Ideological Voting on Federal Courts of Appeals: A Preliminary Investigation', University of Chicago Law & Economics, Olin working paper no. 198 (2003); University of Chicago, Public Law working paper no. 50; AEI-Brookings Joint Center working paper no. 03-9 (2003), available at SSRN: http://ssrn.com/abstract=442480 or http://dx.doi.org/10.2139/ssrn.442480.

33. C. Ferraris and R. Carveth, 'NASA and the Columbia disaster: decision-making by groupthink?', *Proceedings of the 2003 Association for Business Communication Annual Convention*, p. 10.

34. J. Chein, D. Albert, L. O'Brien, K. Uckert and L. Steinberg, 'Peers increase adolescent risk taking by enhancing activity in the brain's reward circuitry', *Developmental Science* 14 (2011), F1–F10. See also Margo Gardner and Laurence Steinberg, 'Peer influence on risk taking, risk preference, and risky decision making in adolescence and adulthood: an experimental study', *Developmental Psychology* 41, 4 (2005), 625–35.

35. The attraction of social rewards also helps explain why young people join criminal gangs, though recent research has uncovered a critical interaction of genes and upbringing that determines why some are more inclined to be drawn in than others. For example, Kevin Beaver and others at Florida State University found that teenage boys who carry a particular variation of the dopamine transporter gene (DAT1) are more likely to associate with antisocial or delinquent peers – but only if they have been brought up in a 'high risk' family environment with a dearth of maternal affection. This is a good example of how behaviour can result from both individual characteristics or experience and group environment. Kevin M. Beaver, John Paul Wright and Matt DeLisi, 'Delinquent peer group formation: evidence of a gene X environment correlation', *Journal of Genetic Psychology* 169 (2008), 227–44.

36. Richard Thaler and Cass Sunstein, *Nudge: Improving Decisions about Health, Wealth, and Happiness* (Yale University Press, 2008).

37. Cass R. Sunstein, *Going to Extremes* (Oxford University Press, 2009), p. 5.

38. Three areas – capital punishment, abortion and national security – appear immune to polarization bias. Apparently judges feel so strongly on these issues that they are immune to persuasion. For further cases studies see Cass Sunstein, David Schkade, Lisa Ellman and Andres Sawicki, *Are Judges Political? An Empirical Investigation of the Federal Judiciary* (Brookings Institution Press, 2006).

39. 'Conservatives remain the largest ideological group in US', published on Gallup.com, 12 January 2012.

40. Data supplied by Bill Bishop and Robert Cushing. See their book *The Big Sort: Why the Clustering of Like-Minded America Is Tearing Us Apart* (Marina Books, 2009).

41. Sunstein, *Going to Extremes*, p. 80.

42. For an in-depth, first-hand analysis of how jihadist groups are radicalized via the Internet, see Mark Sageman, *Leaderless Jihad: Terror Networks in the Twenty-First Century* (University of Pennsylvania Press, 2008).

43. In *Post-Broadcast Democracy* (Cambridge University Press, 2007), political scientist Markus Prior documents how this increasing media choice has polarized America's voters.

44. You'd think that forcing opposed groups to mix and talk would always reduce polarization and cause people to shift their views towards each other. Yet this rarely happens when those views are strongly held, in which case correction leads only to further entrenchment. A different tack is required. Dan Kahan and colleagues at the Cultural Cognition Project at Yale Law School have found that people are less likely to dismiss contradictory information if they feel sympathetic towards the person presenting it – for example, if they share with them certain values, loyalties or a cultural worldview (see http://www.culturalcognition.net). The messenger is more important than the message here: accurate information or well-reasoned argument will fall on deaf ears unless it comes from someone in our own social group.

45. From Barbara Ehrenreich, 'Family values', in *The Worst Years of Our Lives: Irreverent Notes from a Decade of Greed* (Lime Tree, 1991), p. 11.

46. Further reading on brainstorming: N. Kohn and S. Smith, 'Collaborative fixation: effects of others' ideas on brainstorming', *Applied Cognitive Psychology* 25, 3 (2011), 359–71; 'Separating creativity from evaluation', in C. McCauley, 'Group dynamics in Janis's theory of groupthink: backward and forward', *Organizational Behavior and Human Decision Processes* 73 (1998), 142–62, p. 153; Alan R. Dennis, Randall K. Minas and Akshay Bhagwatwar, 'Sparking creativity: improving electronic brainstorming with individual cognitive priming', *System Science (HICSS), 2012 45th Hawaii International Conference on System Sciences* (IEEE, 2012); Nicolas Michinov, 'Is electronic brainstorming or brainwriting the best way to improve creative performance in groups? An overlooked comparison of two idea-generation techniques', *Journal of Applied Social Psychology* 42, S1 (2012), E222–43.

47. See Anthony T. Pescosolido and Richard Saavedra, 'Cohesion and sports teams: a review', *Small Group Research* 43, 6 (2012), 744–58.

48. N. Triplett, 'The dynamogenic factors in pacemaking and competition', *American Journal of Psychology* 9 (1898), 507–33.

49. Sometimes the presence of others can have the opposite effect and reduce motivation, a phenomenon psychologists call 'social loafing'. Social loafing tends to occur during group activities that mask individual effort, such as pulling on a rope or singing in a chorus, causing reduced personal accountability and making it easier for participants to hide in the crowd or feel that their contribution won't count for much. Social loafing was first noted by Max Ringelmann, a professor of agricultural engineering, in 1913.

50. Quoted on www.thecoldestjourney.org blog, 18 June 2013.

CHAPTER 7: THE FEAR THAT BINDS

1. From Joseph Soeters and René Moelker, 'German–Dutch co-operation in the heat of Kabul', in Gerhard Kümmel and Sabine Colmar (eds), *Soldat – Militär – Politik – Gesellschaft* (Nomos, 2003), pp. 63–75.

2. In addition to the German troops, one Afghan bystander was killed and ten wounded in this attack.

3. Mark Dechesne, Coen van den Berg and Joseph Soeters, 'International collaboration under threat: a field study in Kabul', *Conflict Management and Peace Science* 24 (2007), 25–36.

4. Ron Leifer, 'The legacy of Ernest Becker', *Psychnews International* 2, 4 (July–September 1997), available at http://userpage.fu-berlin.de/expert/psychnews/2_4/pn24d.htm.

5. Ernest Becker, *The Denial of Death* (Simon & Schuster, 1973), p. 26.

6. Becker, *Denial of Death*.

7. Leifer, 'Legacy of Ernest Becker'.

8. Directed by Patrick Shen, produced by Greg Bennick and Transcendental Media.

9. www.ratemyprofessors.com.

10. He hasn't lost those culinary skills. He co-founded Esperanto, a multi-ethnic fast-food restaurant in Saratoga Springs, which features among other things the 'doughboy', a baked cheese and chicken-filled dumpling of his own invention that has had rave reviews, including in *The New York Times*.

11. Other psychologists have proposed alternative hypotheses to explain the human tendency to buy into complex worldviews. For example, the Meaning

Maintenance Model championed by Travis Proulx at Tilburg University and Steven Heine at the University of British Columbia states that one of our primary motivations is to find meaning in our lives and make sense of the world, and that fear of death is only one of many sources of cognitive dissonance that force us to find ways of reaffirming our outlook (an unexpected end to a relationship or long-term job might have the same effect). Immo Fritsche at the University of Leipzig and colleagues propose that the reason people become more loyal to their own group and more prejudicial towards outsiders when they feel threatened is to maintain a sense of personal control over an uncertain situation. For a summary of some of these competing views and a reaction from Greenberg, Pyszczynski and Solomon, see Tom Pyszczynski, Jeff Greenberg, Sheldon Solomon and Molly Maxfield, 'On the unique psychological import of the human awareness of mortality: theme and variations', *Psychological Inquiry* 17, 4 (2006), 328–56.

12. A. Rosenblatt, J. Greenberg, S. Solomon, T. Pyszczynski and D. Lyon, 'Evidence for terror management theory: I. The effects of mortality salience on reactions to those who violate or uphold cultural values', *Journal of Personality and Social Psychology* 57, 4 (1989), 681–90.

13. H. McGregor, J.D. Lieberman, S. Solomon, J. Greenberg, J. Arndt, L. Simon and T. Pyszczynski, 'Terror management and aggression: evidence that mortality salience motivates aggression against worldview threatening others', *Journal of Personality and Social Psychology* 74, 3 (1998), 590–605.

14. The threat of violence can actually make us more agreeable towards members of our in-group. Andrew White and colleagues at Arizona State University found that across fifty-four nations, average scores for this personality trait were higher the more a country spent on its military (which the researchers took as a proxy for how threatened it felt). See A. White, D. Kenrick, Y. Li, C. Mortensen, S. Neuberg and A. Cohen, 'When nasty breeds nice: threats of violence amplify agreeableness at national, individual, and situational levels', *Journal of Personality and Social Psychology* 103, 4 (2012), 622–34.

15. Tom Pyszczynski, Sheldon Solomon and Jeff Greenberg, *In the Wake of 9/11: The Psychology of Terror* (American Psychological Association, 2003), p. 5.

16. Ibid.

17. Tom Pyszczynski, 'What are we so afraid of? A terror management theory perspective on the politics of fear', *Social Research* 71, 4 (2004), 827–48, p. 839.

18. Not all terror attacks boost support for the national leadership. The Spanish people responded to the 2004 Madrid train bombings by voting their government out of power in the general election three days later. This could

have been because they believed the government had made the country more vulnerable to terrorism by supporting the American invasion of Iraq – and also because of the government's cynical attempt to blame the attacks on Basque separatists.

19. George Bush's speech to Congress, 20 September 2001, available at http://www.presidency.ucsb.edu/ws/index.php?pid=64731&st=&st1=.

20. Becker, *Denial of Death*, p. 149.

21. These effects are also apparent in experimental studies carried out by Solomon and others in 2003 and 2004. They demonstrated that reminding people of the 9/11 attacks (even subliminally) was equivalent to reminding them of their own deaths, and that both manipulations caused them to increase their support for Bush. See Mark J. Landau *et al.*, 'Deliver us from evil: the effects of mortality salience and reminders of 9/11 on support for President George W. Bush', *Personality and Social Psychology Bulletin* 30, 9 (2004), 1136–50.

22. This principle applies not just to political values but to anything that might be relevant in moments of fear and threat as a bolster against uncertainty. A religious person might adhere more strongly to their faith. A strong family person might draw closer to their loved ones. Someone who sets great store by a scientific understanding of the world might become even more rationalistic, as demonstrated in a 2013 experiment at the University of Oxford. This suggested that for secularists, belief in science appears to serve a similar psychological function in the face of existential anxiety as religious faith does for believers. See M. Farias, A.-K. Newheiser, G. Kahane and Z. de Toledo, 'Scientific faith: belief in science increases in the face of stress and existential anxiety', *Journal of Experimental Social Psychology* 49, 6 (2013), 1210–13. See note 35 for more discussion on the theme of salient value-systems.

23. Landau *et al.*, 'Deliver us from evil', study 4. This result was replicated six weeks before the election. See Florette Cohen, Daniel M. Ogilvie, Sheldon Solomon, Jeff Greenberg and Tom Pyszczynski, 'American roulette: the effect of reminders of death on support for George W. Bush in the 2004 Presidential Election', *Analyses of Social Issues and Public Policy* 5 (2005), 177–87.

24. Drew Westen, *The Political Brain: The Role of Emotion in Deciding the Fate of the Nation* (Public Affairs, 2007), p. xv.

25. See Dan M. Kahan, 'Ideology, motivated reasoning, and cognitive reflection: an experimental study', *Judgment and Decision Making* 8 (2013), 407–24.

26. *Time* magazine, 3 May 2004, p. 32.

27. Delivered to a televised joint session of Congress on 28 January 2003, available at http://www.presidency.ucsb.edu/ws/index.php?pid=29645&st=&st1=.

28. In his opening speech of the debate on Iraq in the House of Commons, 18 March 2003.

29. One example of how irrational fears of terrorism affect everyday life is the vastly disproportionate premiums charged by insurance companies for terrorism cover in residential areas of London where there has never been a terrorist attack – a requirement that many landlords insist on and then pass on to their leaseholders and tenants.

30. Data from Statistical Abstract of the United States, US Census Bureau.

31. Data from Bureau of Labor Statistics, US Department of Labor.

32. Broadcast 15 July 1979, available at http://www.presidency.ucsb.edu/ws/index.php?pid=32596&st=&st1=.

33. Richard M. Doty, Bill E. Peterson and David G. Winter, 'Threat and authoritarianism in the United States, 1978–1987', *Journal of Personality and Social Psychology* 61, 4 (1991), 629–40.

34. Carl Iver Hovland and Robert R. Sears, 'Minor studies of aggression: VI. Correlation of lynchings with economic indices', *Journal of Psychology: Interdisciplinary and Applied* 9, 2 (1940), 301–10. Joseph Hepworth and Stephen West confirmed the correlation when they re-analysed the Hoyland-Sears data-set nearly half a century later, though found it less pronounced: Joseph T. Hepworth and Stephen G. West, 'Lynchings and the economy: a time-series reanalysis of Hovland and Sears (1940)', *Journal of Personality and Social Psychology* 55, 2 (1988), 239–47.

35. The fact that enthusiasm for capital punishment is seen in conservative but not liberal states reflects the prediction from terror management theory that people under threat revert to their dominant cultural worldview – liberals, who champion tolerance, tend to be less favourable towards capital punishment. Indeed the results of one study suggest that in liberal US states during times of threat support for capital punishment *decreases* (Stewart J.H. McCann, 'Societal threat, authoritarianism, conservatism, and US state death penalty sentencing (1977–2004)', *Journal of Personality and Social Psychology* 94, 5 (2008), 913–23).

36. For a classic analysis of the interplay between socioeconomic conditions and psychology in 1930s Germany see *Escape from Freedom* by the German social psychologist Erich Fromm (Rinehart, 1941), ch. 6.

37. Thomas Ohlemacher, 'Public opinion and violence against foreigners in the reunified Germany', *Zeitschrift für Soziologie* 23, 3 (1994), 222–36.

38. *British Social Attitudes 29* (2012), National Centre for Social Research, London, report available at http://www.bsa-29.natcen.ac.uk/.

39. David Goodhart, *The British Dream: Successes and Failures of Post-War Immigration* (Atlantic, 2013), p. xxi.

40. R.D. Putnam, '*E pluribus unum*: diversity and community in the twenty-first century', *Scandinavian Political Studies* 30 (2007), 137–74.

41. See Ashutosh Varshney, *Ethnic Conflict and Civic Life: Hindus and Muslims in India* (Yale University Press, 2002). More recently Varshney has conducted similar studies in cities in Sri Lanka, Indonesia and Malaysia, with mixed results. Early analysis suggests that the Indian model applies in Sri Lanka (Negombo, for example, is exceptionally ethnically integrated and traditionally peaceful) but less so in Malaysia (Kuala Lumpur, where Malay and Chinese communities hardly mix, has been relatively quiet since 1969) – though he has found no example of a deeply integrated community turning violent, so integration would seem to be a sufficient condition for peace if not a necessary one ('Civil society, Islam and ethnocommunal conflict', in Alfred Stepan (ed.), *Democracies in Danger*, Johns Hopkins University Press, 2009).

42. T. Cantle, *Community Cohesion: A Report of the Independent Review Team* (Home Office, London, 2001), p. 9.

43. From Goodhart, *British Dream*, p. 78.

44. Paul Nolan, *The Northern Ireland Peace Monitoring Report* (Community Relations Council, Belfast, 2012).

45. See G.W. Allport, *The Nature of Prejudice* (Perseus Books, 1954).

46. www.theparentscircle.com.

47. www.arikpeace.org.

48. Journal entry 1938, quoted in Susan Shillinglaw's introduction to John Steinbeck, *Of Mice and Men* (Penguin, 1994), p. vii.

49. Zachary K. Rothschild, Abdolhossein Abdollahi and Tom Pyszczynski, 'Does peace have a prayer? The effect of mortality salience, compassionate values, and religious fundamentalism on hostility toward out-groups', *Journal of Experimental Social Psychology* 45, 4 (2009), 816–27.

50. Matt Motyl, Joshua Hart, Tom Pyszczynski, David Weise, Molly Maxfield and Angelika Siedel, 'Subtle priming of shared human experiences eliminates threat-induced negativity toward Arabs, immigrants, and peace-making', *Journal of Experimental Social Psychology* 47, 6 (2011), 1179–84.

51. For a full description of Sherif's experiment see http://psychclassics.yorku.ca/Sherif.

52. For more examples of co-operation between Palestinians and Israelis see Daniel Gavron, *Holy Land Mosaic: Stories of Cooperation and Coexistence between Israelis and Palestinians* (Rowman and Littlefield, 2008).

53. In April 2011, the US ended its much criticized colour-coded alert system introduced in 2002 (green–blue–yellow–orange–red) and replaced it with an advisory system with a simpler hierarchy of threat levels (none–elevated–imminent).

54. Former Metropolitan Police chief Sir Paul Stephenson in a speech at the Royal United Services Institute, London, 24 November 2010, available at http://www.met.police.uk/pressbureau/burspeeches/page03.htm.

55. A notable exception is the Norwegian government, whose response to the massacre of seventy-seven people by the far-right militant Anders Breivik on 22 July 2011 was to ensure that nothing undermined the country's core values. Prime Minister Jens Stoltenberg called for 'more democracy, more openness and greater political participation', for which he received broad political support. No laws were changed and the police received no extra powers. Today in Norway Breivik's type of extremist ideology is more marginalized than ever.

56. One of the common ways political leaders manipulate both public fear and the fluidity of group boundaries to shore up support is by blaming internal instability on outsiders. Note the attempt by Hosni Mubarak's regime during the early days of the 2011 Egyptian revolution to pin the unrest on 'foreign agents' and 'traitors to Egypt', repeated by Egypt's military leaders during their clashes with the Muslim Brotherhood after President Morsi's removal from power in July 2013; and President Obama's efforts in June 2013 to deflect criticism of his government's secret surveillance programme by claiming it was directed only at foreigners.

57. R. Gillespie and D.C. Jessop, 'Do reminders of terrorist events influence acceptance of racial pride? A terror management theory perspective' (unpublished manuscript, 2007).

58. According to data from many sources including the Gallup Center for Muslim Studies (http://www.gallup.com), the Pew Research Center for the People and the Press (http://www.people-press.org/) and the European Muslim Research Centre at the University of Essex (http://centres.exeter.ac.uk/emrc/).

59. There are also health implications. Several studies have found a link between repeated media exposure to distressing events such as 9/11 and the Iraq war, and increased rates of PTSD and other stress-related disorders. See R.C. Silver, E.A. Holman, J.P. Andersen, M. Poulin, D.N. McIntosh and V. Gil-Rivas, 'Mental and physical health effects of acute exposure to media images of the 9/11 attacks and the Iraq War', *Psychological Science* 24 (2013), 1623–34.

60. From *Anti-Muslim Hate Crime and the Far Right*, by the Centre for Fascist,

Anti-Fascist and Post-Fascist Studies at Teesside University, June 2013, using data from the Faith Matters 'Tell Mama' project (www.tellmamauk.org).

61. In Andrew Weaver, *Keeping Our Cool: Canada in a Warming World* (Penguin, 2008).

62. He also found that Arab citizens of Israel, questioned during the Israeli army's invasion of Gaza in January 2009, became more favourable towards peaceful co-existence with Israeli Jews when presented with the climate change scenario – though this applied only to Arabs who already had a strong sense of sharing a common bond with the rest of humanity. Tom Pyszczynski, Matt Motyl, Kenneth E. Vail III, Gilad Hirschberger, Jamie Arndt and Pelin Kesebir, 'Drawing attention to global climate change decreases support for war', *Peace and Conflict: Journal of Peace Psychology* 18, 4 (2012), 354–68. The researchers are pragmatic about how all this might play out on the ground, acknowledging both that climate change is a politically charged issue and that once catastrophic changes have taken place the chances of conflict would rise. The best chance for solidarity, they argue, is before the changes strike and when the threat is imminent.

63. Another possible psychological effect of a superordinate threat like climate change is an increase in authoritarian attitudes towards people within society who might threaten the collective order, such as criminals, radicals or moral transgressors. See Immo Fritsche, J. Christopher Cohrs, Thomas Kessler and Judith Bauer, 'Global warming is breeding social conflict: the subtle impact of climate change threat on authoritarian tendencies', *Journal of Environmental Psychology* 32, 1 (2011), 1–10.

64. Sigmund Freud, *The Future of an Illusion* (1927), p. 16, quoted in Pyszczynski *et al.*, 'Drawing attention'.

65. Cormac McCarthy, *The Road* (Alfred A. Knopf, 2006).

CHAPTER 8: TOGETHER ALONE

1. Recorded in F. Spencer Chapman, *Northern Lights: The Official Account of the British Arctic Air-Route Expedition 1930–1931* (Chatto & Windus, 1932), p. 117.

2. Diary of A. Courtauld, vol. 1, 6 July 1930 to 6 August 1931. Original manuscript. Consulted at Scott Polar Research Institute, Cambridge: MS 123/125/126; BJ.

3. Augustine Courtauld, *Man the Ropes* (Hodder and Stoughton, 1957), p. 65.

4. Diary of A. Courtauld.

5. Ibid.

6. Ibid.

7. Addressed to his fiancée Mollie Montgomerie.

8. Diary of A. Courtauld.

9. Ibid.

10. Worryingly for air and road passengers, visions of this ilk have also been reported by long-distance aviators and truck drivers: giant red spiders crawling across the windscreen, imaginary animals running across the road, etc.

11. For more details of these experiments see Woodburn Heron, 'The pathology of boredom', *Scientific American* 196 (1957), 52–6; and Philip Solomon *et al.* (eds), *Sensory Deprivation: A Symposium Held at Harvard Medical School* (Harvard University Press, 1961).

12. D.O. Hebb, 'The motivating effects of exteroceptive stimulation', *American Psychologist* 13, 3 (1958), 109–13, p. 111.

13. Chapman, *Northern Lights*, p 175.

14. Diary of A. Courtauld.

15. Chapman, *Northern Lights*, p. 176.

16. Ibid., p. 187.

17. You can read about her expedition at http://www.icecapstation.com and watch videos at http://www.gregatkins.tv/productions/ice/index.html.

18. Mollie Butler, *August and Rab: A Memoir* (Weidenfeld and Nicolson, 1987), p. 9.

19. Courtauld, *Man the Ropes*, p. 64.

20. Chapman, *Northern Lights*, p. 186.

21. Nicholas Wollaston, *The Man on the Ice Cap: The Life of August Courtauld* (Constable, 1980), p. 144.

22. J.M. Scott, *Portrait of an Ice Cap* (Chatto & Windus, 1953), p. v.

23. The full quotation is: 'Our language has wisely sensed those two sides of man's being alone. It has created the word "loneliness" to express the pain of being alone. And it has created the word "solitude" to express the glory of being alone.' From Paul Tillich, *The Eternal Now* (SCM Press, 1963), p. 11.

24. John Milton, *Paradise Lost*, book 1, lines 254–5.

25. Richard E. Byrd, *Alone* (Putnam, 1938), pp. 94–6.

26. This was Apsley Cherry-Garrard's 'worst journey in the world' from Cape Evans to Cape Crozier in 1911: see ch. 5.

27. Byrd, *Alone*, p. 226.

28. In Edwin P. Hoyt, *The Last Explorer: The Adventures of Admiral Byrd* (John Day Company, 1968), pp. 327–8.

29. Joe Simpson, *Touching the Void* (Jonathan Cape, 1988), p. 152.

30. From an interview with Messner in John Geiger's *The Third Man Factor* (Canongate, 2009), p. 157. See also www.thirdmanfactor.com.

31. She covered 27,354 miles in 71 days, 14 hours, 18 minutes and 33 seconds.

32. Ellen MacArthur, *Full Circle* (Michael Joseph, 2010), p. 200. MacArthur also acknowledged the psychological importance of her land crew. 'The team was the best thing. Everything we did together: we built the boat together, we trained on the boat together; that atmosphere was phenomenal. We were like a family and that was very powerful' (from an interview with *Engineering & Technology* magazine, July 2013).

33. This yacht, the Giltspur, carried McClean across the Atlantic in 1982. At the time, it was nine feet nine inches long, the smallest vessel to have made the crossing. Three weeks later an American sailor repeated the feat in a yacht eight inches shorter. Not to be outdone, McClean cut two feet off the Giltspur with a chainsaw and reclaimed the record the following year.

34. Diary of A. Courtauld.

35. Byrd, *Alone*, p. 85.

36. 'The greening of the astronauts', *Time* magazine, 11 December 1972, p. 43.

37. Some isolates claim to have kept themselves sane by reading books. The travel writer Sylvain Tesson brought a library of eighty books with him on a six-month retreat in a cabin on Siberia's Lake Baikal. 'A book is a way to have someone with you', he wrote ('Russia: solitude in Siberia', *Guardian*, 31 May 2013, http://www.theguardian.com/travel/2013/may/31/siberia-cabin-lake-baikal-russia). However, he also had two dogs with him, which would have provided similar benefit. See Sylvain Tesson, *Consolations of the Forest: Alone in a Cabin in the Middle Taiga* (Alan Lane, 2013).

38. See Stuart Grassian, 'Psychiatric effects of solitary confinement', *Journal of Law and Policy* 22 (2006), p. 357. Little research has been done on whether couples may be immune to some of these problems, although a study on three married couples ice-locked together on a boat in the Arctic for nine months suggest the added emotional support is an advantage in a small group: Gloria R. Leon and Gro M. Sandal, 'Women and couples in isolated extreme environments: applications for long-duration missions', *Acta Astronautica* 53 (2004), 259–67.

39. Byrd, *Alone*, p. 16.

40. His message, fired from a catapult onto the deck of a passing ship near Cape Town, was reprinted in *The Sunday Times*, 23 March 1969, p. 3, under the title 'Flying Frenchman sails off to Pacific to "save my soul"', by Denis Herbstein.

41. Film released in 1998 starring Jim Carrey depicting a man living his life under constant observation inside a reality television show.

42. Private correspondence between Vanunu and Hounam, 17 April 1997.

43. For further details of pathologies see Craig Haney, 'Mental health issues in long-term solitary and "supermax" confinement', *Crime and Delinquency* 49, 1 (2003), 124–56; *Reforming Punishment: Psychological Limits to the Pains of Imprisonment* (American Psychological Association Books, 2006); Peter Scharff Smith, 'The effects of solitary confinement on prison inmates: a brief history and review of the literature', *Crime and Justice* 34, 1 (2006), 441–528; Stuart Grassian, 'Psychiatric effects of solitary confinement', *Journal of Law and Policy* 22 (2006), 325–83.

44. This range is estimated from a number of studies, including David Lovell, 'Patterns of disturbed behavior in a supermax population', *Criminal Justice and Behavior* 35, 8 (2013), 985–1004. It is important to note that it is not always clear what proportion of prisoners were mentally ill or brain damaged before being locked up.

45. Figures from the California Department of Corrections and Rehabilitation.

46. Grassian, 'Psychiatric effects of solitary confinement', pp. 331–2.

47. Part of this quotation appeared in 'Does solitary confinement breach the Eighth Amendment?', *New Scientist* online, 29 June 2012, available at www.newscientist.com/article/dn21992-does-solitary-confinement-breach-the-eighth-amendment.html.

48. Craig Haney, 'Taming the dynamics of cruelty in supermax prisons', *Criminal Justice and Behavior* 35 (2008), 956–84.

49. From Detention in Afghanistan and Guantanamo Bay: Statement of Shafiq Rasul, Asif Iqbal and Rhuhel Ahmed, issued 26 July 2004, paragraph 199.

50. Where it constitutes 'severe mental pain or suffering', the use of solitary confinement violates the Geneva Conventions and international humanitarian law. In October 2011, the UN Special Rapporteur on Torture called for a worldwide ban on its use in civilian prisons, describing it as 'a harsh measure which is contrary to rehabilitation, the aim of the penitentiary system' ('Solitary confinement should be banned in most cases, UN expert says', UN News Centre, https://www.un.org/apps/news/story.asp?NewsID=40097). The International Committee of the Red Cross, which prefers to decide on a case by case basis whether solitary confinement constitutes abuse, has nonetheless declared that it 'is in principle undesirable and should be avoided' (ICRC Israel/Occupied Territories E-Newsletter, August 2012).

51. Sarah Shourd, 'Tortured by solitude', *New York Times*, 5 November 2011.

52. See 'Saying no to Saddam', *New Scientist*, 26 June 2004, p. 44.

53. She describes her experience and the mental exercises she used to survive it in *Seven Years Solitary* (Hamish Hamilton, 1957).

54. Ahmed Errachidi, *The General: The Ordinary Man who Challenged Guantanamo* (Chatto & Windus, 2013), p. 132.

55. Terry Waite, *Taken on Trust* (Hodder & Stoughton, 1993), p. 241.

56. Brian Keenan, *An Evil Cradling* (Hutchinson, 1992); Terry Anderson, *Den of Lions: Memoirs of Seven Years in Captivity* (Hodder & Stoughton, 1993).

57. John McCain, *Faith of My Fathers: A Family Memoir* (Random House, 2008), p. 201.

58. Field Manual 2-22.3: Human Intelligence Collector Operations. Headquarters, Department of the Army, Washington DC, September 2006.

59. Most of the methods used by interrogators and taught in training have changed little since the Second World War. Scientific research into their effectiveness is virtually non-existent, meaning that interrogators must often 'make it up on the fly', according to forensic psychologist Robert Fein, chair of a US government review into interrogation methods in 2006 (see www.fas.org/irp/dni/educing.pdf). In 2009, the Obama administration moved to change that with the creation of the High Value Detainee Interrogation Group, an intelligence-gathering unit that is using behavioural science to try to improve interviewing techniques and filter out approaches (many of them abusive) that don't work.

60. 'Saying no to Saddam', *New Scientist*, 26 June 2004, p. 44.

61. Part of this paragraph appeared in 'The enforcer', *New Scientist*, 20 November 2004.

62. Tillich, *Eternal Now*, p. 12.

63. Social rejection really does 'hurt': unlike any other emotional response, rejection activates the same areas of the brain as physical pain, such as the dorsal anterior cingulate cortex and the anterior insula. See Ethan Kross, Marc G. Bermana, Walter Mischel, Edward E. Smith and Tor D. Wager, 'Social rejection shares somatosensory representations with physical pain', *PNAS* 108, 15 (2011), 6270–5. One interpretation of this finding is that for our early ancestors, being excluded from one's group or tribe was as much a threat to survival as physical injury.

64. Further reading: S.W. Cole, 'Social regulation of human gene expression', *Current Directions in Psychological Science* 18, 3 (2009), 132–7; John T. Cacioppo and Louise C. Hawkley, 'Perceived social isolation and cognition', *Trends in Cognitive Sciences* 13, 10 (2009), 447–54; John T. Cacioppo, Louise C. Hawkley,

Greg J. Norman and Gary G. Berntson, 'Social isolation', *Annals of the New York Academy of Sciences* 1231 (Social Neuroscience: Gene, Environment, Brain, Body) (2011), 17–22; and Lisa M. Jaremka, 'Loneliness promotes inflammation during acute stress', *Psychological Science* 24, 7 (2013), 1089–97.

65. John T. Cacioppo and William Patrick, *Loneliness: Human Nature and the Need for Social Connection* (W.W. Norton, 2008), p. 5.

66. For research on the effects of institutionalized environment on brain and behavioural development see the Bucharest Early Intervention Project, a collaboration between Tulane University, the University of Maryland and the Children's Hospital Boston: www.bucharestearlyinterventionproject.org.

67. Social deprivation is not just a human affliction. One of the most graphic examples of its crippling effects is psychologist Harry Harlow's experiments on rhesus macaque monkeys at the University of Wisconsin-Madison during the 1960s, in which he deprived them of social contact after birth for months or years. He observed that they became 'enormously disturbed' even after thirty days, and after a year were 'obliterated' socially, incapable of interaction of any kind. After they were let out some refused to eat, a condition the researchers determined as 'emotional anorexia'; others went into a state of shock, clutching and rocking themselves in the corner of their cage. Animals that were isolated later in life appeared to recover their sociality after release but became more aggressive. H.F. Harlow, R.O. Dodsworth and M.K. Harlow, 'Total social isolation in monkeys', *PNAS* 54, 1 (1965), 90–7.

68. For more on Cacioppo's research-based action plan for tackling loneliness, see Cacioppo and Patrick, *Loneliness*, ch. 13.

69. Dave Grossman, *On Killing: The Psychological Cost of Learning to Kill in War and Society* (Little, Brown, 1995), p. 290.

70. This view has been expressed by many analysts including Richard Gabriel, distinguished professor at the Royal Military College of Canada and an expert on the history of military psychiatry. The true number of Vietnam veterans with PTSD has been much debated. The National Vietnam Veterans' Readjustment Study, funded by the US government, estimated that twenty to twenty-five years after returning from the war, 15.2% of veterans (more than 400,000) still showed symptoms of full-blown PTSD, and 35.8% of those veterans who had experienced 'high levels of war zone exposure'. Many psychiatrists consider these figures conservative.

71. Stephani L. Hatch, Samuel B. Harvey, Christopher Dandeker, Howard Burdett, Neil Greenberg, Nicola T. Fear and Simon Wessely, 'Life in and after

the Armed Forces: social networks and mental health in the UK military', *Sociology of Health & Illness* 35, 7 (2013), 1045–64, p. 1048.

72. Deirdre MacManus, Kimberlie Dean, Margaret Jones, Roberto J. Rona, Neil Greenberg, Lisa Hull, Tom Fahy, Simon Wessely and Nicola T. Fear, 'Violent offending by UK military personnel deployed to Iraq and Afghanistan: a data linkage cohort study', *The Lancet* 381, 9870 (2013), 907–17.

73. Roy R. Grinker and John P. Spiegel, *Men Under Stress* (Blackiston, 1945), p. 454.

74. Angus Macqueen, 'Los 33: Chilean miners face up to a strange new world', *Observer*, 17 July 2011. His documentary, *Chilean Miners: 17 Days Buried Alive*, was shown on BBC2 in August 2011.

75. Theodore Kaczynski, 'The Unabomber manifesto: industrial society and its future', available at http://editions-hache.com/essais/pdf/kaczynski2.pdf.

76. Puckett is currently a law enforcement consultant to the Program of Psychiatry and the Law at the University of California in San Francisco. For more detail on her research into lone terrorists see Terry Turchie and Kathleen Puckett, *Hunting the American Terrorist: The FBI's War on Homegrown Terror* (History Publishing Company, 2007).

77. Some psychiatrists have claimed that Harris was a psychopath, a judgement derived almost entirely from their reading of his journal.

78. C. McCauley, S. Moskalenko and B. Van Son, 'Characteristics of lone-wolf violent offenders: a comparison of assassins and school attackers', *Perspectives on Terrorism* 7, 1 (2013), 4–24.

79. Mark R. Leary, Robin M. Kowalski, Laura Smith and Stephen Phillips, 'Teasing, rejection, and violence: case studies of the school shootings', *Aggressive Behavior* 29 (2003), 202–14.

80. The evolutionary explanation would be that for our early ancestors being excluded from the group would have meant a very short life.

81. William James, *The Principles of Psychology* (Henry Holt, 1890), vol. 1, ch. 10, p. 293.

EPILOGUE

1. Matthew D. Lieberman, *Social: Why Our Brains Are Wired to Connect* (Oxford University Press, 2013), p. 9.

2. World Health Organization, International Association for Suicide Prevention, *Preventing Suicide: A Resource for Media Professionals* (2008).

3. In Antonio Damasio, *Self Comes to Mind: Constructing the Conscious Brain* (Pantheon, 2010), p. 23.

Selective Bibliography

Akerlof, George, and Shiller, Robert J., *Animal Spirits* (Princeton University Press, 2009).

Allen, Colonel Ethan, *A Narrative of Colonel Ethan Allen's Captivity Containing His Voyages and Travels Interspersed with Some Political Observations, Written by Himself* (Robert Bell, 1779; The Georgian Press, 1930).

Anderson, Terry, *Den of Lions: Memoirs of Seven Years in Captivity* (Hodder & Stoughton, 1993).

Arendt, Hannah, *The Human Condition* (University of Chicago Press, 1958).

——*Eichmann in Jerusalem: A Report on the Banality of Evil* (Faber and Faber, 1963).

Arthur, Max, *Forgotten Voices of the Great War* (Ebury Press, 2002).

Atran, Scott, *Talking to the Enemy: Faith, Brotherhood, and the (Un)making of Terrorists* (Ecco, 2010).

Barrie, J. M., *Courage* (Hodder and Stoughton, 1922).

Barrows, Susanna, *Distorting Mirrors: Visions of the Crowd in Late Nineteenth-Century France* (Yale University Press, 1981).

Bauman, Zygmunt, *Modernity and the Holocaust* (Polity Press, 1989).

Becker, Ernest, *The Denial of Death* (Simon & Schuster, 1973).

Beharry, Johnson, *Barefoot Soldier: A Story of Extreme Valour* (Sphere, 2006).

Berman, Eli, *Radical, Religious and Violent: The New Economics of Terrorism* (MIT, 2009).

Bishop, Bill, *The Big Sort: Why the Clustering of Like-Minded America Is Tearing Us Apart* (Marina Books, 2009).

Blass, Thomas, ed., *Obedience to Authority: Current Perspectives on the Milgram Paradigm* (Psychology Press, 1999).

Blass, Thomas, *The Man Who Shocked the World* (Basic Books, 2004).

Bone, Edith, *Seven Years Solitary* (Hamish Hamilton, 1957).

Borch, Christian, *The Politics of Crowds: An Alternative History of Sociology* (Cambridge University Press, 2012).

Bourke, Joanna, *An Intimate History of Killing: Face-to-Face Killing in Twentieth-Century Warfare* (Granta, 1999).

Brazier, Kevin, *The Complete Victoria Cross* (Pen & Sword, 2010).

Brownfield, Charles, A., *Isolation: Clinical and Experimental Approaches* (Random House, 1965).

Browning, Christopher R., *Ordinary Men* (Aaron Asher, 1992).

Burney, Christopher, *Solitary Confinement* (Clerke and Cockeran, 1952).

Byrd, Richard E., *Alone* (Putnam, 1938).

Cacioppo, John T., and Patrick, William, *Loneliness: Human Nature and the Need for Social Connection* (W. W. Norton, 2008).

Canetti, Elias, *Crowds and Power* (Claassen Verlag, 1960; in English, Victor Gollancz, 1962).

Cannadine, David, *The Undivided Past: History Beyond Our Differences* (Allen Lane, 2013).

Cesarani, David, *Eichmann: His Life and Crimes* (William Heinemann, 2004).

Cherry-Garrard, Apsley, *The Worst Journey in the World* (Constable, 1922).

Christakis, Nicholas, and Fowler, James, *Connected* (Little, Brown, 2009).

Courtauld, Augustine, *Man the Ropes* (Hodder and Stoughton, 1957).

Croucher, Matt, *Bulletproof* (Random House, 2010).

Damasio, Antonio, *The Feeling of What Happens: Body and Emotion in the Making of Consciousness* (Houghton Mifflin Harcourt, 1999).

Davis, Wade, *Into the Silence: The Great War, Mallory, and the Conquest of Everest* (The Bodley Head, 2011).

Decety, J., and Ickes, W., eds, *The Social Neuroscience of Empathy* (MIT Press, 2009).

DeSteno, David, and Valdesolo, Piercarlo, *Out of Character* (Crown, 2011).

Drury, John, and Stott, Clifford, eds, *Crowds in the 21st Century: Perspectives from Contemporary Social Science* (Routledge, 2013).

Enden, Richard van, *The Soldier's War: The Great War Through Veterans' Eyes* (Bloomsbury, 2008).

Ferguson, Niall, *The Ascent of Money* (Allen Lane, 2008).

Fogelman, Eva, *Conscience and Courage* (Anchor, 1994).

Friedman, Milton, and Jacobson Schwartz, Anna, *A Monetary History of the United States 1867–1960* (Princeton University Press, 1963).

Fromm, Erich, *Escape from Freedom* (Rinehart, 1941).

Fulbrook, Mary, *A Small Town Near Auschwitz: Ordinary Nazis and the Holocaust* (Oxford University Press, 2012).

Gambetta, Diego, ed., *Making Sense of Suicide Missions* (Oxford University Press, 2005).

Gardner, Dan, *Risk: The Science and Politics of Fear* (McClelland and Stewart, 2008).

Geiger, John, *The Third Man Factor: Surviving the Impossible* (Canongate, 2009).

Geras, Norman, *Solidarity in the Conversation of Humanity* (Verso, 1995).

Gerbaudo, Paolo, *Tweets and the Streets* (Pluto Press, 2012).

Ginneken, Jaap van, *Crowds, Psychology, and Politics, 1871–1899* (Cambridge University Press, 1992).

Glover, Jonathan, *Inhumanity: A Moral History of the Twentieth Century* (Jonathan Cape, 1999).

Golway, Terry, *So Others Might Live: A History of New York's Bravest – The FDNY from 1700 to the Present* (Basic Books, 2002).

Goodhart, David, *The British Dream: Successes and Failures of Post-War Immigration* (Atlantic, 2013).

Graffagnino, J. Kevin, Hand, Samuel B., and Sessions, Gene, eds, *Vermont Voices, 1609 through the 1990s: A Documentary History of the Green Mountain State* (Vermont Historical Society, 1999).

Grinker, Roy R., and Spiegel, John P., *Men Under Stress* (Blackiston, 1945).

Grossman, Dave, *On Killing: The Psychological Cost of Learning to Kill in War and Society* (Little, Brown, 1995).

Haidt, Jonathan, *The Righteous Mind: Why Good People Are Divided by Politics and Religion* (Allen Lane, 2012).

Haslam, Alex, *The New Psychology of Leadership* (Psychology Press, 2010).

Hatfield, Elaine, Cacioppo, John, and Rapson, Richard, *Emotional Contagion: Studies in Emotion and Social Interaction* (Cambridge University Press, 1993).

Heller, Robert, and Stephens, Rebecca, *The Seven Summits of Success* (Capstone, 2005).

Hood, Bruce, *The Self Illusion* (Constable, 2012).

Hounam, Peter, *The Woman from Mossad: The Story of Mordechai Vanunu and the Israeli Nuclear Program* (Vision Paperbacks, 1999).

Hull, William L., *The Struggle for a Soul* (Doubleday, 1963).

Jackson, Joe, *A World on Fire: A Heretic, an Aristocrat, and the Race to Discover Oxygen* (Viking, 2005).

Janis, Irving L., *Groupthink* (Houghton Mifflin, 1982).

Keenan, Brian, *An Evil Cradling* (Hutchinson, 1992).

Khalil, Ashraf, *Liberation Square: Inside the Egyptian Revolution and the Rebirth of a Nation* (St Martin's Press, 2011).

Khalil, Karim, *Messages from Tahir: Signs from Egypt's Revolution* (AUC Press, 2011).

Kolk, Bessel van der, *Psychological Trauma* (American Psychiatric Publishing, 1987).

Krakauer, Jon, *Into Thin Air* (Macmillan, 1997).

Lang, Jochen von, ed., in collaboration with Claus Sibyll, *Eichmann Interrogated: Transcripts from the Archives of the Israeli Police* (The Bodley Head, 1983).

Lankford, Adam, *The Myth of Martyrdom* (Palgrave Macmillan, 2013).

Le Bon, Gustave, *The Crowd: A Study of the Popular Mind* (Macmillan, 1896).

Lieberman, Matthew D., *Social: Why Our Brains Are Wired to Connect* (Oxford University Press, 2013).

Lipstadt, Deborah, *The Eichmann Trial* (Schocken Books, 2011).

Logan, Richard, *Alone: A Fascinating Study of Those who Have Survived Long, Solitary Ordeals* (Stackpole, 1993).

Macaulay, J., and Berkowitz, L., eds, *Altruism and Helping Behavior* (Academic Press, 1970).

Mackey, Chris, and Miller, Greg, *The Interrogator's War: Inside the Secret War against Al Qaeda* (John Murray, 2004).

Marshall, S. L. A., *Men Against Fire: The Problem of Battle Command* (William Morrow, 1947).

McCauley, Clark, and Moskalenko, Sophia, *Friction: How Radicalization Happens to Them and Us* (Oxford University Press, 2011).

McClelland, J. S., *The Crowd and the Mob: From Plato to Canetti* (Unwin Hyman, 1989).

McManus, John C., *The Deadly Brotherhood: The American Combat Soldier in World War II* (Presidio Press, 1998).

McNeill, William H., *Keeping Together in Time: Dance and Drill in Human History* (Harvard University Press, 1995).

McPherson, James M., *For Cause and Comrades: Why Men Fought in the Civil War* (Oxford University Press, 1997).

Mear, Roger, and Swan, Robert, *In The Footsteps of Scott* (Jonathan Cape, 1987).

Merari Ariel, *Driven to Death: Psychological and Social Aspects of Suicide Terrorism* (Oxford University Press, 2010).

Michel, Lou, and Herbeck, Dan, *American Terrorist: Timothy McVeigh and the Oklahoma City Bombing* (Regan Books, 2001).

Milgram, Stanley, *Obedience to Authority* (Tavistock, 1974).

Nisbett, Richard, *The Geography of Thought* (Nicholas Brealey, 2003).

Noyce, Wilfrid, *They Survived: A Study of the Will to Live* (Heinemann, 1962).

Oliner, Samuel P., and Oliner, Pearl M., *The Altruistic Personality* (The Free Press, 1988).

Perry, Gina, *Behind the Shock Machine: The Untold Story of the Notorious Milgram Psychology Experiments* (Scribe, 2012).

SELECTIVE BIBLIOGRAPHY

Post, Jerrold M., *The Mind of the Terrorist: The Psychology of Terrorism from the IRA to Al-Qaeda* (Palgrave Macmillan, 2007).

Press, Eyal, *Beautiful Souls* (Farrar, Straus and Giroux, 2012).

Priestley, Joseph, *An Appeal to the Public on the Subject of the Riots in Birmingham* (J. Thomson, 1791).

——*An Appeal to the Public on the Subject of the Riots in Birmingham* (J. Johnson, 1792).

——*Memoirs of the Rev. Dr. Joseph Priestley, to the Year 1795* (James Belcher, 1810).

Pyszczynski, Tom, Solomon, Sheldon, and Greenberg, Jeff, *In the Wake of 9/11: The Psychology of Terror* (American Psychological Association, 2003).

Randall, Willard Sterne, *Ethan Allen: His Life and Times* (Norton, 2011).

Reading the Riots: Investigating England's Summer of Discontent (Guardian Shorts e-book, 2011).

The Register of the Victoria Cross (This England Books, 1981).

Reicher, Stephen, and Stott, Clifford, *Mad Mobs and Englishmen: Myths and Realities of the 2011 Riots* (Constable & Robinson e-book, 2011).

Renwick Monroe, Kristen, *The Heart of Altruism: Perceptions of a Common Humanity* (Princeton University Press, 1996).

Rorty, Richard, *Contingency, Irony and Solidarity* (Cambridge University Press, 1989).

Rudé, George, *The Crowd in History: A Study of Popular Disturbances in France and England 1730–1848* (John Wiley, 1964).

Rusesabagina, Paul, *An Ordinary Man* (Bloomsbury, 2006).

Sageman, Mark, *Leaderless Jihad: Terror Networks in the Twenty-First Century* (University of Pennsylvania Press, 2008).

Schofield, Robert, *The Enlightenment of Joseph Priestley: A Study of His Life and Work from 1733 to 1773* (Pennsylvania State University Press, 1997).

——*The Enlightened Joseph Priestley: A Study of His Life and Work from 1773 to 1804* (Pennsylvania State University Press, 2004).

Scott, J. M., *Portrait of an Ice Cap* (Chatto & Windus, 1953).

Scott, Jeremy, *Dancing on Ice* (Old Street Publishing, 2008).

Sennett, Richard, *Together: The Rituals, Pleasures and Politics of Cooperation* (Yale University Press, 2012).

Shephard, Ben, *A War of Nerves: Soldiers and Psychiatrists 1914–1994* (Jonathan Cape, 2000).

Shiller, Robert J., *Irrational Exuberance* (Princeton University Press, 2000).

——*The Subprime Solution: How Today's Global Financial Crisis Happened, and What to Do About It* (Princeton University Press, 2008).

Sighele, Scipio, *La foule criminelle: essai de psychologie collective* (Felix Alcan, 1901).

Smith, Joanna, and Haslam, Alexander, eds, *Social Psychology: Revisiting the Classic Studies* (Sage, 2012).

Smith, Richard B., *Ethan Allen and the Capture of Fort Ticonderoga* (The History Press, 2010).

Spencer Chapman, F., *Northern Lights: The Official Account of the British Arctic Air-Route Expedition 1930–1931* (Chatto & Windus, 1932).

——*Watkins' Last Expedition* (Vanguard Library, 1953).

Staub, Ervin, *The Roots of Evil* (Cambridge University Press, 1989).

——*Overcoming Evil: Genocide, Violent Conflict, and Terrorism* (Oxford University Press, 2011).

Stott, Clifford, and Pearson, Geoff, *Football Hooliganism: Policing and the War on the English Disease* (Pennant Books, 2007).

Streatfeild, Dominic, *Brainwash: The Secret History of Mind Control* (Hodder & Stoughton, 2006).

Stroud, Mike, *Shadows on the Wasteland* (Jonathan Cape, 1993).

Sunstein, Cass R., *Why Societies Need Dissent* (Harvard University Press, 2003).

——*On Rumors* (Farrar, Straus and Giroux, 2009).

——*Going to Extremes* (Oxford University Press, 2009).

Thaler, Richard, and Sunstein, Cass, *Nudge: Improving Decisions about Health, Wealth, and Happiness* (Yale University Press, 2008).

Tillich, Paul, *The Eternal Now* (SCM Press, 1963).

Todorov, Tzvetan, *The Fragility of Goodness* (Weidenfeld and Nicolson, 2001).

Turchie, Terry, and Puckett, Kathleen, *Hunting the American Terrorist: The FBI's War on Homegrown Terror* (History Publishing Company, 2007).

Varshney, Ashutosh, *Ethnic Conflict and Civic Life: Hindus and Muslims in India* (Yale University Press, 2002).

Waite, Terry, *Taken on Trust* (Hodder & Stoughton, 1993).

Watts, Duncan, *Everything Is Obvious: How Common Sense Fails* (Atlantic Books, 2011).

Westen, Drew, *The Political Brain: The Role of Emotion in Deciding the Fate of the Nation* (Public Affairs, 2007).

Wollaston, Nicholas, *The Man on the Ice Cap: The Life of August Courtauld* (Constable, 1980).

Zillmer, Eric, Harrower, Molly, Ritzler, Barry and Archer, Robert, *The Quest for the Nazi Personality: A Psychological Investigation of Nazi War Criminals* (Lawrence Erlbaum, 1995).

Zimbardo, Philip, *The Lucifer Effect* (Random House, 2007).

Index

___

287

INDEX

INDEX